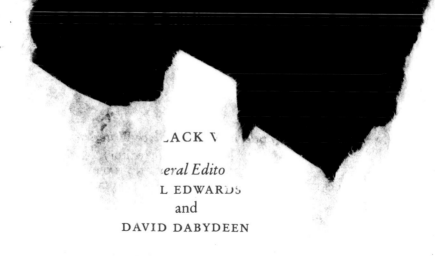

ACK V

eral Edito

L EDWARDS

and

DAVID DABYDEEN

D1639239

...atles in the Early Black Writers Series:
Christopher Fyfe (editor)
'OUR CHILDREN FREE AND HAPPY':
LETTERS FROM BLACK SETTLERS IN AFRICA IN THE 1790S

Forthcoming:
Iain McCalman (editor)
THE HORRORS OF SLAVERY AND OTHER WRITINGS
BY ROBERT WEDDERBURN
Paul Jefferson (editor)
THE TRAVELS OF WILLIAM WELLS BROWN

Black Writers in Britain
1760–1890

Selected and introduced by
PAUL EDWARDS
and
DAVID DABYDEEN

EDINBURGH UNIVERSITY PRESS

© Edinburgh University Press 1991
Reprinted 1995
22 George Square, Edinburgh

Typeset in Linotron Garamond Stempel
by Nene Phototypesetters, Northampton.
Printed and bound in Great Britain by
Hartnolls Limited, Bodmin, Cornwall

British Library Cataloguing
  in Publication Data
Black writers in Britain 1760-1890.
—(Early black writers series)
    I. Edwards, Paul   II. Dabydeen, David
    III. Series
    820.9

ISBN 0 7486 0267 4

Contents

Acknowledgements

Acknowledgements of permission to quote manuscript sources such as the letters of Philip Quaque or those of the Sierra Leone Settlers will be found at the end of the introductions to the individual authors.

We wish to thank the University of Warwick (D.D.), the British Academy and the University of Edinburgh (P.E.) for their assistance.

For their affection and encouragement, we should also like to offer thanks to Anna, Nancy Bennett and Joe Harte (D.D.) and to Ingbritt, Kristina and Birgitta (P.E.).

Introduction

The plan for this volume was essentially laid down in an earlier collaboration between us, a chapter on 'Black writers of the 18th and 19th centuries' in David Dabydeen (ed.) *The Black Presence in English Literature* (1985), 50–67. We had in mind courses for students at both school and university level, our aim being to draw attention to the considerable volume of such writing 'if only to dispel the idea that black people have in the past simply been written about, and have not spoken for themselves.'

The words of black people in Britain have come down to us in several forms. Indeed, the first words of an African on record in English were spoken by a South African called Coorie who had been kidnapped *circa* 1615 and brought to England to learn the language and so be useful as an interpreter. It is said that 'when he had learned a little of our Language, he would daily lye upon the ground and cry very often this in broken English, *Coorie home goe* ...'[1] The earliest accounts here, such as those of Briton Hammon and Ukawsaw Gronniosaw, were recorded from oral accounts, taken down for instance, like Gronniosaw's, 'by the elegant pen of a young lady of Leominster'. The spoken word must have been a force amongst the Afro-British of this period, and two of the authors included here also made names for themselves as public speakers, Equiano and Wedderburn. We include three speeches here, one made by John Henry Naimbanna on hearing a debate on slavery in the House of Commons and noted down by a companion, another the verbatim record of a speech from the dock in his own defence made by William Davidson, at his trial for sedition in 1820, and Wedderburn's defence against a charge of blasphemy, also in 1820. Then there are the letters, some published, many still in manuscript, ranging from the stylish personal correspondence of Ignatius Sancho and the politically influential letters of Olaudah Equiano, to the clumsy but often moving and revealing letters of the early settlers of the Sierra Leone colony to John Clarkson. By the late 18th century, there was a considerable literate black population. Some, like Equiano, were educated in the schools on board the larger warships on which he served, and by the tuition received from friends. Some were educated at their employer's expense, like Dr Samuel Johnson's servant, Francis Barber,[2] who was sent to school at Bishop's Stortford, or Julius Soubise the favourite of the Duchess of Queensberry, whose education included a short period at Eton. Some are known to have received tuition in the households where they were employed as we learn from the account books of, for example, the Duke of Gordon and the Duke of Marlborough.[3] Sancho, as a protégé of the Duke of Montagu, was provided with books and assistance as a teenager, and a small number, like Philip Quaque, who was ordained a minister in 1765, received a full time education, and indeed two, a Jamaican, William Fergusson, and a Trinidadian, John Baptist Philip, were awarded Doctorates of Medicine by Edinburgh University in 1814 and 1815 respectively. It should not be surprising, then, that by the end of the 18th century and into the 19th, a considerable body of Afro-British writing, autobiographical and polemical, had been published.

Literacy in English among black slaves, while encouraged by a few missionaries and sympathetic individuals, was fiercely opposed by most planters and slave-owners, who feared that demands for emancipation would be encouraged and given a voice. Not only would instruction 'render them less fit or less willing to labour' but according to William Knox, writing in the 1760's, it would also lead to 'a general insurrection of the Negroes and the massacre of their owners.'[4] Frederick Douglass, the great American slave-narrator, describes how his master tried to prevent him from learning to read:

> Very soon after I went to live with Mr. and Mrs. Auld, she commenced to teach me the A, B, C. After I had learned this, she assisted me in learning to spell words of three or four letters. Just at this point in my progress, Mr. Auld found out what was going on, and at once forbade Mrs. Auld to instruct me further, telling her, among other things, it was unlawful, as well as unsafe to teach a slave to read. To use his own words, further, he said, 'If you give a nigger an inch, he will, take an ell. A nigger should know nothing but to obey his master – to do as he is told to do. Learning would *spoil* the best nigger in the world.' 'Now,' said he, 'if you teach that nigger (speaking of myself) how to read, there would be no keeping him. It

would forever unfit him to be a slave. He would at once become unmanageable, and of no value to his master. As to himself, it could do him no good, but a great deal of harm. It would make him discontented and unhappy.'[5]

That the power of white over black was the power of the English language was a lesson many slaves had to learn at first hand. Hence those with opportunity set out to master the master's language. Equiano found his possession of the spoken language both a threat and a protective skill:

'Then,' said he, 'you are now my slave.' I told him my master could not sell me ... 'and by the law of the land no man has the right to sell me.' And I added, that I had heard a lawyer and others at different times tell my master so ... Upon this Captain Doran said I talked too much English.

On this they made up to me, and were about to handle me; but I told them to be still and keep off; for I had seen those kind of tricks played upon other free blacks, and they must not think to serve me so. At this they paused a little, and the one said to the other – it will not do; and the other answered that I talked too good English.[6]

Personal survival and advancement apart, the literate black contributed directly to the liberation of his fellow Africans. Black autobiographies and testimonies formed an essential weapon in the arsenal of the Abolitionists who were mobilising public opinion against the slave trade. Equiano travelled all over Britain reading from his book and speaking against the trade. His addresses to the public as well as his lobbying in Parliament made him, in the estimation of the Irish abolitionist Thomas Digges, 'a principal instrument in bringing about the motion for a repeal of the Slave-act.'[7]

Black people had moved from being packed 'like books upon a shelf' aboard the slave ship, to being authors, an extraordinary transformation and achievement, but even so, in terms of personal cost, a time of misery and confusion. Highly intelligent and articulate people such as Equiano were able to depict these sufferings of the many and express the frustration they as individuals felt at the racist treatment constantly received from mean-spirited, insensitive and ignorant whites. Educated or not, the African slaves were to construct their own culture from the wreckage of the past, but it is clear that this process was crucially aided by those of them

in England and America who became literate in English. Exposure
to other people's books such as in Equiano's case the English Bible,
and Milton, both gave depth to their despair and expression to
the experience of their loss. So Equiano finds words in *Paradise
Lost* which seem to articulate with dignity and passion his own
condition,

> Regions of sorrow, doleful shades, where peace
> And rest can rarely dwell. Hope never comes
> That comes to all, but torture without end
> Still urges.[8]

Quoting presumably from memory, Equiano misquotes slightly,
introducing the merest hint of hope: for Milton's 'rest can never
dwell', he has 'rest can rarely dwell'.

And Frederick Douglass tells us of the torments he endured after
reading books that vindicated human rights:

> The reading of these documents helped me to utter my
> thoughts, and to meet the arguments brought forward to
> sustain slavery; but while they relieved me of one difficulty,
> they brought on another even more painful than the one of
> which I was relieved. The more I read, the more I was led to
> abhor and detest my enslavers. I could regard them in no other
> light than a band of successful robbers who had left their
> homes, and gone to Africa, and stolen us from our homes, and
> in a strange land reduced us to slavery. I loathed them as being
> the meanest as well as the most wicked of men. As I read and
> contemplated the subject, behold! that very discontentment
> which Master Hugh had predicted would follow my learning
> to read had already come, to torment and sting my soul to
> unutterable anguish. As I writhed under it, I would at times
> feel that learning to read had been a curse rather than a blessing.
> It had given me a view of my wretched condition, without the
> remedy. It opened my eyes to the horrible pit, but no ladder
> upon which to get out. In moments of agony, I envied my
> fellow-slaves for their stupidity.[9]

Such frustrations and despair result from conflicting attitudes to
white society. Mastery of the English language meant exposure not
only to the books of British civilization but to its history, arts and
sciences. Black writers responded to the best of the civilization,
expressing genuine admiration for the way the society had developed culturally and scientifically. In addition they were befriended

whilst living in Britain by kind and thoughtful white people, and the experience of such kindness deepened their appreciation of the country. Simultaneously, the bigotry of other whites and the existence of slavery made them detest the society. However free black writers were as individuals, there were constant reminders of the greed and cruelty of white people who continued to enslave Africans. There was too the memory of loss of family which no amount of individual freedom or material acquisition could eradicate. The childhood experience of separation from his sister haunts Equiano's life:

> Yes, thou dear partner of all my childish sports! thou sharer of my joys and sorrows! happy should I have ever esteemed myself to encounter every misery for you, and to procure your freedom by the sacrifice of my own. Though you were early forced from my arms, your image has been always rivetted in my heart, from which neither time nor fortune have been able to remove it: so that, while the thoughts of your sufferings have damped my prosperity, they have mingled with adversity and increased its bitterness. To that Heaven which protects the weak from the strong, I commit the care of your innocence and virtues, if they have not already received their full reward, and if your youth and delicacy have not long fallen victims to the violence of the African trader, the pestilential stench of a Guinea ship, the lash and lust of a brutal and unrelenting overseer.[10]

Already isolated by colour, the sense of the absence of family would have deepened the loneliness of black writers living in Britain. Acquiring a British education had already removed them, intellectually, from the mass of black slaves in the Caribbean and North America, and culturally from their own communities in Africa. There could be no going back to the condition of slavery, hence the concerted campaign by British-based blacks to prevent their owners returning them to the West Indies or Africa. Nor was there any easy homecoming to Africa: what was in Coorie a simple desire for repatriation to a loved and clearly remembered homeland, became in later authors less immediate and realisable. 'Home' became any place that they found themselves in, and different writers identified with different places. Ultimately the only security was in writing, in rooting the experience in words, hence the extraordinary efforts people such as Equiano made to record their lives:

I had resolved to keep a journal of this singular and interesting voyage; and I had no other place for this purpose but a little cabin, or the doctor's store-room, where I slept. This little place was stuffed with all manner of combustibles, particularly with tow and aquafortis, and many other dangerous things. Unfortunately it happened in the evening as I was writing my journal, that I had occasion to take the candle out of the lanthorn, and a spark having touched a single thread of the tow, all the rest caught the flame, and immediately the whole was in blaze. I saw nothing but present death before me, and expected to be the first to perish in the flames. In a moment the alarm was spread, and many people who were near ran to assist in putting out the fire. All this time I was in the very midst of the flames; my shirt, and the handkerchief on my neck were burnt, and I was almost smothered with the smoke. However, through God's mercy, as I was nearly giving up all hopes, some people brought blankets and mattresses and threw them on the flames, by which means in a short time the fire was put out. I was severely reprimanded and menaced by such of the officers who knew it, and strictly charged never more to go there with a light: and, indeed, even my own fears made me give heed to this command for a little time; but at last, not being able to write my journal in any other part of the ship, I was tempted again to venture by stealth with a light in the same cabin though not without considerable fear and dread on my mind.[11]

This episode demonstrates the effort of will, sometimes involving what appears to be not simply a challenge to authority, but to reason itself, that must have been a feature of the heroism of these early black writers. The immediate record of the embryonic autobiography is all that matters, and he is ready to risk his own life, and the ship's too, to ensure its survival.

DAVID DABYDEEN, Warwick
PAUL EDWARDS, Edinburgh

Notes

1. Edward Terry, *A Voyage to East India*, London 1655, for the history of Coorie. The passage referred to is quoted in Paul Edwards and James Walvin, *Black Personalities in the Era of the Slave Trade*, London 1983,

11–12. A summary of his life is to be found in H. W. Debrunner, *Presence and Prestige: Africans in Europe*, Basel 1979, 58.

2. A. L. Reade, *Johnsonian Gleanings, Part II: Francis Barber*, London 1912.

3. The Duke of Gordon's accounts, in the accounts book of William Bell, his factor, July 27, 1762, Scottish Record Office G. D. 44/51/80, payments made to a schoolmaster for 'Teaching the Black Boy Harry', quoted in Gates and Davis (eds), *The Slaves Narrative*, Oxford and New York 1985, 175. For the Duke of Marlborough's accounts recording payments for books for a black servant, see David Green, 'A Cupful o' Crabs' in *Countryman*, XLVIII, 1953, 40.

4. Cited in Peter Fryer, *Staying Power*, Pluto Press, London 1984, 154.

5. *Narrative of the Life of Frederick Douglass*, New American Library edn., 1968, 49.

6. Paul Edwards ed., *The Life of Olaudah Equiano*, Longmans, Harlow 1989, 58–9; 117.

7. Letter included in the facsimile of the first edition in the Dawson Colonial History Series, *The Life of Olaudah Equiano*, ed. Paul Edwards, Dawson of Pall Mall, London 1969, Appendix A, I. xii.

8. *Paradise Lost*, I 65–8; Equiano (1789) I.189.

9. Douglass, op. cit. 55.

10. Equiano (1989) ed. Edwards, 18–19.

11. ibid., 130.

The Writers

1

BRITON HAMMON

A Narrative of the Uncommon Sufferings and Surprising Deliverance of Briton Hammon, a Negro Man

Boston 1760

This was the first published work by a Black author in English, though it was written not by his own hand, but 'taken down' by a white amanuensis from his own oral account. It has features in common with other British and American slave narratives. Several of these describe capture by Indians, though we have not included this section of the narrative here; and a central theme, as in the narratives of Gronniosaw and Equiano below, is the demonstration of divine providence. It bears a superficial similarity in some respects to Equiano's narrative, but rather more, in its self-denying piety, to that of Gronniosaw, though even so there are notable differences. Gronniosaw's humility has its ironic potential and can occasionally burst into something like an angry blaze, while Equiano, despite his ambivalent respect for the values of the 'old England' for which he sailed and fought as a seaman, was a representative of heroic independence, selfhood and survival, a committed abolitionist leader, and a principal spokesman for the slaves and the black poor. Hammon shows little of such independent spirit.

Hammon's book concludes with his joyful return to the house of his owner and master in Boston, 'to my own native land', and if there are villains in Hammon's world they are not the slave traders and estate managers of Equiano's account, but the Red Indians and Spanish, traditional enemies, respectively, of the white American settlers and the British Navy. In incidents occurring earlier than the passage included here, first the Indians, then the Spanish, capture and imprison him after he is shipwrecked whilst on a private venture for which he had been temporarily released by his master. At the time of these events, the American states were still part of the English colonial possessions and his patriotism towards Britain is made apparent, in his account of his rescue by the Royal Navy from the Spanish in Havana after the latter had imprisoned him for

3

refusing to serve on Spanish ships. The Spanish try to remove him from a British man-of-war, but 'the Captain, who was a true Englishman, refus'd them, and said he could not answer it, to deliver up any Englishman under English colours.'

Hammon saw action, as did large numbers of black seamen, on British warships, and was wounded in battle, recuperating at Greenwich Hospital, in London, after which he worked as a sea-cook on merchant ships. Little or no reference is made to slavery or the slave trade, and the climax of the narrative is his providential re-uniting with his beloved master, a passenger aboard one of the ships on which he happens to be working, and their happy return together 'home' to Boston. The pattern of the narrative seems designed to reinforce the sentimental and convenient stereotype of the loving and trusting slave which, though it may have been a minor aspect of slave experience, is placed in perspective by accounts such as Equiano's of the brutalisation of most slaves, and of his own complex relationships with his white 'masters'.

The text is that of the first edition, as reissued by Kraus Reprints, Nendeln, 1972.

After being on Shore [*in Havana*] another Twelvemonth, I endeavour'd to make my Escape the second Time, by trying to get on board of a Sloop bound to *Jamaica*, and as I was going from the City to the Sloop, was unhappily taken by the Guard, and ordered back to the Castle, and there confined. – However, in a short time I was set at Liberty, and order'd with a Number of others to carry the *Bishop* from the Castle, thro' the Country, to confirm the old People, baptize Children, &c. for which he receives large Sums of Money. – I was employ'd in this Service about Seven Months, during which Time I lived very well, and then returned to the Castle again, where I had my Liberty to walk about the City, and do Work for my self; – The *Beaver, an English* Man of War then lay in the Harbour, and having been informed by some of the Ship's Crew that she was to sail in a few Days, I had nothing now to do, but to seek an Opportunity how I should make my Escape.

Accordingly one Sunday Night the Lieutenant of the Ship with a Number of the Barge Crew were in a Tavern, and Mrs. *Howard* who had before been a Friend to me, interceded with the Lieutenant to carry me on board: the Lieutenant said he would with all his Heart, and immediately I went on board in the Barge. The next Day the *Spaniards* came along side the *Beaver*, and demanded me again, with a Number of others who had made their Escape from them, and got on board the Ship but just before I did; but the Captain, who was a true *Englishman*, refus'd them, and said he could not answer it, to deliver up any *Englishmen* under *English* Colours. – In a few Days we set Sail for *Jamaica*, where we arrived safe, after a short and pleasant Passage.

After being at *Jamaica* a short Time we sail'd for *London*, as convoy to a Fleet of Merchantmen, who all arrived safe in the *Downs*, I was turned over to another Ship, the *Arcenceil*, and there remained about a Month. From this Ship I went on board the *Sandwich* of 90 Guns; on board the *Sandwich*, I tarry'd 6 Weeks, and then was order'd on board the *Hercules*, Capt. *John Porter*, a 74 Gun Ship, we sail'd on a Cruize, and met with a *French* 84 Gun Ship, and had a very smart Engagement, in which about 70 of our Hands were Kill'd and Wounded, the Captain lost his Leg in the Engagement, and I was Wounded in the Head by a small Shot. We should have taken this Ship, if they had not cut away the most of our Rigging; however, in about three Hours after, a 64 Gun Ship, came up with and took her. – I was discharged from the *Hercules* the 12th Day of *May* 1759 (having been on board of that Ship 3 Months) on account of my being disabled in the Arm, and render'd incapable of Service, after being honourably paid the Wages due to me. I was put into the *Greenwich* Hospital where I stay'd and soon recovered. – I then ship'd myself a Cook on board Captain *Martyn*, an arm'd Ship in the King's Service. I was on board this Ship almost Two Months, and after being paid my Wages, was discharg'd in the Month of *October*. – After my discharge from Captain *Martyn*, I was taken sick in *London* of a fever, and was confin'd about 6 Weeks, where I expended all my Money, and left in very poor Circumstances; and unhappy for me I knew nothing of my *good Master's* being in *London* at this my very difficult Time. After I got well of my sickness, I ship'd myself on board of a large Ship bound to *Guinea*, and being in a publick House one Evening, I overheard a Number of Persons talking about Rigging a Vessel bound to *New-England*, I ask'd them to what Part of *New-England* this Vessel was bound? they told me, to *Boston*; and having ask'd them who was Commander? they told me, Capt. *Watt*; in a few Minutes after this the Mate of the Ship came in, and I ask'd him if Captain *Watt* did not want a Cook, who told me he did, and that the

Captain would be in, in a few Minutes; and in about Half an Hour the Captain came in, and then I ship'd myself at once, after begging off from the Ship bound to *Guinea*; I work'd on board Captain *Watt's* Ship almost Three Months, before she sail'd, and one Day being at Work in the Hold, I overheard some Persons on board mention the Name of *Winslow*, at the Name of which I was very inquisitive, and having ask'd what *Winslow* they were talking about? They told me it was *General Winslow*; and that he was one of the Passengers, I ask'd them what *General Winslow*? For I never knew *my good Master*, by that Title before; but after enquiring more particularly I found it must be my *Master*, and in a few Days Time the Truth was joyfully verify'd by a happy Sight of his Person, which so overcame me, that I could not speak to him for some Time – *My good Master* was exceeding glad to see me, telling me that I was like one arose from the Dead, for he thought I had been Dead a great many Years, having heard nothing of me for almost Thirteen Years.

I think I have not deviated from Truth, in any particular of this my Narrative, and tho' I have omitted a great many Things, yet what is wrote may suffice to convince the Reader, that I have been most grievously afflicted, and yet thro' the Divine Goodness, as miraculously preserved, and delivered out of many Dangers; of which I desire to retain a *grateful Remembrance*, as long as I live in the World.

And now, That in the Providence of that GOD, who delivered his Servant David out of the Paw of the Lion and out of the Paw of the Bear, *I am freed from a* long *and* dreadful Captivity, among worse Savages than they; *And am return'd to my* own Native Land, to Shew how Great Things the Lord hoth done for Me; *I would call upon all Men. and Say*, O Magnifie the Lord with Me, and let us Exalt his Name together! – O that Men would Praise the Lord for His Goodness, and for his Wonderful Works to the Children of Men!

(10–14)

2

UKAWSAW GRONNIOSAW
(known as James Albert)
born c.1710, Bornu

A Narrative of the Remarkable Particulars in the Life of James Albert Ukawsaw Gronniosaw, An African Prince, related by himself

c.1770, various editions

The tone of obsequious humility which characterises much of this narrative might lead some readers to think Gronniosaw something of a 'Holy Willie', particularly since his self-approving sense of superiority from an early age to his family, who must have found him rather a pain in the neck, makes such claims to humility suspect:

> I had, from my infancy, a curious turn of mind, and was more grave and reserved in my disposition than either of my brothers and sisters. I often teased them with questions they could not answer; for which reason they disliked me, as they thought I was either foolish or insane. (Narr. 3)

Other readers may find in his narrative evidence of his 'amiable and tender disposition ... well attested ... by many creditable persons in London and other places', noted by W. Shirley in the original introduction. Since the narrative was 'taken from his own mouth, and committed to paper by the elegant pen of a young lady of the town of Leominster', we cannot be sure whether or not the more self-satisfied pieties might have come from her, rather than Gronniosaw, but we must also bear in mind the pious audience for which the narrative is intended, and the 'holier than thou' quality of many of the conversion narratives of the period. The reader might also be on the watch for the possible presence of the now widely recognised strategy of slave narrative, the placing of an ironic sting in the tail of apparently innocent and humble protestations of admiration for the virtues of the white Christian world, a device highly developed in the narrative of Olaudah Equiano.

Both Equiano and his friend Ottobah Cugoano (see below)

would have read Gronniosaw. Cugoano mentions him in his own book, *Thoughts and Sentiments on the Evil of Slavery*, in which there is evidence of Equiano's own revising hand, and Equiano himself clearly echoes Gronniosaw's story of the talking book, included here and in another version, at the end of the second of the Equiano extracts.

The narrative tells of his childhood in Bornu, his kidnapping as a teenager, his experience as a house slave in America, his manumission and his adventures at sea aboard a privateer. After ending this voyage in New York, he signed up with Admiral Pocock's fleet, and came to England, where he found himself to his surprise and disappointment amongst rogues and sinners. Next, he travelled to Amsterdam, where

> The Calvinist ministers in Holland desired to hear my experience from myself. I stood before thirty-eight ministers every Tuesday, for seven weeks altogether, and they were all very well satisfied, and were persuaded that I was what I pretended to be ... the Lord Almighty was with me at that time in a remarkable manner, and gave me words, and enabled me to, answer them, so great was his mercy in taking me in hand, a poor blind heathen. (19)

Gronniosaw met and married a white girl, and scenes from their life together with their children, often in extreme poverty, are strikingly recorded.

Four episodes of the narrative are included here. (a) His journey with a merchant to the coast of Africa, at the end of which he is betrayed by those to whom he had been entrusted. There are some implausibilities in this account, which seems to embroider the narrative with the features of popular sensational and sentimental fiction. The section ends with his early experience of American slavery and includes the stories of the talking book; and of the punishment by whipping of old Ned, on the orders of his mistress, 'a fine young lady, and very good to me', told in the ambivalent terms so characteristic of slave narrative. (b) The second extract describes his growing sense of belonging to God's elect, and the death of his master who 'left me by his will, ten pounds and my freedom'. (c) Next comes his first unhappy experience of English 'Christian' society, and his meeting with his future wife. (d) The final section describes his married life and its grim burden of poverty, with underlying rage bursting out from beneath the mask of humility when the clergyman refuses to bury his dead child.

The only conveniently available full text, used here, is that of 1840, reprinted in a collection of early black texts published by Kraus Reprints, Nendeln 1972. This text differs slightly, but insignificantly, from earlier editions.

a. Enslavement in Africa and America

I was now more than a thousand miles from home, without a friend, or means to procure one. Soon after I came to the merchant's house, I heard the drums beat remarkably loud, and the trumpets blow. The persons accustomed to this employ are obliged to go on a very high structure, appointed for that purpose, that the sound may be heard at a great distance. They are higher than the steeples in England. I was mightily pleased with sounds so entirely new to me, and was very inquisitive to know the cause of this rejoicing, and asked many questions concerning it. I was answered that it was meant as a compliment to me, because I was grandson to the King of Bournou.

This account gave me a secret pleasure, but I was not suffered long to enjoy this satisfaction; for in the evening of the same day, two of the merchant's sons, boys about my own age, came running to me, and told me that the next day I was to die, for the king intended to behead me. I replied, that I was sure it could not be true, for I came there to play with them, and to see houses walk upon the water with wings to them, and to see the white folks; but I was soon informed that their king imagined I was sent by my father as a spy, and would make such discoveries at my return home as would enable them to make war with great advantage to ourselves; and for these reasons he had resolved that I should never return to my native country. When I heard this, I suffered misery that cannot be described. I wished a thousand times that I had never left my friends and country. But still the Almighty was pleased to work miracles for me.

The morning I was to die, I was washed, and all my gold ornaments made bright and shining, and then carried to the palace, where the king was to behead me himself, as is the custom of the place. He was seated, upon a throne at the top of an exceeding large yard, or court, which you must go through to enter the palace. It is as wide and spacious as a large field in England. I had a lane of lifeguards to go through, which I guessed to be about three hundred paces.

I was conducted by my friend, the merchant, about half way up, then he durst proceed no farther. I went up to the king alone. I advanced with an undaunted courage, and it pleased God to melt the heart of the king, who sat with his cimeter in his hand ready to behead me; yet, being himself so affected, he dropped it out of his hand, and took me upon his knees, and wept over me. I put my right hand round his neck, and pressed him to my heart. He set me down and blessed me, and added, that he would not kill me, that I should not go home, but be sold for a slave. I was then conducted back again to the merchant's house.

The next day he took me on board a French brig; but the captain did not choose to buy me. He said I was too small; so the merchant took me home with him again.

The partner, whom I have spoken of as my enemy, was very angry to see me return, and again proposed putting an end to my life; for he represented to the other that I should bring them into troubles and difficulties, and that I was so little that no person would buy me. The merchant's resolution began to waver, and I was indeed afraid that I should be put to death. But, however, he said he would try me once more.

A few days after, a Dutch ship came into the harbour, and they carried me on board, in hopes that the captain would purchase me. As they went, I heard them agree, that if they could not sell me then, they would throw me overboard. I was in extreme agony when I heard this, and as soon as ever I saw the Dutch captain, I ran to him, and put my arms round him, and said, 'Father, save me,' for I knew that if he did not buy me I should be treated very ill, or possibly murdered. And though he did not understand my language, yet it pleased the Almighty to influence him in my behalf, and he bought me for two yards of check, which is of more value there than in England.

When I left my dear mother, I had a large quantity of gold about me, as is the custom of our country. It was made into rings, and they were linked one into another, and formed into a kind of chain, and so put round my neck, and arms, and legs, and a large piece hanging at one ear, almost in the shape of a pear. I found all this troublesome, and was glad when my new master took it from me. I was now washed, and clothed in the Dutch or English manner. My master grew very fond of me, and I loved him exceedingly. I watched every look, was always ready when he wanted me, and endeavoured to convince him by every action that my only pleasure was to serve him well. I have since thought that he must have been a serious man. His actions corresponded very well with such a character. He used to read prayers in public to the ship's crew every Sabbath day; and when I first saw him read, I was never so surprised in my life, as when I saw the book talk to my master, for I thought it did, as I observed him to look upon it, and move his lips. I wished it would do so with me. As soon as my master had done reading, I followed him to the place where he put the book, being mightily delighted with it, and when nobody saw me, I opened it, and put my ear down close upon it, in great hopes that it would say something to me; but I was very sorry, and greatly disappointed, when I found that it would not speak. This thought immediately presented itself to me, that every body and every thing despised me because I was black.

I was exceedingly sea-sick at first; but when I became more accustomed to the sea, it wore off. My master's ship was bound for Barbadoes. When we arrived there, he thought fit to speak of me to several gentlemen of his acquaintance, and one of them expressed a particular desire to see me. He had a great mind to buy me; but the captain could not immediately be prevailed upon to part with me. However, as the gentleman seemed very solicitous, he at length let me go, and I was sold for fifty dollars (*four-and-sixpenny pieces in English*.) My new master's name was Vanhorn, a young gentleman. His home was in New England, in the city of New York, to which place he took me with him. He dressed me in his livery, and was very good to me. My chief business was to wait at table and tea, and clean knives, and I had a very easy place; but the servants used to curse and swear surprisingly, which I learned faster than anything; indeed, it was almost the first English I could speak. If any of them affronted me, I was sure to call upon God to damn them immediately; but I was broken off it all at once, occasioned by the correction of an old black servant that lived in the family. One day I had just cleaned the knives for dinner, when one of the maids took one to cut bread and butter with; at which I was very angry, and immediately called upon God to damn her, when this old black man told me that I must not say so. I asked him why? He replied that there was a wicked man called the devil, who lived in hell, and would take all who said these words, and put them into the fire, and burn them. This terrified me greatly, and I was entirely broken off swearing. Soon after this, as I was placing the china for tea, my mistress came into the room just as the maid had been cleaning it, and the girl had unfortunately sprinkled the wainscot with the mop, at which my mistress was very angry. The girl very foolishly answered her again, which made her worse, and she called upon

God to damn her. I was vastly concerned to hear this, as she was a fine young lady, and was very good to me, insomuch that I could not help speaking to her; 'Madam,' said I, 'you must not say so.' 'Why?' said she. 'Because there is a black man called the devil, that lives in hell, and he will put you into the fire and burn you, and I shall be very sorry for that.' 'Who told you this?' replied my lady. 'Old Ned,' said I. 'Very well,' was all her answer; but she told my master of it, and he ordered that old Ned should be tied up and whipped, and he was never suffered to come into the kitchen with the rest of the servants afterwards. My mistress was not angry with me, but rather diverted with my simplicity, and by way of talk, she repeated what I had said to many of her acquaintances that visited her; and among the rest, Mr. Freelandhouse, a very gracious, good minister, heard it, who took a great deal of notice of me, and desired my master to part with me to him. He would not hear of it at first, but being greatly persuaded, he let me go, and Mr. Freelandhouse gave fifty pounds for me. He took me home with him, and made me kneel down, and put my two hands together, and prayed for me, and every night and morning he did the same. I could not make out what he did this for, nor the meaning of it, nor what they spoke to when they talked. I thought it comical, but I liked it very well. After I had been a little while with my new master, I grew more familiar, and asked him the meaning of prayer. (I could hardly speak English to be understood.) He took great pains with me, and made me understand that he prayed to God, who lived in heaven; that he was my Father and best Friend. I told him that this must be a mistake, that my father lived at Bournou, and that I wanted very much to see him, and likewise my dear mother and sister, and I wished he would be so good as to send me home to them; and I added all that I could think of to induce him to convey me back. I appeared in great trouble, and my good master was so affected, that the tears ran down his face. He told me that God was a great and good Spirit, that he created all the world, and every person and thing in it, in Ethiopia, Africa, and America, and everywhere. I was delighted when I heard this. 'There,' said I, 'I always thought so when I lived at home. Now if I had wings like an eagle, I would fly to tell my dear mother that God is greater than the sun, moon, and stars, and that they were made by him.' I was exceedingly pleased with this information of my master's, because it corresponded so well with my own opinion. I thought, now if I could but get home, I should be wiser than all my country-folks, my grandfather, or father, or mother, or any of them. 'But though I was somewhat enlightened by this information of my master's, yet I had no other knowledge of God but that he was a good Spirit, and created every body, and every thing. I never was sensible in myself, nor had any one ever told me, that he would punish the wicked and love the just. I was only glad that I had been told there was a God, because I had always thought so.

My dear kind master grew very fond of me, as was his lady. She put me to school, but I was uneasy at that, and did not like to go; but my master and mistress, in the gentlest terms, requested me to learn, and persuaded me to attend my school without any anger at all; so that at last I began to like it better, and learnt to read pretty well. My schoolmaster was a good man, and was very indulgent to me; his name was Vanosdore. I was in this state when, one Sunday, I heard my master preach from these words out of the Revelation (i. 7); 'Behold, he cometh in the clouds, and every eye shall see him, and they that pierced him.' These words affected me excessively. I was in great agony, because I thought my master directed them to me only; and I fancied that he observed me with unusual earnestness. I was farther confirmed in this belief, as I looked round the church and could see no one person besides myself in such grief and distress as I was. I began to think that my master hated me, and was very desirous to go home to my own country; for I thought that if God did come, as he said, he would certainly be most angry with *me*, as I did not know what he was, nor had ever heard of him before.

I went home in great trouble, but said nothing to anybody. I was somewhat afraid of my master; for I thought he disliked me. The next text I heard him preach from was, 'Follow peace with all men, and holiness, without which no man shall see the Lord.' (Heb. xii. 14.) He preached the law so severely, that it made me tremble. He said that God would judge the whole world, Ethiopia, Asia, Africa, and everywhere. I was now excessively perplexed, and undetermined what to do, as I had now reason to believe that my situation would be equally bad, to go as to stay. I kept these thoughts to myself, and said nothing to any person whatever.

(6–10)

b. The Pains of Conversion; Freedom

I could find no relief, nor the least shadow of comfort, and the extreme distress of my mind so affected my health that I continued ill for three days and nights, and would admit of no means to be taken for my recovery, though my lady was very kind, and sent many things to me. I rejected every means of relief, and wished to die. I would not go into my bed, but lay in the stable upon some straw. I felt all the horrors of a troubled conscience, so hard to be borne, and saw all the vengeance of God ready to overtake me. I was sensible that there was no way for me to be saved unless I came to Christ, and I could not come to him; for I thought it was impossible that he should receive such a sinner as I.

The last night that I continued in this place, in the midst of my distress, these words were brought home upon my mind; 'Behold the Lamb of God.' I was something comforted at this, and began to grow easier, and wished for day, that I might find these words in my Bible. I rose very early the following morning, and went to my schoolmaster, Mr. Vanosdore, and communicated the situation of my mind to him. He was greatly rejoiced to find me inquiring the way to Zion, and blessed the Lord who had worked so wonderfully for me, a poor heathen. I was more familiar with this good gentleman than with my master, or any other person; and found myself more at liberty to talk to him. He encouraged me greatly, and prayed with me frequently, and I was always benefited by his discourse.

About a quarter of a mile from my master's house stood a large and remarkably fine oak tree, in the midst of a wood. I often used to be employed there in cutting down trees, (a work I was very fond of,) and I seldom failed going to this place every day, sometimes twice a day, if I could be spared. It was the greatest pleasure I ever experienced to sit under this oak, for there I used to pour out my complaints before the Lord; and when I had any particular grievance, I used to go there, and talk to the tree, and tell my sorrows as if it were to a friend. Here I often lamented my own wicked heart and undone state, and found more comfort and consolation than I ever was sensible of before. Whenever I was treated with ridicule and contempt, I used to come here and find peace. I was glad to be employed in cutting wood; it was a great part of my business, and I followed it with delight, as I was then quite alone, and my heart lifted up to God, and I was enabled to pray continually; and, blessed for ever by his holy name, he mercifully answered my prayers. I can never be thankful enough to almighty God for the many comfortable opportunities I experienced there.

It is possible that the circumstance I am going to relate will not gain credit with many; but this I know, that the joy and comfort it conveyed to me cannot be expressed, and only conceived by those who have experienced the like.

I was one day in a most delightful frame of mind, and my heart overflowed with love and gratitude to the Author of all my comforts. I was so drawn out of myself, and so filled and awed by the presence of God, that I saw (or thought I saw) light inexpressible dart down from heaven upon me, and shine around me for the space of a minute. I continued on my knees, and joy unspeakable took possession of my soul. The peace and serenity which filled my mind after this was wonderful, and cannot be told. I would not have changed situations with any person, or been any one but myself for the world. I blessed God for my poverty, and that I had no worldly riches or grandeur to draw my heart from him. I wished at that time, if it had been possible, to have continued on that spot for ever. I felt an unwillingness in myself to have anything more to do with the world, or to mix with society again. I seemed to possess a full assurance that my sins were forgiven me. I went home, all my way rejoicing, when this text of Scripture came full upon my mind; 'And I will make an everlasting covenant with them, that I will not turn away from them to do them good; but I will put my fear in their hearts, that they shall not depart from me.' The first opportunity that presented itself, I went to my old schoolmaster, and made known to him the happy state of my soul, who joined with me in praise to God for his mercy to me, the vilest of sinners. I was now perfectly easy, and had scarcely a wish to make beyond what I possessed, when my temporal comforts were all blasted by the death of Mr. Freelandhouse, who was taken from this world rather suddenly. He died of a fever, after a very short illness. Before he died he told me that he had given me my freedom, and that I was at liberty to go where I would. He added, that he had always prayed for me, and he hoped that I should be kept unto the end. My master left me, by his will, ten pounds and my freedom.

(12–13)

c. The Shortcomings of Christian England

I never knew how to set a proper value on money. If I had but a little meat and drink to supply the present necessities of life, I never wished for more; and when I had any, I always gave it where I saw an object in distress. If it was not for my dear wife and children, I should pay as little regard to money now as I did at that time. I continued some time with Mr. Dunscum as his servant, and he was very kind to me. But I had a vast inclination to visit England, and wished continually that it would please Providence to make a clear way for me to see this island. I entertained a notion that if I could get to England, I should never more experience either cruelty or ingratitude; so that I was very desirous to get among Christians. I knew Mr. Whitfield very well. I had often heard him preach at New York. In this disposition I enlisted in the 28th regiment of foot, who were designed for Martinico, in the late war. We went in Admiral Pocock's fleet from New York to Barbadoes, and from thence to Martinico. When that was taken, we proceeded to the Havannah, and took that place likewise. There I got discharged. I was at that time worth about thirty pounds, but I never regarded money in the least. I would not tarry for my prize-money, lest I should lose my chance of going to England. I went with the Spanish prisoners to Spain, and came to Old England with the English prisoners. I cannot describe my joy when we arrived within sight of Portsmouth. But I was astonished, when we landed, to hear the inhabitants of that place curse and swear, and be otherwise profane. I expected to find nothing but goodness, gentleness, and meekness in this Christian land, and I suffered great perplexity of mind at seeing so much wickedness.

I inquired if any serious Christian people resided there, and the woman I made the inquiry of answered me in the affirmative, and added that she was one of them. I was heartily glad to hear her say so. I thought I could give her my whole heart. She kept a public house. I deposited with her all the money that I had not an immediate occasion for, as I thought it would be safer with her. I gave her twenty-five guineas, six of which I desired her to lay out to the best advantage, in buying me some shirts, a hat, and some other necessaries. I made her a present of a very handsome large looking glass that I brought with me from Martinico, in order to recompense her for the trouble I had given her. I must do this woman the justice to acknowledge that she did lay out some little for my use, but the nineteen guineas, and part of the six guineas, with my watch, she would not return, but denied that I ever gave them to her.

I soon perceived that I had got amongst bad people, who defrauded me of money and watch, and that all my promised happiness was blasted. I had no friend but God, and I prayed to him earnestly. I could scarcely believe it possible that the place where so many eminent Christians had lived and preached could abound with so much wickedness and deceit. I thought it worse than Sodom, considering the great advantage they possessed. I cried like a child, and that almost continually. At length God heard my prayers, and raised me up a friend indeed.

This publican had a brother who lived on Portsmouth Common, whose wife was a very serious, good woman. When she heard of the treatment I had met with, she came and inquired into my real situation, and was greatly troubled at the ill usage I had received, and she took me home to her own house. I now began to rejoice, and my prayer was turned into praise. She made use of all the arguments in her power to prevail upon her who had wronged me to return my watch and money, but it was to no purpose, as she had given me no receipt, and I had nothing to show for it; so that I could not demand it. My good friend was excessively angry with her, and obliged her to give me back four guineas, which she said she gave me out of charity, though, in fact, it was my own, and a great deal more. She would have employed other means to oblige her to give up my money, but I would not suffer her. 'Let it go,' said I; 'my God is in heaven.' I did not mind my loss in the least. All that grieved me was that I had been disappointed in finding some Christian friends, with whom I hoped to enjoy a little sweet and comfortable society.

I thought the best method that I could take now was to go to London, and find out Mr. Whitfield, who was the only living soul that I knew in England, and get him to direct me how to procure a living without being troublesome to any person. I took leave of my Christian friends at Portsmouth, and went in the stage to London. A creditable tradesman in the city, who went up with me in the stage, offered to show me the way to Mr. Whitfield's tabernacle, knowing that I was a perfect stranger. I thought it very kind, and accepted his offer; but he obliged me to give him half-a-crown for going with me, and likewise insisted on my giving him five shillings more for conducting me to Dr. Gifford's meeting.

I began now to entertain a very different idea of the inhabitants of England to what I had figured to myself before I came among them. Mr. Whitfield received me very friendly, was heartily glad to see me, and directed me to a proper place to board and lodge, in Petticoat-lane, till he could think of some way to settle me in, and paid for my lodging, and all my expenses. The morning after I came to my new lodgings, as I was at breakfast with the gentlewoman of the house, I heard the noise of some looms over our heads, and upon inquiring what it was, she told me that a person was weaving silk. I expressed a great desire to see it, and asked if I might. She told me that she would go up with me, for she was sure that I should be very welcome; and she was as good as her word. As soon as we entered the room, the person that was weaving looked about and smiled upon us, and I loved her from that moment. She asked me many questions, and I, in return, talked a great deal to her. I found that she was a member of Mr. Allen's meeting, and I began to entertain a good opinion of her, though I was almost afraid to indulge this inclination, lest she should prove like the rest that I had met with, at Portsmouth, &c., and which had almost given me a dislike to all white women. But after a short acquaintance, I had the happiness to find that she was very different, and quite sincere, and I was not without hopes that she entertained some esteem for me. We often went together to hear Dr. Gifford. As I had always a propensity to relieve every object in distress as far as I was able, I used to give to all that complained to me, sometimes half a guinea at a time, as I did not understand the real value of it. But this good woman took great pains to correct and advise me in that and many other respects.

After I had been in London about six weeks, I was recommended to the notice of some acquaintances of my late master, Mr. Freelandhouse, who had heard him speak frequently of me. I was much persuaded by them to go to Holland, as my master lived there before he bought me, and he used to speak of me so respectfully among his friends there, that it raised in them a curiosity to see me, particularly the gentlemen engaged in the ministry, who expressed a desire to hear my experience and to examine me. I found that it was my good old master's design that I should have gone if he had lived, for which reason I resolved upon going to Holland, and informed my dear friend Mr. Whitfield of my intention. He was much averse to my going at first; but after I gave him my reasons he appeared very well satisfied. I likewise informed my Betty (the good woman that I have just named) of my determination to go to Holland, and told her I believed she was to be my wife; and if it was the Lord's will I desired it, but not else. She made me very little answer, but has since told me that she did not think it at that time.

(16–18)

d. Hard Times

The boundless goodness of God to me has been so very great, that with the most humble gratitude I desire to prostrate myself before him; for I have been wonderfully supported in every affliction. My God never left me.

My dear wife and I were now both unemployed, and we could get nothing to do. The winter proved remarkably severe, and we were reduced to the greatest distress imaginable. I was always very shy at asking for anything, and could never beg; neither did I choose to make known our wants to any person, for fear of offending, as we were entire strangers; but our last bit of bread was gone, and I was obliged to think of something to do for our support. I did not mind for myself at all, but to see my dear wife and children in want, pierced me to the heart. I now blamed myself for bringing her from London, as, doubtless, had we continued there, we might have found friends to have kept us from starving. The snow was at this season remarkably deep, so that we could see no prospect of being relieved. In this melancholy situation, not knowing what step to pursue, I resolved to make my case known to a gentleman's gardener that lived near us, and entreat him to employ me; but when I came to him my courage failed me, and I was ashamed to make known our real situation. I endeavoured all that I could to prevail on him to set me to work, but to no purpose, for he assured me that it was not in his power. But just when I was about to leave him, he asked me if I would accept of some carrots. I took them with great thankfulness, and carried them home. He gave me four, and they were very large and fine. We had nothing to make a fire with, consequently we could not boil them, but we were glad to have them to eat raw. Our youngest child was then an infant, so that my wife was obliged to chew it, and feed her in that manner for several days. We allowed ourselves but one every day, lest they should not last till we could get some other supply. I was unwilling to eat at all myself, nor would I take any the last day that we continued in this situation, as I could not bear the thought that my wife and children should be in want of the means of support. We lived in this manner till our carrots were gone, and then my wife began to lament because of our poor babes. I comforted her all that I could, still hoping and believing that my God would not let us die, but that it would please him to relieve us, which he did almost by a miracle. We went to bed as usual, before it was quite dark, as we had neither fire nor candle; but we had not been there long before some person knocked at the door and inquired if James Albert lived there. I answered in the affirmative, and rose immediately. As soon as I opened the door, I found that it was the servant of an eminent attorney who resided at Colchester. He asked how it was with me, and if I was almost starved. I burst out into crying, and told him that I was indeed. He said that his master supposed so, and that he wanted to speak with me, and I must return with him. This gentleman's name was Danniel. When I came to his house, he told me that he had thought a great deal about me of late, and was apprehensive that I must be in want, and could not be satisfied till he had sent to inquire after me. I made known my distress to him, at which he was greatly affected, and generously gave me a guinea, and promised to be kind to me in future. I could not help exclaiming, 'O the boundless mercies of my God! I prayed unto him, and he has heard me. I trusted in him, and he has preserved me. Where shall I begin to praise him, or how shall I love him enough?'

I immediately went and bought some bread and cheese, and some coal, and carried them home. My dear wife was rejoiced to see me return with something to eat. She instantly got up and dressed our babes, whilst I made a fire; and the first nobility in the land never made a better meal. We did not forget to thank the Lord for all his goodness to us. Soon after this, as the spring came on, Mr. Peter Danniel employed me in helping to pull down a house, and to rebuild it. I had then very good work, and full employ. He sent for my wife and children to Colchester, and provided a house for us, where we lived very comfortably. I worked at his house for more than a year, till it was finished, and after that I was employed by several successively.

I had at this time an offer made me of going to Norwich, and having constant employ. My wife seemed pleased with this pro-posal, as she supposed that she might get work there in the weaving manufactory; that being the business she was brought up to, and more likely to succeed there than in any other place; and we thought as we had an opportunity of moving to a town where we might both be employed, it was most advisable to do so, and that probably we might settle there for our lives. When this step was resolved upon, I went first alone, to see how it would answer, which I afterwards very much repented; for it was not in my power immediately to send my wife any supply, as I fell into the hands of a master that was neither kind nor considerate. She was reduced to great distress, so that she was obliged to sell the few goods that we had; and when I sent for her, she was under the necessity of parting with our bed.

When she came to Norwich, I hired a room ready furnished. I experienced a great deal of difference in the carriage of my master from what I had been accustomed to from some of my other masters, and he was very irregular in his payments to me. My wife hired a loom, and wove all the leisure time that she had, and we began to do very well, till we were overtaken by fresh misfortunes. Our three poor children fell ill of the smallpox, which was a great trial to us; but still I was persuaded in myself that we should not be forsaken. I did all in my power to keep my dear partner's spirits from sinking. As her whole attention was now taken up by the children, she could mind nothing else, and all that I could get was but little to support a family in such a situation, besides paying for the hire of our room, which I was obliged to omit doing for several weeks; but the woman to whom we were indebted threatened that if we did not pay her immediately, she would turn us all into the street. The apprehension of this plunged me into the deepest distress, considering the situation of my poor babes. But my God, still faithful to his promise, raised me up a friend. Mr. Henry Gurdney, a Quaker, heard of our distress, and sent a servant to the woman we hired our room from, who paid our rent, and bought all the goods, with my wife's loom, and gave us them all.

Some other gentlemen hearing of his design, were pleased to assist him in these generous acts, for which we can never be sufficiently thankful. After this my children soon came about, and we began to do pretty well again. My dear wife worked hard and constantly when she could get work, but it was very disagreeable, her employ being so uncertain. I was far from being happy with my master, as he did not use me well. I could scarcely ever get my money from him; yet I continued patient till it pleased God to alter my situation.

My worthy friend Mr. Gurdney advised me to follow the employment of chopping chaff, and bought me an instrument for that purpose. There were but few persons in the town that made this their business besides myself, so that I did very well indeed, and we became quite easy and happy. But we did not continue long in this comfortable state, as many of the inferior people were envious and ill natured, and they commenced the same employ, and worked under price on purpose to get my business from me; and they succeeded so well that I could scarcely get anything to do, and we became again unfortunate. Nor did this misfortune come alone, for just at this time we lost one of our little girls, who died of a fever. This circumstance occasioned us new troubles, for the Baptist minister refused to bury her because we were not their members, and the parson of the parish denied because she had never been baptized. I applied to the Quakers, but met with no success. At length I resolved to dig a grave in the garden behind the house, and bury her there, when the parson of the parish sent to tell me that he would bury the child, but did not choose to read the burial service over her. I told him that I did not care whether he would or no, *as the child could not hear it.*

We met with a great deal of ill treatment after this, and we found it very difficult to live. We could scarcely get work to do, and were obliged to pawn our clothes. We were ready to sink under our troubles, when I proposed to my wife to go to Kidderminister, and try if we could succeed any better there.

I left my wife once more, and set out for Kidderminster, in order to judge if the situation would suit us. As soon as I arrived there I waited upon Mr. Fawcett, who was pleased to receive me very kindly, and recommended me to Mr. Watson, who employed me in twisting silk and worsted together. I continued here about a fortnight, and when I thought that it would answer our expectation, I returned to Norwich to fetch my wife. She was then near her time, and too much indisposed, so that we were obliged to tarry until she was brought to bed; and as soon as she could conveniently travel, we came to Kidderminster; but we brought nothing with us, as we were obliged to sell all that we had to pay our debts, and the expenses of my wife's illness, &c.

Such is our situation. My wife, by hard labour at the loom, does everything that can be expected from her towards the maintenance of our family, and God is pleased to incline his people to yield us their charitable assistance, being myself, through age and infirmities, able to contribute but little to their support. And as poor pilgrims, we are travelling through many difficulties, waiting for the call, when the Lord shall deliver us out of the evils of this world, and bring us to the everlasting glories of the world to come. To him be praise for ever and ever. Amen.

3

IGNATIUS SANCHO
1729–1780

The Letters of the late Ignatius Sancho

London, 1782

Igantius Sancho, who was to become the most urbane and mannered of the 18th century Afro-British authors, suffered from one of the unhappiest starts in life. He was born on a slave ship, separated from his parents in infancy, then sold to three maiden ladies 'resident in Greenwich, whose prejudices had unhappily taught them, that African ignorance was the only security for obedience, and that to enlarge the mind of their slave would go near to emancipate his person' (James Jekyll's, 'The Life of Ignatius Sancho' i–ii, a memoir written as a preface to the 1782 edition of the *Letters*). But the Duke of Montagu, well-known for his anti-slavery and anti-racist views, by chance meeting the teenage Sancho, found in him 'a native frankness of manner as yet unbroken by servitude and unrefined by education' (Jekyll iii). The Duke looked on Sancho as his protégé, loaned him books, and urged the three ugly sisters to do something about his education: but they continued to see him merely as their slave, and, Jekyll says, even threatened to re-sell him into American slavery. At this he ran away and sought the protection of the Montagus.

All this took place before the Mansfield Decision of 1772,[1] and according to the law at this time, the three ladies were within their rights. The Duchess of Montagu took him into service, where he was to become a respected and admired servant over many years during which he had the opportunity to enjoy the friendship of the novelist Sterne and the actor David Garrick.

The circumstances of his birth and upbringing meant that he had no direct memories of Africa, and he gives a first impression of having been wholly assimilated into the styles and values of polite English society. But closer consideration of the *Letters* leads to the conclusion that there are tensions and paradoxes of feeling in them which need to be recognised and

24

have recently even been seen as conscious strategies of protest (for books and articles discussing this see the bibliography under Edwards and Sandiford). Though for much of his life he was not subjected to the worst brutalities of slavery, the very fact of the colour of his skin, and the prejudiced attitudes to race adopted by many in his society would have made him conscious of his African origins: this emerges in his letters in a more muted fashion than in the writings of his near contemporaries, Equiano and Cugoano, whose early youth was spent in Africa.

Jekyll's memoir tells us that in middle life Sancho grew over-fond of gambling. However, he had many less frivolous interests. He became a devotee of the theatre, and gained a reputation as a sound judge of the arts, in particular painting and music. His correspondence with the novelist, Sterne, was well known, and though Sancho failed to impress as an actor, he became a friend of Garrick, wrote music, some examples of which have survived, and befriended a number of painters and sculptors. He married, and settled into domesticity, his wife, Anne, giving birth to six children. By 1773, gout and corpulence had made it impossible for him to continue as a senior household servant to the family of his patron, the late Duke, and he settled down in London to run a grocery business in Charles St., Mayfair. His children, the 'Sanchonets' as he himself called them, became the recurring subjects of his affectionate letters. His son, William, who had worked as a librarian for the great botanist, Sir Joseph Banks, continued to run the store after his father's death as a bookshop, and Sancho's letters continued to be widely read, sufficiently so for William to re-issue them in an edition of 1803. The letters cover a wide range of topics, but his affection for his family, particularly young William, is a recurrent theme, which brings out the more engaging aspects of Sancho's stylistic debt to the sentimental novelist, his friend Sterne:

> You cannot imagine what hold little Billy gets of me – he grows prattles – every day learns something new – and by his good-will would be ever in the shop with me – The monkey! he clings round my legs – and if I chide him or look sour, he holds up his little mouth to kiss me. – I know I am the fool – for parents' weakness is child's strength: – truth orthodox – which will hold good between lover and lovee ... Mrs. Sancho is so-so – The virgins are as well as youth and innocence – souls void of care and consciences [consciousness?] of offence can be. Dame Sancho would be better if she cared less. – I am her barometer – If a sigh escapes me, it is answered by a tear in her eye. – I oft assume a gaiety to illume her dear

sensibility with a smile – which twenty years ago almost
bewitched me: – and MARK! – after twenty years enjoyment constitutes my highest pleasure! (Letter LIV, 111–
115)

Of Sancho's letters, by far the best known in his own day,
and included here, was the one written to Sterne praising his
words against slavery and published in the 1775 edition of the
novelist's letters, as well as in Fitzgerald's *Life of Sterne*, in
both instances along with Sterne's reply, a facsimile of the
latter being included as an appendix in early editions of
Sancho. We also include two letters to his friend Julius
Soubise, an African 'man about town' and favourite of the
Duchess of Queensbury. The sole survivor of Soubise's own
letters will be found with a brief account of his life, on
pp. 81–2. Sancho's letter describing the Gordon Riots in
London in 1780 displays the anti-radical feeling of an English
gentleman in business, but, combined with Sancho's nervous
conservatism, a strong sense of human comedy; and we include
one letter to a young man, Jack Wingrave, son of one of
Sancho's English friends, who had gone out to India and
written home in a prejudiced way about the conduct of the
natives, which provides Sancho with a platform for an attack
on the savagery and greed of the 'Christian navigators', the
European East-India traders, as well as a defence of Christian
commerce. Such seemingly contradictory responses to the
commercial impulse are to be found elsewhere in the black
writers of the period, notably in Equiano.

The text is taken from the so-called 5th edition, published in
1802/3 by Sancho's son William, reissued with an introduction
by P. Edwards, in Dawson's Colonial History series, London
1968. We have not been able to trace third and fourth editions,
and in claiming that his edition was the fifth, William may have
been trying to give the impression that interest in his father's
letters had remained as high in the intervening years, as it had
been on the publication of the first and second editions.

a. To Mr. Sterne

July, 1776.

REVEREND SIR,

IT would be an insult on your humanity (or perhaps look like it) to
apologize for the liberty I am taking. – I am one of those people
whom the vulgar and illiberal call '*Negurs*.' – The first part of my
life was rather unlucky, as I was placed in a family who judged

ignorance the best and only security for obedience. – A little reading
and writing I got by unwearied application. – The latter part of my
life has been – thro' God's blessing, truly fortunate, having spent it
in the service of one of the best families in the kingdom. – My chief
pleasure has been books. – Philanthropy I adore. – How very much,
good Sir, am I (amongst millions) indebted to you for the character
of your amiable uncle Toby! – I declare, I would walk ten miles in
the dog-days, to shake hands with the honest corporal. – Your
Sermons have touch'd me to the heart, and I hope have amended it,
which brings me to the point. – In your tenth discourse, page
seventy-eight, in the second volume – is the very affecting passage –
'Consider how great a part of our species – in all ages down to this –
have been trod under the feet of cruel and capricious tyrants, who
would neither hear their cries, nor pity their distresses, – Consider
slavery – what it is – how bitter a draught and how many millions
are made to drink it!' – Of all my favourite authors, not one has
drawn a tear in favour of my miserable black brethren – excepting
yourself, and the humane author of Sir George Ellison. – I think
you will forgive me; – I am sure you will applaud me for beseeching
you to give one half-hour's attention to slavery, as it is at this day
practised in our West Indies. – That subject, handled in your
striking manner, would ease the yoke (perhaps) of many – but if
only of one – Gracious God! – what a feast to a benevolent heart! –
and, sure I am, you are an epicurean in acts of charity. – You, who
are universally read, and as universally admired – you could not fail
– Dear Sir, think in me you behold the uplifted hands of thousands
of my brother Moors. – Grief you pathetically observe is eloquent;
– figure to yourself their attitudes; – hear their supplicating
addresses! – alas! – you cannot refuse. – Humanity must comply –
in which hope I beg permission to subscribe myself,

Reverend Sir, &c.

IGN. SANCHO.

b. To Mr. F—: On Phillis Wheatley[2]

Charles Street, January 27, 1778.

FULL heartily and most cordially do I thank thee, good Mr. F—, for
your kindness in sending the books – That upon the unchristian and
most diabolical usage of my brother Negroes – the illegality – the
horrid wickedness of the traffic – the cruel carnage and depopula-

tion of the human species – is painted in such strong colours – that I should think would (if duly attended to) flash conviction – and produce remorse in every enlightened and candid reader. – The perusal affected me more than I can express; – and indeed I felt a double or mixt sensation – for while my heart was torn for the sufferings – which, for aught I know – some of my nearest kin might have undergone – my bosom, at the same time, glowed with gratitude – and praise toward the humane – the Christian – the friendly and learned Author of that most valuable book. – Blest be your feet! – and Heaven's peace be ever upon them! – I, who, thank God! am no bigot – but honour virtue – and the practise of the great moral duties – equally in the turban – or the lawn-sleeves – who think Heaven big enough for all the race of man – and hope to see and mix amongst the whole family of Adam in bliss hereafter – I with these notions (which, perhaps, some may style absurd) look upon the friendly Author – as being far superior to any great name upon your continent. – I could wish that every member of each house of parliament had one of these books. – And if his Majesty perused one through the breakfast – though it might spoil his appetite – yet the consciousness of having it in his power to facilitate the great work – would give an additional sweetness to his tea. – Phyllis's poems do credit to nature – and put art – merely as art – to the blush. – It reflects nothing either to the glory or generosity of her master – if she is still his slave – except he glories in the *low vanity* of having in his wanton power a mind animated by Heaven – a genius superior to himself. – The list of splendid – titled – learned names, in confirmation of her being the real authoress – alas! shows how very poor the acquisition of wealth and knowledge is – without generosity – feeling – and humanity. – These good great folks – all know – and perhaps admired – nay, praised Genius in bondage – and then, like the Priests and the Levites in sacred writ, passed by – not one good Samaritan amongst them. – I shall be ever glad to see you – and am, with many thanks,

                                        Your most humble servant,
                                        IGNATIUS SANCHO.

c. To Mr. J— W—e [Jack Wingrave]: On India, Trade and a Good Library

1778

YOUR good father insists on my scribbling a sheet of absurdities, and gives me a notable reason for it, that is, 'Jack will be pleased with it.' – Now be it known to you – I have a respect both for father and son – yea for the whole family, who are every soul (that I have the honor or pleasure to know any thing of) tinctured – and leavened with all the obsolete goodness of old times – so that a man runs some hazard in being seen in the W—'s society of being biassed to Christianity. – I never see your poor father but his eyes betray his feelings for the hopeful youth in India – A tear of joy dancing upon the lids is a plaudit not to be equalled this side death! – See the effects of right-doing, my worthy friend – Continue in the track of rectitude – and despite poor paltry Europeans – titled, Nabobs – Read your Bible – As day follows night, God's blessing follows virtue – honor and riches bring up the rear – and the end is peace. – Courage, my boy – I have done preaching. – Old folks love to seem wise – and if you are silly enough to correspond with gray hairs, take the consequence. – I have had the pleasure of reading most of your letters, through the kindness of your father. – Youth is naturally prone to vanity – Such is the weakness of human nature, that pride has a fortress in the best of hearts – I know no person that possesses a better than Johnny W—e: – but although flattery is poison to youth, yet truth obliges me to confess that your correspondence betrays no symptom of vanity – but seems with truths of an honest affection, which merits praise – and commands esteem.

In some one of your letters which I do not recollect – you speak (with honest indignation) of the treachery and chicanery of the Natives[3]. – My good friend, you should remember from whom they learnt those vices: – The first Christian visitors found them a simple, harmless people – but the cursed avidity for wealth urged these first visitors (and all the succeeding ones) to such acts of deception – and even wanton cruelty – that the poor ignorant Natives soon learnt to turn the knavish and diabolical arts – which they too soon imbibed – upon their teachers.

I am sorry to observe that the practice of your country (which as a resident I love – and for its freedom, and for the many blessings I enjoy in it, shall ever have my warmest wishes, prayers, and blessings): I say it is with reluctance that I must observe your country's conduct has been uniformly wicked in the East – West-Indies – and even on the coast of Guinea. – The grand object of English navigators – indeed of all Christian navigators – is money – money – money – for which I do not pretend to blame them – Commerce was meant by the goodness of the Deity to diffuse the various goods of the earth into every part – to unite mankind in the blessed chains of brotherly love, society, and mutual dependence: – the enlightened Christian should diffuse the Riches of the Gospel of peace, with the commodities of his respective land – Commerce attended with strict honesty, and with Religion for its companion, would be a blessing to every shore it touched at. – In Africa, the poor, wretched natives – blessed with the most fertile and luxuriant soil – are rendered so much the more miserable for what Providence meant as a blessing: – the Christians' abominable Traffic for slaves – and the horrid cruelty and treachery of the petty Kings – encouraged by their Christian customers – who carry them strong liquors, to enflame their national madness – and powder and bad fire-arms, to furnish them with the hellish means of killing and kidnapping. – But enough – it is a subject that sours my blood – and I am sure it will not please the friendly bent of your social affections. – I mentioned these only to guard my friend against being too hasty in condemning the knavery of a people who, bad as they may be – possibly – were made worse by their Christian visitors. – Make human nature thy study, whereever thou residest – whatever the religion, or the complexion, study their hearts. – Simplicity, kindness, and charity be thy guide! With these even Savages will respect you – and God will bless you.

Your father, who sees every improvement of his boy with delight, observes that your handwriting is much for the better – In truth, I think it is as well as any modest man can wish. – If my long epistles do not frighten you – and I live till the return of next spring – perhaps I shall be enabled to judge how much you are improved since your last favor – Write me a deal about the natives – the soil and produce – the domestic and interior manners of the people – customs – prejudices – fashions – and follies. – Alas! we have plenty of the two last here – and, what is worse, we have politics – and a detestable Brothers' war trumpets – shouts of combatants – and thunder of cannon – All these he can bear with soldier-like fortitude – with now and then a secret wish for the society of his London friends – in the sweet blessed security of peace and friendship.

This, young man, is my second letter – I have wrote till I am stupid, I perceive – I ought to have found it out two pages back. – Mrs. Sancho joins me in good wishes – I join her in the same – in which double sense believe me,

Yours, &c. &c.

I. SANCHO.

Very short.

[POSTSCRIPT]

It is with sincere pleasure I hear you have a lucrative establishment – which will enable you to appear and act with decency – Your good sense will naturally lead you to proper economy – as distant from frigid parsimony, as from a heedless extravagancy – But as you may possibly have some time to spare upon your hands for necessary recreation, give me leave to obtrude my poor advice. – I have heard it more than once observed of fortunate adventurers – they have come home enriched in purse, but wretchedly barren in intellects – The mind, my dear Jack, wants food – as well as the stomach – Why then should not one wish to increase in knowledge as well as money? – Young says – 'Books are fair Virtue's advocates and friends' – Now my advice is – to preserve about £20 a year for two or three seasons – by which means you may gradually form a useful, elegant, little library – Suppose now the first year you send the order, and the money, to your father, for the following books – which I recommend from my own superficial knowledge as useful. – A man should know a little of Geography – History – nothing more useful, or pleasant.

Robertson's Charles the Fifth, 4 vols.

Goldsmith's History of Greece, 2 vols.

Ditto, of Rome, 2 vols.

Ditto, of England, 4 vols.

Two small volumes of Sermons useful – and very sensible – by one Mr. Williams, a dissenting minister – which are as well as fifty – for I love not a multiplicity of doctrines – A few plain tenets, easy, simple, and directed to the heart, are better than volumes of controversial nonsense. – Spectators – Guardians – and Tatlers – you have of course. – Young's Night-Thoughts – Milton – and Thomson's Seasons were my summer companions for near twenty years – They mended my heart – they improved my veneration of the Deity – and increased my love to my neighbours.

You have to thank God for strong natural parts – a feeling humane heart – You write with sense and judicious discernment – Improve yourself, my dear Jack, that, if it should please God to return you to your friends with the fortune of a man in upper rank, the embellishments of your mind may be ever considered as greatly superior to your riches – and only inferior to the goodness of your heart. I give you the above as a sketch – Your father and other of your friends will improve upon it in the course of time – I do indeed judge that the above is enough at first – in conformity with the old adage – 'A few Books and a few Friends, and those well chosen.'

Adieu, Yours,

I. SANCHO.

d. To J— S—, Esq. [John Spink]: On the Gordon Riots[4]

Charles Street, June 6, 1780.

DEAR AND MOST RESPECTED SIR,

In the midst of the most cruel and ridiculous confusion, I am now set down to give you a very imperfect sketch of the maddest people that the maddest times were ever plagued with. – The public prints have informed you (without doubt) of last Friday's transactions; – the insanity of Lord George Gordon, and the worse than Negro barbarity of the populace; – the burnings and devastations of each night you will also see in the prints: – This day, by consent, was set apart for the further consideration of the wished-for-repeal; – The people (who had their proper cue from his lordship) assembled by ten o'clock in the morning – Lord N[orth], who had been up in Council at home till four in the morning, got to the house before eleven, just a quarter of an hour before the associators reached Palace-yard: – But I should tell you, in Council there was a deputation from all parties; – The S[helburne] party was for prosecuting Ld G—, and leaving him at large; – the At[torne]y G[enera]l laughed at the idea, and declared it was doing just nothing; – The M[inorit]y were for his expulsion, and so dropping him gently into insignificancy; – that was thought wrong, as he would still be industrious in mischief; – The R[ockingha]m party, I should suppose, you will think counselled best, which is, this day to expel him from the house – commit him to the Tower – and then prosecute him at leisure – by which means he will lose the opportunity of getting a seat in the next parliament, and have decent leisure to repent him of the heavy evils he has occasioned. – There is at this present moment at least a hundred thousand poor, miserable, ragged rabble, from twelve to sixty years of age, with blue cockades in their hats – besides half as many women and children, all parading the streets – the bridge – the Park – ready for any and every mischief. – Gracious God! what's the matter now? I was obliged to leave off – the shouts of the mob – the horrid clashing of swords – and the clutter of a multitude in swiftest motion – drew me to the door – when every one in the street was employed in shutting up shop. – It is now just five o'clock – the ballad-singers are exhausting their musical talents with, the downfall of Popery, S[andwic]h, and N—h. – Lord S—h narrowly escaped with life about an hour since; the mob seized his chariot going to the house, broke his glasses, and, in struggling to get his lordship out, they somehow have cut his face – The guards flew to his assistance – the light-horse scowered the road, got his chariot, escorted him from the coffee-house, where he had fled for protection, to his carriage, and guarded him bleeding very fast home. This – this – is liberty! genuine British liberty! – This instant about two thousand liberty boys are swearing and swaggering by with large sticks – thus armed, in hopes of meeting with the Irish chairmen and labourers – All the guards are out – and all the horse; – the poor fellows are just worn out for want of rest, having been on duty ever since Friday. – Thank heaven, it rains; may it increase, so as to send these deluded wretches safe to their homes, their families, and wives! About two this afternoon, a large party took it into their heads to visit the King and Queen, and entered the Park for that purpose – but found the guard too numerous to be forced, and after some useless attempts gave it up. – It is reported, the house will either be prorogued, or parliament dissolved, this evening, as it is in vain to think of attending any business while this anarchy lasts.

I cannot but felicitate you, my good friend, upon the happy distance you are placed from our scene of confusion. May foul Discord and her cursed train never approach your blessed abode! Tell Mrs. S—, her good heart would ache, did she see the anxiety, the woe, in the faces of mothers, wives, and sweethearts, each equally anxious for the object of their wishes, the beloved of their hearts. – Mrs. Sancho and self both cordially join in love and gratitude, and every good wish – crowned with the peace of God, which passeth all understanding, &c.

I am, dear Sir,

Yours ever by inclination,

IGN. SANCHO.

[POSTSCRIPT,]

The Sardinian ambassador offered 500 guineas to the rabble to save a painting of our Saviour from the flames, and 1000 guineas not to destroy an exceeding fine organ: The gentry told him, they would burn him if they could get at him, and destroyed the picture and organ directly. – I am not sorry I was born in Afric. – I shall tire you, I fear – and, if I cannot get a frank, make you pay dear for bad news. – There is about a thousand mad men, armed with clubs, bludgeons, and crows, just now set off for Newgate, to liberate, they say, their honest comrades. – I wish they do not some of them lose their lives of liberty before morning. It is thought by many who discern deeply, that there is more at the bottom of this business than merely the repeal of an act which has as yet produced no bad consequences, and perhaps never might. – I am forced to own that I am for an universal toleration. Let us convert by our example, and conquer by our meekness and brotherly love!

Eight o'clock. – Lord George Gordon has this moment announced to my Lords the mob – that the act shall be repealed this evening: – Upon this, they gave a hundred cheers – took the horses from his hackney-coach – and rolled him full jollily away: They are huzzaing now ready to crack their throats.

Huzzah.

I am forced to conclude for want of room – The remainder in our next.

e. To Mr. S—e [Soubise]: Good Advice to a Fellow Sufferer

Richmond, Oct. 11, 1772.

YOUR letter gave me more pleasure than in truth I ever expected from your hands – but thou art a flatterer; – why dost thou demand advice of me? Young man, thou canst not discern wood from trees; – with awe and reverence look up to thy more than parents – look up to thy almost divine benefactors – search into the motive of every glorious action – retrace thine own history – and when you are convinced that they (like the All-gracious Power they serve) go

about in mercy doing good – retire abashed at the number of their
virtues – and humbly beg the Almighty to inspire and give you
strength to imitate them. – Happy, happy lad! what a fortune is
thine! – Look round upon the miserable fate of almost all of our
unfortunate colour – superadded to ignorance, – see slavery, and the
contempt of those very wretches who roll in affluence from our
labours. Superadded to this woeful catalogue – hear the ill-bred and
heart-racking abuse of the foollish vulgar – You, S—e, tread as
cautiously as the strictest rectitude can guide ye – yet must you
suffer from this – but armed with truth – honesty – and conscious
integrity – you will be sure of the plaudit and countenance of the
good. – If, therefore, thy repentance is sincere – I congratulate thee
as sincerely upon it – it is thy birth-day to real happiness. –
Providence has been very lavish of her bounty to you – and you are
deeply in arrears to her – your parts are as quick as most men's; urge
but your speed in the race of virtue with the same ardency of zeal
as you have exhibited in error – and you will recover, to the
satisfaction of your noble patrons – and to the glory of yourself. –
Some philosopher – I forget who – wished for a window in his
breast – that the world might see his heart; – he could only be a
great fool, or a very good man: – I will believe the latter, and
recommend him to your imitation. – Vice is a coward; to be truly
brave, a man must be truly good; you hate the name of cowardice –
then, S—e, avoid it – detest a lye – and shun lyars – be above
revenge; – if any have taken advantage either of your guilt or
distress, punish them with forgiveness – and not only so – but, if
you can serve them any future time, do it – You have experienced
mercy and long-sufferance in your own person – therefore gratefully remember it, and shew mercy likewise.

I am pleased with the subject of your last – and if your conversion
is real, I shall ever be happy in your correspondence – But at the
same time I cannot afford to pay five pence for the honour of your
letters; – five pence is the twelfth part of five shillings – the
forty-eighth part of a pound – it would keep my girls in potatoes
two days. – The time may come, when it may be necessary for you
to study calculations; – in the mean while, if you cannot get a frank,
direct to me under cover to his Grace the Duke of ——. You have the
best wishes of your sincere friend (as long as you are your own
friend)

IGNATIUS SANCHO.

You must excuse blots and blunders – for I am under the dominion of a cruel head-ach – and a cough, which seems too fond of me.

f. To Mr. S— [Soubise]: More Good Advice

Charles Street, Westm. Nov. 29, 1778.

DEAR S—,

YOURS, dated from Madras, came safe to hand – I need not tell you that your account pleased me – and the style of your letter indicated a mind purged from its follies – and a better habit of thinking, which I trust happily preceded a steadier course of action – I know not whether or not Providence may not in your instance produce much good out of evil – I flatter myself you will yet recover, and stand the firmer in your future life from the reflection (bitter as it is) of your former. – I have no doubt but you received my letter charged with the heavy loss of your great, your noble, friendly benefactress, and patroness, the good duchess of Q—y; she entered into bliss, July 17, 1777, just two days after you sailed from Portsmouth. – I have now to inform you, that his Grace followed her October 21st this year; just fifteen months after his good duchess – full of years and honors – He is gone to join his duchess, and share in the rewards of a righteous God, who alone knew their merits, and alone could reward them.

Thus it has pleased God to take your props to himself – teaching you a lesson at the same time, to depend upon an honest exertion of your own industry – and humbly to trust in the Almighty.

You may safely conclude now, that you have not many friends in England – Be it your study, with attention, kindness, humility, and industry, to make friends where you are – Industry with good-nature and honesty is the road to wealth. – A wise œconomy – without avaricious meanness, or dirty rapacity, will in a few years render you decently independent.

I hope you cultivate the good-will and friendship of L—.[5] He is a jewel – prize him – love him – and place him next your heart – He will not flatter or fear you – So much the better – the fitter for your friend – He has a spirit of generosity – Such are never ungrateful – He sent us a token of his affection, which we shall never forget. – Let me counsel you for your character's sake, and as bound in honor, the first money you can spare, to send over 20l. to discharge your debt at Mr. P—'s, the sadler – It was borrowed money, you know. – As for me, I am wholly at your service to the extent of my power – But whatever commissions you send over to me – send money – or I stir none – Thou well knowest my poverty – but 'tis an honest poverty – and I need not blush or counceal it. – You also are indebted to Mr. O—, Bond-street – What little things of that kind you can recollect – pay as soon as you are able – It will spunge out many evil traces of things past, from the hearts and heads of your enemies – create you a better name – and pave the way for your return some years hence into England – with credit and reputation. – Before I conclude, let me, as your true friend, recommend seriously to you to make yourself acquainted with your Bible. – Believe me, the more you study the word of God, your peace and happiness will increase the more with it. – Fools may deride you – and wanton youth throw out their frothy gibes: – but as you are not to be a boy at all your life – and I trust would not be reckoned a fool – use your every endeavour to be a good man – and leave the rest to God. – Your letters from the Cape, and one from Madeira, I received; they were both good letters, and descriptions of things and places. – I wish to have your description of the fort and town of Madras – country adjacent – people – manner of living – value of money – religion – laws – animals – fashions – taste, &c. &c. – In short, write any thing – every thing – and above all, improve your mind with good reading – converse with men of sense, rather than with fools of fashion and riches – be humble to the rich – affable, open, and good-natured to your equals – and compassionately kind to the poor. – I have treated you freely in proof of my friendship – Mrs. S—, under the persuasion that you are really a good man, sends her best wishes – When her handkerchief is washed, you will send it home – The girls wish to be remembered to you, and all to friend Lincoln.

Yours, &c. &c.

I. SANCHO.

Notes

1. Granville Sharp had taken up the case of James Somerset, a runaway slave, and in 1772 Lord Chief Justice Mansfield declared that in such cases slaves could not be returned to American slavery, but were legally entitled to remain in England. He did not, as is sometimes said, declare them to be free, but the decision gave them greater security.

2. The black American poet, whose verse was published in 1773.
3. Extracts of two letters from Mr. W—e to his father, dated Bombay, 1776 and 1777: (Sancho's note)

   '1776. I have introduced myself to Mr. G—., who behaved very friendly in giving me some advice, which was very necessary, as the inhabitants, who are chiefly Blacks, are a set of canting, deceitful people, and of whom one must have great caution.'

   '1777. I am now thoroughly convinced, that the account which Mr. G— gave me of the natives of this country is just and true, that they are a set of deceitful people, and have not such a word as Gratitude in their language, neither do they know what it is – and as to their dealings in trade, they are like unto Jews.'
4. The Gordon Riots of 1780 were engineered by Lord George Gordon, leader of the Protestant Association and a fierce anti-Catholic, against the leniency of certain clauses in the Catholic Relief Act of 1778, which relaxed restrictions on Roman Catholics.
5. L— appears to be the 'Lincoln' referred to later in the letter. He was a friend of Sancho who had also gone to India. In a letter of May 4 1799, Sancho calls him 'a seasoned creole of St. Kitts', and a list of Sancho's correspondents by his friend Stevenson refers to him as 'an Affrican'. *Slavery and Abolition*, 1.3. (1980). 356–7.

4

OTTOBAH CUGOANO (JOHN STUART)
Born Adjumako c.1757

Thoughts and Sentiments on the Evil and Wicked Traffic of the Slavery and Commerce of the Human Species

London, 1787

Ottobah Cugoano was born in the mid 1750s in the region of
the town of 'Agimaque [mod. Adjumako], in the country of
Fantyn' [mod. Fanti], part of modern Ghana. He was captured
and enslaved around 1770, and brought to England from the
West Indies by his purchaser, Alexander Campbell. By 1788 he
was a free man and personal servant to Cosway, court painter
to the Prince of Wales. In *An Island in the Moon*, William
Blake refers to Cosway (whom he calls Mr Jacko) as having
black servants in his house. Cugoano shows a more overt and
assertive black radicalism than anything that can be seen in
such contemporaries as Hammon, Gronniosaw and Sancho,
and though he acknowledges the good fortune that attended
him under divine benevolence after his enslavement, he never
allows his argument to slip into the common hypocrisy of the
slave owners, and some churchmen, even of some slaves, that
the benefits of Christian conversion outweighed the sufferings
of slavery, and that slavery was itself part of a divine scheme of
benevolence. Like his friend Equiano, having no high expectations of white benevolence, he embraces the contemporary
view that hopes for the immediate future lie in the virtuous
self-interest of Christian trade, and in benevolent alleviation of
the worst miseries of slavery rather than full abolition. His
recognition that the British fleet would be required to enforce
any future Bill of Abolition shows eminent commonsense, as
does his recognition that the development of education and
trade skills must go hand in hand with abolition, though his
plans for post-abolition training are rather less than radical.
Though he abhors the practice of slavery and asks for legisla-
tion 'to hinder and prohibit all men under British government
to traffic either in buying or selling men', he assumes pessimis-
tically and with reason to that slave ownership will continue in

39

the British colonies, suspecting that the establishment of the Freetown colony for freed slaves in 1787 to be yet another piece of white duplicity, and anticipates that little more can be proposed as a practical aim than humane treatment, Christian teaching, instruction in trades, and freedom, (subject to good conduct) after seven years: what might constitute bad conduct is not made clear, and what might happen to those slaves who did not pass the seventh year test is not discussed. Nevertheless, his book represents in its aggressive and often bitter urgency of tone, a considerable advance in radical sentiments.

One further problem with Cugoano is the disparity between the language of his book, and that of a surviving holograph letter, included here as item 5. It seems clear that though he may well have drafted the book largely on his own, it must have been extensively revised by another hand. There is evidence that the hand may have been that of his friend Equiano. The matter is discussed in the introduction to the 1969 reprint.

The text is taken from the first edition. This was reprinted in Dawson's Colonial History series, ed. Paul Edwards, London 1969. The letter to Granville Sharp is from the Granville Sharp papers at the Gloucester County Record Office. There is an excellent chapter on Cugoano in Keith A. Sandiford, *Measuring the Moment* (1988).

a. Capture

I was born in the city of Agimaque, on the coast of Fantyn; my father was a companion to the chief in that part of the country of Fantee, and when the old king died I was left in his house with his family; soon after I was sent for by his nephew, Ambro Accasa, who succeeded the old king in the chiefdom of that part of Fantee known by the name of Agimaque and Assinee. I lived with his children, enjoying peace and tranquillity, about twenty moons, which, according to their way of reckoning time, is two years. I was sent for to visit an uncle, who lived at a considerable distance from Agimaque. The first day after we set out we arrived at Assinee, and the third day at my uncle's habitation, where I lived about three months, and was then thinking of returning to my father and young companion at Agimaque; but by this time I had got well acquainted with some of the children of my uncle's hundreds of relations, and we were some days too ventursome in going into the woods to gather fruit and catch birds, and such amusements as pleased us. One day I refused to go with the rest, being rather apprehensive that something might happen to us; till one of my play-fellows said to me, because you belong to the great men, you are afraid to venture your carcase, or else of the *bounsam*,[1] which is the devil. This enraged me so much, that I set a resolution to join the rest, and we went into the woods as usual; but we had not been above two hours before our troubles began, when several great ruffians came upon us suddenly, and said we had committed a fault against their lord, and we must go and answer for it ourselves before him.

Some of us attempted in vain to run away, but pistols and cutlasses were soon introduced, threatening, that if we offered to stir we should all lie dead on the spot. One of them pretended to be more friendly than the rest, and said, that he would speak to their lord to get us clear, and desired that we should follow him; we were then immediately divided into different parties, and drove after him. We were soon led out of the way which we knew, and towards the evening, as we came in sight of a town, they told us that this great man of theirs lived there, but pretended it was too late to go and see him that night. Next morning there came three other men, whose language differed from ours, and spoke to some of those who watched us all the night, but he that pretended to be our friend with the great man, and some others, were gone away. We asked our keepers what these men had been saying to them, and they answered, that they had been asking them, and us together, to go and feast with them that day, and that we must put off seeing the great man till after; little thinking that our doom was so nigh, or that these villains meant to feast on us as their prey. We went with them again about half a day's journey, and came to a great multitude of people, having different music playing; and all the day after we got there, we were very merry with the music, dancing and singing. Towards the evening, we were again persuaded that we could not get back to where the great man lived till next day; and when bedtime came, we were separated into different houses with different people. When the next morning came, I asked for the men that brought me there, and for the rest of my companions; and I was told that they were gone to the sea side to bring home some rum, guns and powder, and that some of my companions were gone with them, and that some were gone to the fields to do something or other. This gave me strong suspicion that there was some treachery in the case, and I began to think that my hopes of returning home again were all over. I soon became very uneasy, not knowing what to do, and refused to eat or drink for whole days together, till the man of the house told me that he would do all in his power to get me back to my uncle; then I eat a little fruit with him, and had some thoughts that I should be sought after, as I would be then missing at home about five or six days. I enquired every day if the men had come back, and for the rest of my companions, but could get no answer of any satisfaction. I was kept about six days at this man's house, and in the evening there was another man came and talked with him a good while, and I heard the one say to the other he must go, and the other said the sooner the better; that man came out and told me that he knew my relations at Agimaque, and that we must set out to-morrow morning, and he would convey me there. Accordingly we set out next day, and travelled till dark, when we came to a place where we had some supper and slept. He carried a large bag with some gold dust, which he said he had to buy some goods at the sea side to take with him to Agimaque. Next day we travelled on, and in the evening came to a town, where I saw several white people, which made me afraid that they would eat me, according to our notion as children in the inland parts of the country. This made me rest very uneasy all the night, and next morning I had some victuals brought, desiring me to eat and make haste, as my guide and kid-napper told me that he had to go to the castle with some company that were going there, as he had told me before, to get some goods. After I was ordered out, the horrors I soon saw and felt, cannot be well described; I saw many of my miserable countrymen chained two and two, some hand-cuffed, and some with their hands tied behind. We were conducted along by a guard, and when we arrived at the castle, I asked my guide what I was brought there for, he told me to learn the ways of the *browfow*,[2] that is the white faced people. I saw him take a gun, a piece of cloth, and some lead for me, and then he told me that he must now leave me there, and went off. This made me cry bitterly, but I was soon conducted to a prison, for three days, where I heard the groans and cries of many, and saw some of my fellow-captives. But when a vessel arrived to conduct us away to the ship, it was a most horrible scene; there was nothing to be heard but rattling of chains, smacking of whips, and the groans and cries of our fellow-men. Some would not stir from the ground, when they were lashed and beat in the most horrible manner. I have forgot the name of this infernal fort; but we were taken in the ship that came for us, to another that was ready to sail from Cape Coast. When we were put into the ship, we saw several black merchants coming on board, but we were all drove into our holes, and not suffered to speak to any of them. In this situation we continued several days in sight of our native land; but I could find no good person to give any information of my situation to Accasa at Agimaque. And when we found ourselves at last taken away, death was more preferable than life, and a plan was concerted amongst us, that we might burn and blow up the ship, and to perish all together in the flames; but we were betrayed by one of our own countrywomen, who slept with some of the head men of the ship, for it was common for the dirty filthy sailors to take the African women and lie upon their bodies; but the men were chained and pent up in holes. It was the women and boys which were to burn the ship, with the approbation and groans of the rest; though that was prevented, the discovery was likewise a cruel bloody scene.

But it would be needless to give a description of all the horrible scenes which we saw, and the base treatment which we met with in this dreadful captive situation, as the similar cases of thousands, which suffer by this infernal traffic, are well known. Let it suffice to say, that I was thus lost to my dear indulgent parents and relations, and they to me. All my help was cries and tears, and these could not avail; nor suffered long, till one succeeding woe, and dread, swelled up another. Brought from a state of innocence and freedom, and, in a barbarous and cruel manner, conveyed to a state of horror and slavery: This abandoned situation may be easier conceived than described. From the time that I was kidnapped and conducted to a factory, and from thence in the brutish, base, but fashionable way of traffic, consigned to Grenada, the grievous thoughts which I then felt, still pant in my heart; though my fears and tears have long since subsided. And yet it is still grievous to think that thousands more have suffered in similar and greater distress, under the hands of barbarous robbers, and merciless task-masters; and that many even now are suffering in all the extreme bitterness of grief and woe, that no language can describe. The cries of some, and the sight of their misery, may be seen and heard afar; but the deep sounding groans of thousands, and the great sadness of their misery and woe, under the heavy load of oppressions and calamities inflicted upon them, are such as can only be distinctly known to the ears of Jehovah Sabaoth.

This Lord of Hosts, in his great Providence, and in great mercy to me, made a way for my deliverance from Grenada. – Being in this dreadful captivity and horrible slavery, without any hope of deliverance, for about eight or nine months, beholding the most dreadful scenes of misery and cruelty, and seeing my miserable companions often cruelly lashed, and as it were cut to pieces, for the most trifling faults; this made me often tremble and weep, but I escaped better than many of them. For eating a piece of sugarcane, some were cruelly lashed, or struck over the face to knock their teeth out. Some of the stouter ones, I suppose often reproved, and grown hardened and stupid with many cruel beatings and lashings, or perhaps faint and pressed with hunger and hard labour, were often committing trespasses of this kind, and when detected, they met with exemplary punishment. Some told me they had their teeth pulled out to deter others, and to prevent them from eating any cane in future. Thus seeing my miserable companions and countrymen in this pitiful, distressed and horrible situation, with all the brutish baseness and barbarity attending it, could not but fill my little mind with horror and indignation. But I must own, to the shame of my own countrymen, that I was first kid-napped and betrayed by some of my own complexion, who were the first cause of my exile and slavery; but if there were no buyers there would be no sellers. So far as I can remember, some of the Africans in my country keep slaves, which they take in war, or for debt; but those which they keep are well fed, and good care taken of them, and treated well; and, as to their cloathing, they differ according to the custom of the country. But I may safely say, that all the poverty and misery that any of the inhabitants of Africa meet with among themselves, is far inferior to those inhospitable regions of misery which they meet with in the West-Indies, where their hard-hearted overseers have neither regard to the laws of God, nor the life of their fellow-men.

Thanks be to God, I was delivered from Grenada, and that horrid brutal slavery. – A gentleman coming to England, took me for his servant, and brought me away, where I soon found my situation become more agreeable. After coming to England, and seeing others write and read, I had a strong desire to learn, and getting what assistance I could, I applied myself to learn reading and writing, which soon became my recreation, pleasure, and delight; and when my master perceived that I could write some, he sent me to a proper school for that purpose to learn. Since, I have endeavoured to improve my mind in reading, and have sought to get all the intelligence I could, in my situation of life, towards the state of my brethren and countrymen in complexion, and of the miserable situation of those who are barbarously sold into captivity, and unlawfully held in slavery.

But, among other observations, one great duty I owe to Almighty God, (the thankful acknowlegement I would not omit for any consideration) that, although I have been brought away from my native country, in that torrent of robbery and wickedness, thanks be to God for his good providence towards me; I have both obtained liberty, and acquired the great advantages of some little learning, in being able to read and write, and, what is still infinitely of greater advantage, I trust, to know something of Him *who is that God whose providence rules over all, and who is the only Potent One that rules in the nations over the children of men. It is unto Him, who is the Prince of the Kings of the earth, that I would give all thanks.* And, in some manner, I may say with Joseph, as he did with respect to the evil intention of his brethren, when they sold him into Egypt, that whatever evil intentions and bad motives those insidious robbers had in carrying me away from my native country and friends, I trust, was what the Lord intended for my good. In this respect, I am highly indebted to many of the good people of England for learning and principles unknown to the people of my native country. But, above all, what have I obtained from the Lord God of Hosts, the God of the Christians! in the divine revelation of the only true God, and the Saviour of men, what a treasure of wisdom and blessings are involved? How wonderful is the divine goodness displayed in those invaluable books the Old and New Testaments, that inestimable compilation of books, the Bible? And, O what a treasure to have, and one of the greatest advantages to be able to read therein, and a divine blessing to understand!

(6–13)

b. Proposals

And now that blessings may come instead of a curse, and that many beneficent purposes of good might speedily arise and flow from it, and be more readily promoted: I would hereby presume to offer the following considerations, as some outlines of a general reformation which ought to be established and carried on. And first, I would propose, that there ought to be days of mourning and fasting appointed, to make enquiry into that great and pre-eminent evil for many years past carried on against the Heathen nations, and the horrible iniquity of making merchandize of us, and cruelly enslaving the poor Africans: and that you might seek grace and repentance, and find mercy and forgiveness before God Omnipotent; and that he may give you wisdom and understanding to devise what ought to be done.

Secondly, I would propose that a total abolition of slavery should be made and proclaimed; and that an univeral emancipation of slaves should begin from the date thereof, and be carried on in the following manner: That a proclamation should be caused to be made, setting forth the Antichristian unlawfulness of the slavery and commerce of the human species; and that it should be sent to all the courts and nations in Europe, to require their advice and assistance, and as they may find it unlawful to carry it on, let them whosoever will join to prohibit it. And if such a proclamation be found advisable to the British legislature, let them publish it, and cause it to be published, throughout all the British empire, to hinder and prohibit all men under their government to traffic either in buying or selling men; and, to prevent it, a penalty might be made against it of one thousand pounds, for any man either to buy or sell another man. And that it should require all slave-holders, upon the immediate information thereof, to mitigate the labour of their slaves to that of a lawful servitude, without tortures or oppression; and that they should not hinder, but cause and procure some suitable means of instruction for them in the knowledge of the Christian religion. And agreeable to the late *royal Proclamation, for the Encouragement of Piety and Virtue, and for the preventing and punishing of Vice, Profaneness and Immorality*; that by no means, under any pretence whatsoever, either for themselves or their masters,the slaves under their subjection should not be suffered to work on the Sabbath days, unless it be such works as necessity and mercy may require. But that those days, as well as some other hours selected for the purpose, should be appropriated for the time of their instruction; and that if any of their owners should not provide such suitable instructors for them, that those slaves should be taken away from them and given to others who would maintain and instruct them for their labour. And that it should be made known to the slaves, that those who had been above seven years in the islands or elsewhere, if they had obtained any competent degree of knowledge of the Christian religion, and the laws of civilization, and had behaved themselves honestly and decently, that they should immediately become free; and that their owners should give them reasonable wages and maintenance for their labour, and not cause them to go away unless they could find some suitable employment elsewhere. And accordingly, from the date of their arrival to seven years, as they arrive at some suitable progress in knowledge, and behaved themselves honestly, that they should be getting free in the course of that time, and at the end of seven years to let every honest man and woman become free; for in the course of that time, they would have sufficiently paid their owners by their labour, both for their first purpose, and for the expenses attending their education. By being thus instructed in the course of seven years, they would become tractable and obedient, useful labourers, dutiful servants and good subjects; and Christian men might have the honor and happiness to see many of them vieing with themselves to praise the God of their salvation. And it might be another necessary duty for Christians, in the course of that time, to make enquiry concerning some of their friends and relations in Africa: and if they found any intelligent persons amongst them, to give them as good education as they could, and find out a way of recourse to their friends; that as soon as they had made any progress in useful learning and the knowledge of the Christian religion, they might be sent back to Africa, to be made useful there as soon, and as many of them as could be made fit for instructing others. The rest would become useful residentors in the colonies; where there might be employment enough given to all free people, with suitable wages according to their usefulness, in the improvement of land; and the more encouragement that could be given to agriculture, and every other branch of useful industry, would thereby encrease the number of the inhabitants; without which any country, however blessed by nature, must continue poor.

And, thirdly, I would propose, that a fleet of some ships of war should be immediately sent to the coast of Africa, and particularly where the slave trade is carried on, with faithful men to direct that none should be brought from the coast of Africa without their own consent and the approbation of their friends, and to intercept all merchant ships that were bringing them away, until such a scrutiny was made, whatever nation they belonged to. And I would suppose, in Great-Britain was to do any thing of this kind, that it would meet with the general approbation and assistance of other Christian nations; but whether it did or not, it could be very lawfully done at all the British forts and settlements on the coast of Africa; and particular remonstrances could be given to all the rest, to warn them of the consequences of such an evil and enormous wicked traffic as is now carried on. The Dutch have some crocodile settlers at the Cape, that should be called to a particular account for their murders and inhuman babarities. But all the present governors of the British forts and factories should be dismissed, and faithful and good men appointed in their room; and those forts and factories, which at present are a den of thieves, might be turned into shepherd's tents, and have good shepherds sent to call the flocks to feed beside them. Then would doors of hospitality in abundance be opened in Africa to supply the weary travellers, and that immense abundance which they are enriched with, might be diffused afar; but the character of the inhabitants on the west coast of Africa, and the rich produce of their country, have been too long misrepresented by avaricious plunderers and merchants who deal in slaves; and if that country was not annually ravished and laid waste, there might be a very considerable and profitable trade carried on with the Africans. And, should the noble Britons, who have often supported their own liberties with their lives and fortunes, extend their philanthropy to abolish the slavery and oppression of the Africans, they might have settlements and many kingdoms united in a friendly alliance with themselves, which might be made greatly to their own advantage, as well as they might have the happiness of being useful to promoting the prosperity and felicity of others, who have been cruelly injured and wrongfully dealt with. Were the Africans to be dealt with in a friendly manner, and kind instructions to be administered unto them, as by degrees they became to love learning, there would be nothing in their power, but what they would wish to render their service in return for the means of improving their understanding; and the present British factories, and other settlements, might be enlarged to a very great extent. And as Great-Britain has been remarkable for ages past, for encouraging arts and sciences, and may now be put in competition with any nation in the known world, if they would take compassion on the inhabitants of the coast of Guinea, and to make use of such means as would be needful to enlighten their minds in the knowledge of Christianity, their virtue, in this respect, would have its own reward. And as the Africans became refined and established in light and knowledge, they would imitate their noble British friends, to improve their lands, and make use of that industry as the nature of their country might require, and to supply those that would trade with them, with such productions as the nature of their climate would produce; and, in every respect, the fair Britons would have the preference with them to a very great extent; and, in another respect, they would become a kind of first ornament to Great-Britain for her tender and compassionate care of such a set of distressed poor ignorant people. And were the noble Britons, and their august Sovereign, to cause protection and encouragement to be given to those Africans, they might expect in a short time, if need required it, to receive from thence great supplies of men in a lawful way, either for industry or defence; and of other things in abundance from so great a source, where every thing is luxurious and plenty, if not laid waste by barbarity and gross ignorance. Due encouragement being given to so great, so just, and such a noble undertaking, would soon bring more revenue in a righteous way to the British nation, than ten times its share in all the profits that slavery can produce*; and such a laudable example would inspire every generous and enterprizing mind to imitate so great and worthy a nation, for establishing religion, justice, and equity to the Africans, and, in doing this, would be held in the highest esteem by all men, and be admired by all the world.

*A gentleman of my acquaintance told me that, if ever he hears tell of any thing of this kind taking place, he has a plan in contemplation, which would, in some equitable manner, produce for one million to fifteen millions sterling to the British government annually, as it might be required; of which a due proportion of that revenue would be paid by the Africans; and that it would prevent all smuggling and illicit traffic; in a great measure, prevent running into debt, long imprisonment, and all unlawful bankruptcies; effectually prevent all dishonesty and swindling, and almost put an end to all robbery, fraud and theft.

(129–35)

c. The Sierra Leone Expedition, 1786–7

Particular thanks is due to every one of that humane society of worthy and respectful gentlemen, whose liberality hath supported many of the Black Poor about London. *Those that honor their*

Maker have mercy on the poor; and many blessings are upon the head of the just: may the fear of the Lord prolong their days, and cause their memory to be blessed, and may their number be encreased to fill their expectations with gladness; for they have not only commiserated the poor in general, *but even those which are accounted as beasts, and imputed as vile in the sight of others.* The part that the British government has taken, to co-operate with them, has certainly a flattering and laudable appearance of doing some good; and the fitting out ships to supply a company of Black People with clothes and provisions, and to carry them to settle at Sierra Leona, in the West coast of Africa, as a free colony to Great-Britain, in a peaceable alliance with the inhabitants, has every appearance of honour, and the approbation of friends. According to the plan, humanity hath made its appearance in a more honorable way of colonization, than any Christian nation have ever done before, and may be productive of much good, if they continue to encourage and support them. But after all, there is some doubt whether their own flattering expectation in the manner as set forth to them, and the hope of their friends may not be defeated and rendered abortive; and there is some reason to fear, that they never will be settled as intended, in any permanent and peaceable way at Sierra Leona.

This prospect of settling a free colony to Great-Britain in a peaceable alliance with the inhabitants of Africa at Sierra Leona, has neither altogether met with the credulous approbation of the Africans here, nor yet been sought after with any prudent and right plan by the promoters of it. Had a treaty of agreement been first made with the inhabitants of Africa, and the terms and nature of such a settlement fixed upon, and its situation and boundary pointed out; then might the Africans, and others here, have embarked with a good prospect of enjoying happiness and prosperity themselves, and have gone with a hope of being able to render their services, in return, of some advantage to their friends and benefactors of Great-Britain. But as this was not done, and as they were to be hurried away at all events, some of them after what would; and yet, after all, to be delayed in the ships before they were set out from the coast, until many of them have perished with cold, and other disorders, and several of the most intelligent among them are dead, and others that, in all probability, would have been most useful for them were hindered from going, by means of some disagreeable jealousy of those who were appointed as governors, the great prospect of doing good seems all to be blown away. And so it appeared to some of those who are now gone, and at last, hap hazard, were obliged to go; who endeavoured in vain to get away by plunging into the water, that they might, if possible wade ashore, as dreading the prospect of their wretched fate, as beholding their perilous situation, having every prospect of difficulty and surrounding danger.

What with the death of some of the original promoters and proposers of this charitable undertaking, and the death and deprivation of others that were to share the benefit of it, and by the adverse motives of those employed to be the conductors thereof, we think it will be more than what can be well expected, if we ever hear of any good in proportion to so great, well-designed, laudable and expensive charity. Many more of the Black People still in this country would have, with great gladness, embraced the opportunity, longing to reach their native land; but as the old saying is, A burnt child dreads the fire, some of these unfortunate sons and daughters of Africa have been severally unlawfully dragged away from their native abodes, under various pretences, by the insidious treachery of others, and have been brought into the hands of barbarous robbers and pirates, and, like sheep to the market, have been sold into captivity and slavery, and thereby have been deprived of their natural liberty and property, and every connection that they held dear and valuable, and subjected to the cruel service of the hard-hearted brutes called planters. But some of them, by various services either to the public or to individuals, as more particularly in the course of last war, have gotten their liberty again in this free country. They are thankful for the respite, but afraid of being ensnared again; for the European seafaring people in general, who trade to foreign parts, have such a prejudice against Black People, that they use them more like asses than men, so that a Black Man is scarcely ever safe among them. Much assiduity was made use to perswade the Black People in general to embrace the opportunity of going with this company of transports; but the wiser sort declined from all thoughts of it, unless they could hear of some better plan taking place for their security and safety. For as it seemed prudent and obvious to many of them taking heed to that sacred enquiry, *Doth a fountain send forth at the same place sweet water and bitter?* They were afraid that their doom would be to drink of the bitter water. For can it be readily conceived that government would establish a free colony for them nearly on the spot, while it supports its forts and garrisons, to ensnare, merchandize, and to carry others into captivity and slavery.

(138–42)

d. Letter written by Cugoano to Granville Sharp, about arrangements for the transport of the free blacks settled in Nova Scotia after the American War of Independence, to the new colony at Freetown, Sierra Leone. It almost certainly dates from early in 1791.

Honoured Sir,

Pardon the liberty taken in troubling you with this few lines but as there is Several Ships now going to New Brunswick I could wish to have your answer that I might be able to give the black-settlers there some kind of answer to their request, the generality of them are mediately natives of africa who Join the british forces Last war, they are consisting of Different Macanicks such as Carpenters, Smiths, Masons and farmers, this are the people that we have immediate use for in the Provence of freedom. Most of them are people of property and able to pay their own Passages, and the family, as well as the Country been by far the cheapest market for victualling vessels, I am of opinion that connections with them will be immediate service – should think it proper to make lest interest for me I shall go over with Cap. Younghusband who will sale for that province in a few days my motive is this, I should endeavour to know who is able to pay their ways, and they that might be thought useful to the free african settlers. This may be Complicated in three months and then youll be able to Judge wether or no, would be worthwhile to send out to a ship for that purpose; the spruce is the native of these Country, which will be Immediately valuable in african Climate, a tree which Produce sugar equall with that which many thousands are murdered for, is, here only by Cuting down its branches and setting a tubb under it, which is only Boild with every little trouble, equally with that of our West india brown sugar. but what encouragement has the poor unfortunate sables those Under sanction of freedom are worse off than slaves. Eight months severe winter, to incounter and when bringh their little stock market oblidge sell for little or nothing at a white mans Price. these inhuman Disinctions of Colours, has in every point, and in every view, spread its Predominant Power over all the northern Climes, that it puts me in the mind of the leaned Bollingbrook, who was some times at lost to known Distinction betwixt a man and a stone.

I have, within this last three months b[een] after upwards of fifty places but, Complexion is a Predominant Prejudice for a man to starve for want in a christian Country be will be a folly. I shall Call for your Answer to morrow.

I am Sincerly your Dutifull Ser
    John Stuart

(xxi–xxiii)

Notes

1. bounsam: modern Fanti *abunsam*, devil or monster.
2. browfow: modern Fanti *abrofo* (pl.), white men.

5

OLAUDAH EQUIANO

1745–1797

*The Interesting Narrative of the Life of
Olaudah Equiano, or Gustavus Vassa the African,
written by himself*

London, 1789

Equiano's autobiography was a best seller in its day, being
published in eight English editions and one American in his
own lifetime as well as translations into Dutch (1790), German
(1792) and Russian (1794). A number of posthumous editions
appeared in the 19th century. After a lapse of nearly a century,
interest in the book revived during the 1950s and after, the
period of African independence and the emergence of an
African literature in English. The *Narrative* is now generally
recognised to be a work of major importance in African
literature, and its author has been hailed as founder of the slave
narrative, a genre which has claimed increasing critical attention particularly in the United States, and is acknowledged to
be central to Black American Literature.

Equiano was born about 1745 in an Igbo village, Essaka,
probably the modern Iseke in Nigeria. His *Narrative* is the
first authentic account in English and from his own hand, of
the life of an African during the period of the Slave Trade.
Equiano gives a detailed account of Igbo life and customs in
the 1750s, his kidnapping by local Africans, his sale to white
slave traders in the Niger Delta, and his experience of the
Middle Passage across the Atlantic to the West Indies. First
sold to a slave-owner in the American colonies, he was bought
by an English naval officer, Michael Pascal, who gave him the
name Gustavus Vassa, in the condescending tradition of
renaming slaves as European heroes. At first he objected to the
name, but in time embraced it with pride, signing all his books
and letters with it, though he returned to the use of his Igbo
name on the title page of his own book, an acknowledgement
of his homeland and its values, which as he tells us many times
he had never forgotten.

He served Pascal for many years during which he received an education both ashore and aboard ship. Cruelly disappointed when Pascal resold him into American slavery, he refused to lose hope, and working for his new owner as a seaman, he managed by petty trading on his own account to save the money to purchase back his freedom. Much of his life was spent at sea, during which time he fought in the British Navy in the Mediterranean with Admiral Boscawen's fleet, with General Wolfe's forces in Canada, and as a free man sailed on many voyages: on an expedition to the Arctic in 1772 as surgeon's mate; as valet to a gentleman on a tour of the Mediterranean spending some time amongst the Turks in Smyrna; and later, back in the Caribbean, living amongst the Miskito Indians in Nicaragua. After publishing his book he married, his wife coming from Soham near Cambridge. One of his two daughters survived to receive a substantial legacy from her father on her 21st birthday, the other is remembered on a memorial verse-inscription at the Parish Church, Chesterton, near Cambridge. The Admiralty appointed him Commissary for Stores to the Expedition for Freed Slaves settling in Freetown in 1787, but after conflicts with the organisers, he travelled no further than Plymouth, where he was dismissed as a troublemaker for inflaming the Black settlers. His dismissal appears to have been less than just, and is discussed in the introduction to the facsimile edition of 1969, xxx–xlv: we might however feel thankful for this dismissal, since otherwise we might not have had his autobiography.

When he died in 1797, he had become a moderately prosperous moneylender in London. However, much of his later life was devoted to work for the abolitionist movement, as he travelled throughout Britain, selling his book and speaking against the slave trade.

We include four sections of the autobiography. First there is Equiano's dramatic account of his experience of the slave-ship which carried him from Africa to Barbados. Characteristic of the *Narrative* is the skill with which Equiano is able simultaneously to convey the innocence of the boy he once was, and the mature self-awareness of the adult he had become by the time he wrote the book, so that the reader experiences something of the unity of the complete life from childhood to maturity. Next comes his first voyage to England. The third shows the Equiano who has learnt the hard way that commodity rules, believing if he is to survive he can only do so by pursuing his own fortune and trusting in divine justice and his energies and good luck. The fourth section shows that Equiano is not without a sense of humour despite his sufferings, and aware of his touches of vanity and the driving power of his acquisitive instincts, in his eagerness, for the suit of superfine

clothes to dance with at his freedom, and the approval of the
'sable females' who begin to cast a more friendly eye on him;
above all in the amused parody of the language of his own
Christian piety in the story of the dying man on shipboard.
This extract closes with the scene in which he at last gains his
freedom. We end with three of the letters which illustrate his
activities on behalf of the movement for the abolition of
slavery, first one of his letters to the press against James Tobin,
the author of a pro-planter book *Cursory Remarks upon the
Rev. Mr Ramsey's Essay* (1785) which had attacked the
Scottish abolitionist James Ramsey, much admired by
Equiano; the second, his letter to Lord Hawkesbury, included
in the evidence of the Parliamentary Enquiry into the Slave
Trade, 1789, in which his economic arguments for trade with
Africa repeat those of the last chapter of his book. The third
letter is private, one of a few surviving in manuscript, written
in great haste (and as a result showing a few minor slips of the
pen but demonstrating Equiano's fluency in English) to abolitionist friends in Nottingham, and revealing yet another
insight into both his commercial and his abolitionist drives, as
he announces his impending marriage to Miss Cullen, 'and
when I have given her 8 or 10 Days Comfort, I mean Directly
to go to Scotland and sell my 5th Editions.'

The text is from the first edition of 1789, reprinted in facsimile
with an introduction and notes by P. Edwards in the Dawson
Colonial History series, London 1969. Paperbacks edited by
Paul Edwards and by Henry L. Gates are in print (see
bibliography).

a. The Middle Passage

The first object which saluted my eyes when I arrived on the coast
was the sea, and a slave ship, which was then riding at anchor, and
waiting for its cargo. These filled me with astonishment, which was
soon coverted into terror when I was carried on board. I was
immediately handled and tossed up to see if I were sound by some
of the crew; and I was now persuaded that I had gotten into a world
of bad spirits, and that they were going to kill me. Their com-
plexions too differing so much from ours, their long hair, and the
language they spoke, (which was very different from any I had ever
heard) united to confirm me in this belief. Indeed such were the
horrors of my views and fears at the moment, that, if ten thousand
worlds had been my own, I would have freely parted with them all
to have exchanged my condition with that of the meanest slave in

my own country. When I looked round the ship too and saw a large furnace or copper boiling, and a multitude of black people of every description chained together, every one of their countenances expressing dejection and sorrow, I no longer doubted of my fate; and, quite overpowered with horror and anguish, I fell motionless on the deck and fainted. When I recovered a little I found some black people about me, who I believed were some of those who brought me on board, and had been receiving their pay; they talked to me in order to cheer me, but all in vain. I asked them if we were not to be eaten by those white men with horrible looks, red faces, and loose hair. They told me I was not; and one of the crew brought me a small portion of spirituous liquor in a wine glass; but, being afraid of him, I would not take it out of his hand. One of the blacks therefore took it from him and gave it to me, and I took a little down my palate, which, instead of reviving me, as they thought it would, threw me into the greatest consternation at the strange feeling it produced, having never tasted any such liquor before. Soon after this the blacks who brought me on board went off, and left me abandoned to despair. I now saw myself deprived of all chance of returning to my native country, or even the least glimpse of hope of gaining the shore, which I now considered as friendly; and I even wished for my former slavery in preference to my present situation, which was filled with horrors of every kind, still heightened by my ignorance of what I was to undergo. I was not long suffered to indulge my grief; I was soon put down under the decks, and there I received such a salutation in my nostrils as I had never experienced in my life: so that, with the loathsomeness of the stench, and crying together, I became so sick and low that I was not able to eat, nor had I the least desire to taste anything. I now wished for the last friend, death, to relieve me; but soon, to my grief, two of the white men offered me eatables; and, on my refusing to eat, one of them held me fast by the hands, and laid me across I think the windlass, and tied my feet, while the other flogged me severely. I had never experienced any thing of this kind before; and although, not being used to the water, I naturally feared that element the first time I saw it, yet nevertheless, could I have got over the nettings, I would have jumped over the side, but I could not; and, besides, the crew used to watch us very closely who were not chained down to the decks, lest we should leap into the water: and I have seen some of these poor African prisoners most severely cut for attempting to do so, and hourly whipped for not eating. This indeed was often the case with myself. In a little time after, amongst the poor chained men, I found some of my own nation, which in a small degree gave ease to my mind. I inquired of these what was to be done with us; they gave me to understand we were to be carried to these white people's country to work for them. I then was a little revived, and thought, if it were no worse than working, my situation was not so desperate: but still I feared I should be put to death, the white people looked and acted, as I thought, in so savage a manner; for I had never seen among any people such instances of brutal cruelty; and this not only shewn towards us blacks, but also to some of the whites themselves. One white man in particular I saw, when we were permitted to be on deck, flogged so unmercifully with a large rope near the foremast, that he died in consequence of it and they tossed him over the side as they would have done a brute. This made me fear these people the more; and I expected nothing less than to be treated in the same manner. I could not help expressing my fears and apprehensions to some of my countrymen: I asked them if these people had no country, but lived in this hollow place (the ship): they told me they did not, but came from a distant one. 'Then,' said I, 'how comes it in all our country we never heard of them?' They told me because they lived so very far off. I then asked where were their women? had they any like themselves? I was told they had: 'and why,' said I, 'do we not see them?' they answered, because they were left behind. I asked how the vessel could go? they told me they could not tell; but that there were cloths put upon the masts by the help of the ropes I saw, and then the vessel went on; and the white men had some spell or magic they put in the water when they liked in order to stop the vessel. I was exceedingly amazed at this account, and really thought they were spirits. I therefore wished much to be from amongst them, for I expected they would sacrifice me: but my wishes were vain; for we were so quartered that it was impossible for any of us to make our escape. While we stayed on the coast I was mostly on deck; and one day, to my great astonishment, I saw one of these vessels coming in with the sails up. As soon as the whites saw it, they gave a great shout, at which we were amazed; and the more so as the vessel appeared larger by approaching nearer. At last she came to an anchor in my sight, and when the anchor was let go I and my countrymen who saw it were lost in astonishment to observe the vessel stop; and were now convinced it was done by magic. Soon after this the other ship got her boats out, and they came on board of us, and the people of both ships seemed very glad to see each other. Several of the strangers also shook hands with us black people, and made motions with their hands, signifying I suppose we were to go to their country; but we did not understand them. At last, when the ship we were in had got in all her cargo, they made ready with many fearful noises, and we were all put under the deck, so that we could not see how they managed the vessel. But this disappointment was the least of my sorrow. The stench of the hold while we were on the coast was so intolerably loathsome, that it was dangerous to remain there for any time, and some of us had been permitted to stay on the deck for the fresh air; but now that the whole ship's cargo were confined together, it became absolutely pestilential. The closeness of the place, and the heat of the climate, added to the number in the ship, which was so crowded that each had scarcely room to turn himself, almost suffocated us. This produced copious perspirations, so that the air soon became unfit for respiration, from a variety of loathsome smells, and brought on a sickness among the slaves, of which many died, thus falling victims to the improvident avarice, as I may call it, of their purchasers. This wretched situation was again aggravated by the galling of the chains, now became insupportable; and the filth of the necessary tubs, into which the children often fell, and were almost suffocated. The shrieks of the women, and the groans of the dying, rendered the whole a scene of horror almost inconceivable. Happily perhaps for myself I was soon reduced so low here that it was thought necessary to keep me almost always on deck; and from my extreme youth I was not put in fetters. In this situation I expected every hour to share the fate of my companions, some of whom were almost daily brought upon deck at the point of death, which I began to hope would soon put an end to my miseries. Often did I think many of the inhabitants of the deep much more happy than myself. I envied them the freedom they enjoyed, and as often wished I could change my condition for theirs. Every circumstance I met with served only to render my state more painful, and heighten my apprehensions, and my opinion of the cruelty of the whites. One day they had taken a number of fishes; and when they had killed and satisfied themselves with as many as they thought fit, to our astonishment who were on the deck, rather than give any of them to us to eat as we expected, they tossed the remaining fish into the sea again, although we begged and prayed for some as well as we could, but in vain; and some of my countrymen, being pressed by hunger, took an opportunity, when they thought no one saw them, of trying to get a little privately; but they were discovered, and the attempt procured them some very severe floggings. One day, when we had a smooth sea and moderate wind, two of my wearied countrymen who were chained together (I was near them at the time), preferring death to such a life of misery, somehow made through the nettings and jumped into the sea: immediately another quite dejected fellow, who, on account of his illness, was suffered to be out of irons, also followed their example; and I believe many more would very soon have done the same if they had not been prevented by the ship's crew, who were instantly alarmed. Those of us that were the most active were in a moment put down under the deck, and there was such a noise and confusion amongst the people of the ship as I never heard before, to stop her, and get the boat out to go after the slaves. However two of the wretches were drowned, but they got the other, and afterwards flogged him unmercifully for thus attempting to prefer death to slavery. In this manner we continued to undergo more hardships than I can now relate, hardships which are inseparable from this accursed trade. Many a time we were near suffocation from the want of fresh air, which we were often without for whole days together. This, and the stench of the necessary tubs, carried off many. During our passage I first saw flying fishes, which surprised me very much: they used frequently to fly across the ship, and many of them fell on the deck. I also now first saw the use of the quadrant; I had often with astonishment seen the mariners make observations with it, and I could not think what it meant. They at last took notice of my surprise; and one of them, willing to increase it, as well as to gratify my curiosity, made me one day look through it. The clouds appeared to me to be land, which disappeared as they passed along. This heightened my wonder; and I was now more persuaded than ever that I was in another world, and that every thing about me was magic. At last we came in sight of the island of Barbadoes, at which the whites on board gave a great shout, and made many signs of joy to us. We did not know what to think of this; but as the vessel drew nearer we plainly saw the harbour, and other ships of different kinds and sizes; and we soon anchored amongst them off Bridge Town. Many merchants and planters now came on board, though it was in the evening. They put us in separate parcels, and examined us attentively. They also made us jump, and pointed to the land, signifying we were to go there. We thought by this we should be eaten by these ugly men, as they appeared to us; and, when soon after we were all put down under the deck again, there was much dread and trembling among us, and nothing but bitter cries to be heard all the night from these apprehensions, insomuch that at last the white people got some old slaves from the land to pacify us. They told us we were not to be eaten, but to work, and were soon to go on land, where we should see many of our country people. This report eased us much; and sure enough, soon after we were landed, there came to us Africans of all languages. We were conducted immediately to the merchant's yard, where we were all pent up together like so many sheep in a fold, without regard to sex or age. As every object was new to me every thing I saw filled me with surprise. What struck me first was that the houses were built with stories, and in every other respect different from those in Africa: but I was still more astonished on seeing people on horseback. I did not know what this could mean; and indeed I thought these people were full of nothing but magical arts.

(I, 70–85)

b. Voyage to England

I stayed in this island for a few days; I believe it could not be above a fortnight; when I and some few more slaves, that were not saleable amongst the rest, from very much fretting, were shipped off in a sloop for North America. On the passage we were better treated than when we were coming from Africa, and we had plenty of rice and fat pork. We were landed up a river a good way from the sea, about Virginia county, where we saw few or none of our native Africans, and not one soul who could talk to me. I was a few weeks weeding grass, and gathering stones in a plantation; and at last all my companions were distributed different ways, and only myself was left. I was now exceedingly miserable, and thought myself worse off than any of the rest of my companions; for they could talk to each other, but I had no person to speak to that I could understand. In this state I was constantly grieving and pining, and wishing for death rather than any thing else. While I was in this plantation the gentleman, to whom I suppose the estate belonged, being unwell, I was one day sent for to his dwelling house to fan him; when I came into the room where he was I was very much affrighted at some things I saw, and the more so as I had seen a black woman slave as I came through the house, who was cooking the dinner, and the poor creature was cruelly loaded with various kinds of iron machines; she had one particularly on her head, which locked her mouth so fast that she could scarcely speak; and could not eat nor drink. I was much astonished and shocked at this contrivance, which I afterwards learned was called the iron muzzle. Soon after I had a fan put into my hand, to fan the gentleman while he slept; and so I did indeed with great fear. While he was fast asleep I indulged myself a great deal in looking about the room, which to me appeared very fine and curious. The first object that engaged my attention was a watch which hung on the chimney, and was going. I was quite surprised at the noise it made, and was afraid it would tell the gentleman any thing I might do amiss: and when I immediately after observed a picture hanging in the room, which appeared constantly to look at me, I was still more affrighted, having never seen such things as these before. At one time I thought it was something relative to magic; and not seeing it move I thought it might be some way the whites had to keep their great men when they died, and offer them libation as we used to do to our friendly spirits. In this state of anxiety I remained till my master awoke, when I was dismissed out of the room, to my no small satisfaction and relief; for I thought that these people were all made up of wonders. In this place I was called Jacob; but on board the African ship I was called Michael. I had been some time in this miserable, forlorn, and much dejected state, without having any one to talk to, which made my life a burden, when the kind and unknown hand of the Creator (who in very deed leads the blind in a way they know not) now began to appear, to my comfort; for one day the captain of a merchant ship, called the Industrious Bee, came on some business to my master's house. This gentleman, whose name was Michael Henry Pascal, was a lieutenant in the royal navy, but now commanded this trading ship, which was somewhere in the confines of the county many miles off. While he was at my master's house it happened that he saw me, and liked me so well that he made a purchase of me. I think I have often heard him say he gave thirty or forty pounds sterling for me; but I do not now remember which. However, he meant me for a present to some of his friends in England: and I was sent accordingly from the house of my then master, one Mr. Campbell, to the place where the ship lay; I was conducted on horseback by an elderly black man, (a mode of travelling which appeared very odd to me). When I arrived I was carried on board a fine large ship, loaded with tobacco, &c. and just ready to sail for England. I now thought my condition much mended; I had sails to lie on, and plenty of good victuals to eat; and every body on board used me very kindly, quite contrary to what I had seen of any white people before; I therefore began to think that they were not all of the same disposition. A few days after I was on board we sailed for England. I was still at a loss to conjecture my destiny. By this time, however, I could smatter a little imperfect English; and I wanted to know as well as I could where we were going. Some of the people of the ship used to tell me they were going to carry me back to my own country, and this made me very happy. I was quite rejoiced at the sound of going back; and thought if I should get home what wonders I should have to tell. But I was reserved for another fate, and was soon undeceived when we came within sight of the English coast. While I was on board this ship, my captain and master named me *Gustavus Vasa*. I at that time began to understand him a little, and refused to be called so, and told him as well as I could that I would be called Jacob; but he said I should not, and still called me Gustavus; and when I refused to answer to my new name, which at first I did, it gained me many a cuff; so at length I submitted, and was obliged to bear the present name, by which I have been known ever since. The ship had a very long passage; and on that account we had very short allowance of provisions. Towards the last we had only one pound and a half of bread per week, and about the same quantity of meat, and one quart of water a day. We spoke with only one vessel the whole time we were at sea, and but once we caught a few fishes. In our extremities the captain and people told me in jest they would kill and eat me; but I thought them in earnest, and was depressed beyond measure, expecting every moment to be my last. While I was in this situation one evening they caught, with a good deal of trouble, a large shark, and got it on board. This gladdened my poor heart exceedingly, as I thought it would serve the people to eat instead of their eating me; but very soon, to my astonishment, they cut off a small part of the tail, and tossed the rest over the side. This renewed my consternation; and I did not know what to think of these white people, though I very much feared they would kill and eat me. There was on board the ship a young lad who had never been at sea before, about four or five years older than myself: his name was Richard Baker. He was a native of America, had received an excellent education, and was of a most amiable temper. Soon after I went on board he shewed me a great deal of partiality and attention, and in return I grew extremely fond of him. We at length became inseparable; and, for the space of two years, he was of very great use to me, and was my constant companion and instructor. Although this dear youth had many slaves of his own, yet he and I have gone through many sufferings together on shipboard; and we have many nights lain in each other's bosoms when we were in great distress. Thus such a friendship was cemented between us as we cherished till his death, which, to my very great sorrow, happened in the year 1759, when he was up the Archipelago, on board his majesty's ship the Preston: an event which I have never ceased to regret, as I lost at once a kind interpreter, an agreeable companion, and a faithful friend; who, at the age of fifteen, discovered a mind superior to prejudice; and who was not ashamed to notice, to associate with, and to be the friend and instructor of one who was ignorant, a stranger, of a different complexion, and a slave! My master had lodged in his mother's house in America: he respected him very much, and made him always eat with him in the cabin. He used often to tell him jocularly that he would kill me to eat. Sometimes he would say to me – the black people were not good to eat, and would ask me if we did not eat people in my country. I said, No: then he said he would kill Dick (as he always called him) first, and afterwards me. Though this hearing relieved my mind a little as to myself, I was alarmed for Dick and whenever he was called I used to be very much afraid he was to be killed; and I would peep and watch to see if they were going to kill him: nor was I free from this consternation till we made the land. One night we lost a man over-board; and the cries and noise were so great and confused, in stopping the ship, that I, who did not know what was the matter, began, as usual, to be very much afraid, and to think they were going to make an offering with me, and perform some magic; which I still believed they dealt in. As the waves were very high I thought the Ruler of the seas was angry, and I expected to be offered up to appease him. This filled my mind with agony, and I could not any more that night close my eyes again to rest. However, when daylight appeared I was a little eased in my mind; but still every time I was called I used to think it was to be killed. Some time after this we saw some very large fish, which I afterwards found were called grampusses. They looked to me extremely terrible, and made their appearance just at dusk; and were so near as to blow the water on the ship's deck. I believed them to be the rulers of the sea; and, as the white people did not make any offerings at any time, I thought they were angry with them: and, at last, what confirmed my belief was, the wind just then died away, and a calm ensued, and in consequence of it the ship stopped going. I supposed that the fish had performed this, and I hid myself in the fore part of the ship, through fear of being offered up to appease them, every minute peeping and quaking: but my good friend Dick came shortly towards me, and I took an opportunity to ask him, as well as I could, what these fish were. Not being able to talk much English, I could but just make him understand my question; and not at all, when I asked him if any offerings were to be made to them: however, he told me these fish would swallow any body; which sufficiently alarmed me. Here he was called away by the captain, who was leaning over the quarter-deck railing and looking at the fish; and most of the people were busied in getting a barrel of pitch to light, for them to play with. The captain now called me to him, having learned some of my apprehensions from Dick; and having diverted himself and others for some time with my fears, which appeared ludicrous enough in my crying and trembling, he dismissed me. The barrel of pitch was now lighted and put over the side into the water: by this time it was just dark, and the fish went after it; and, to my great joy, I saw them no more.

However, all my alarms began to subside when we got sight of land; and at last the ship arrived at Falmouth, after a passage of thirteen weeks. Every heart on board seemed gladdened on our reaching the shore, and none more than mine. The captain immediately went on shore, and sent on board some fresh provisions, which we wanted very much: we made good use of them, and our famine was soon turned into feasting, almost without ending. It was about the beginning of the spring 1757 when I arrived in England, and I was near twelve years of age at that time. I was very much struck with the buildings and the pavement of the streets in Falmouth; and, indeed, any object I saw filled me with new surprise. One morning, when I got upon deck, I saw it covered all over with the snow that fell over-night: as I had never seen any thing of the kind before, I thought it was salt; so I immediately ran down to the mate and desired him, as well as I could, to come and see how somebody in the night had thrown salt all over the deck. He, knowing what it was, desired me to bring some of it down to him: accordingly I took up a handful of it, which I found very cold indeed; and when I brought it to him he desired me to taste it. I did so, and I was surprised beyond measure. I then asked him what it was; he told me it was snow: but I could not in anywise understand him. He asked me if we had no such thing in my country; and I told him, No. I then asked him the use of it, and who made it; he told me a great man in the heavens, called God: but here again I was to all intents and purposes at a loss to understand him; and the more so, when a little after I saw the air filled with it, in a heavy shower, which fell down on the same day. After this I went to church; and having never been at such a place before, I was again amazed at seeing and hearing the service. I asked all I could about it; and they gave me to understand it was worshipping God, who made us and all things. I was still at a great loss, and soon got into an endless field of inquiries, as well as I was able to speak and ask about things. However, my little friend Dick used to be my best interpreter; for I could make free with him, and he always instructed me with pleasure: and from what I could understand by him of this God, and in seeing these white people did not sell one another, as we did, I was much pleased; and in this I thought they were much happier than we Africans. I was astonished at the wisdom of the white people in all things I saw; but was amazed at their not sacrificing; or making any offerings, and eating with unwashed hands, and touching the dead. I likewise could not help remarking the particular slenderness of their women, which I did not at first like; and I thought they were not so modest and shamefaced as the African women.

I had often seen my master and Dick employed in reading; and I had a great curiosity to talk to the books, as I thought they did; and so to learn how all things had a beginning: for that purpose I have often taken up a book, and have talked to it, and then put my ears to it, when alone, in hopes it would answer me; and I have been very much concerned when I found it remained silent.

(I, 90–107)

c. Petty Trading

A poor Creole negro I knew well, who, after having been often thus transported from island to island, at last resided in Montserrat. This man used to tell me many melancholy tales of himself. Generally, after he had done working for his master, he used to employ his few leisure moments to go a fishing. When he had caught any fish, his master would frequently take them from him without paying him; and at other times some other white people would serve him in the same manner. One day he said to me, very movingly, 'Sometimes when a white man take away my fish I go to my master, and he get me my right; and when my master by strength take away my fishes, what me must do? I can't go to any body to be righted: then,' said the poor man, looking up above, 'I must look up to God Mighty in the top for right.' This artless tale moved me much, and I could not help feeling the just cause Moses had in redressing his brother against the Egyptian. I exhorted the man to look up still to the God on the top, since there was no redress below. Though I little thought then that I myself should more than once experience such imposition, and read the same exhortation hereafter, in my own transactions in the islands; and that even this poor man and I should some time after suffer together in the same manner, as shall be related hereafter.

After I had been sailing for some time with this captain, at length I endeavoured to try my luck and commence merchant. I had but a very small capital to begin with; for one single half bit, which is equal to three pence in England, made up my whole stock. However I trusted to the Lord to be with me; and at one of our trips to St. Eustatia, a Dutch island, I bought a glass tumbler with my half bit, and when I came to Montserrat I sold it for a bit, or sixpence. Luckily we made several successive trips to St. Eustatia (which was a general mart for the West Indies, about twenty leagues from Montserrat); and in our next, finding my tumbler so profitable, with this one bit I bought two tumblers more; and when I came back I sold them for two bits, equal to a shilling sterling. When we went again I bought with these two bits four more of these glasses, which I sold for four bits on our return to Montserrat: and in our next voyage to St. Eustatia I bought two glasses with one bit, and with the other three I bought a jug of Geneva, nearly about three pints in measure. When we came to Montserrat I sold the gin for eight bits, and the tumblers for two, so that my capital now amounted in all to a dollar, well husbanded and acquired in the space of a month or six weeks, when I blessed the Lord that I was so rich. As we sailed to different islands, I laid this money out in various things occasionally, and it used to turn out to very good account, especially when we went to Guadaloupe, Grenada, and the rest of the French islands. Thus was I going all about the islands upwards of four years, and ever trading as I went, during which I experienced many instances of ill usage, and have seen many injuries done to other negroes in our dealings with Europeans: and, amidst our recreations, when we have been dancing and merry-making, they, without cause, have molested and insulted us. Indeed I was more than once obliged to look up to God on high, as I had advised the poor fisherman some time before. And I had not been long trading for myself in the manner I have related above, when I experienced the like trial in company with him as follows. This man being used to the water, was upon an emergency put on board of us by his master to work as another hand, on a voyage to Santa Cruz; and at our sailing he had brought his little all for a venture, which consisted of six bits' worth of limes and oranges in a bag; I had also my whole stock, which was about twelve bits' worth of the same kind of goods separate in two bags; for we had heard these fruits sold well in that island. When we came there, in some little convenient time he and I went ashore with fruits to sell them; but we had scarcely landed when we were met by two white men who presently took our three bags from us. We could not at first guess what they meant to do; and for some time we thought they were jesting with us; but they too soon let us know otherwise, for they took our ventures immediately to a house hard by, and adjoining the fort, while we followed all the way begging of them to give us our fruits, but in vain. They not only refused to return them, but swore at us, and threatened if we did not immediately depart they would flog us well. We told them these three bags were all we were worth in the world, and that we brought them with us to sell when we came from Montserrat, and shewed them the vessel. But this was rather against us, as they now saw we were strangers as well as slaves. They still therefore swore, and desired us to be gone, and even took sticks to beat us; while we, seeing they meant what they said, went off in the greatest confusion and despair. Thus, in the very minute of gaining more by three times than I ever did by any venture in my life before, was I deprived of every farthing I was worth. An insupportable misfortune! but how to help ourselves we knew not. In our consternation we went to the commanding officer of the fort and told him how we had been served by some of his people; but we obtained not the least redress: he answered our complaints only by a volley of imprecations against us, and immediately took a horse-whip, in order to chastise us, so that we were obliged to turn out much faster than we came in. I now, in the agony of distress and indignation, wished that the ire of God in his forked lightning might transfix the cruel oppressors among the dead. Still however we persevered; went back again to the house, and begged and besought them again and again for our fruits, till at last some other people that were in the house asked if we would be contented if they kept one bag and gave us the other two. We, seeing no remedy whatever, consented to this; and they, observing one bag to have both kinds of fruit in it, which belonged to my companion, kept that; and the other two, which were mine, they gave us back. As soon as I got them, I ran as fast as I could, and got the first negro man I could to help me off; my companion, however, stayed a little longer to plead; he told them the bag they had was his, and likewise all that he was worth in the world; but this was of no avail, and he was obliged to return without it. The poor old man, wringing his hands, cried bitterly for his loss; and, indeed, he then did look up to God on high, which so moved me with pity for him, that I gave him nearly one third of my fruits. We then proceeded to the markets to sell them; and Providence was more favourable to us than we could have expected, for we sold our fruits uncommonly well; I got for mine about thirty-seven bits. Such a surprising reverse of fortune in so short a space of time seemed like a dream to me, and proved no small encouragement for me to trust the Lord in any situation. My captain afterwards frequently used to take my part, and get me my right, when I have been plundered or used ill by these tender Christian depredators; among whom I have shuddered to observe the unceasing blasphemous execrations which are wantonly thrown out by persons of all ages and conditions, not only without occasion, but even as if they were indulgences and pleasure.

(I. 221–2; 233–240)

d. Disappointment and Freedom

A silversmith, whom we had brought to this place some voyages before, agreed with the Captain to return with us to the West

Indies, and promised at the same time to give the Captain a great deal of money, having pretended to take 'a liking to him, and being, as we thought, very rich. But while we stayed to load our vessel this man was taken ill in a house where he worked, and in a week's time became very bad. The worse he grew the more he used to speak of giving the Captain what he had promised him, so that he expected something considerable from the death of this man, who had no wife or child, and he attended him day and night. I used also to go with the Captain, at his own desire, to attend him; especially when we saw there was no appearance of his recovery: and, in order to recompense me for my trouble, the Captain promised me ten pounds, when he should get the man's property. I thought this would be of great service to me, although I had nearly money enough to purchase my freedom, if I should get safe this voyage to Montserrat. In this expectation I laid out above eight pounds of my money for a suit of superfine clothes to dance with at my freedom, which I hoped was then at hand. We still continued to attend this man, and were with him even on the last day he lived, till very late at night, when we went on board. After we were got to bed, about one or two o'clock in the morning, the Captain was sent for, and informed the man was dead. On this he came to my bed, and waking me, informed me of it, and desired me to get up and procure a light, and immediately go to him. I told him I was very sleepy, and wished he would take somebody else with him; or else, as the man was dead, and could want no farther attendance, to let all things remain as they were till the next morning. 'No, no,' said he, 'we will have the money to-night, I cannot wait till to-morrow; so let us go.' Accordingly I got up and struck a light, and away we both went and saw the man as dead as we could wish. The Captain said he would give him a grand burial, in gratitude for the promised treasure; and desired that all the things belonging to the deceased might be brought forth. Among others, there was a nest of trunks of which he had kept the keys whilst the man was ill, and when they were produced we opened them with no small eagerness and expectation; and as there were a great number within one another, with much impatience we took them one out of the other. At last, when we came to the smallest, and had opened it, we saw it was full of papers, which we supposed to be notes; at the sight of which our hearts leapt for joy; and that instant the Captain, clapping his hands, cried out, 'Thank God, here it is.' But when we took up the trunk, and

began to examine the supposed treasure and long-looked-for bounty, (alas! alas! how uncertain and deceitful are all human affairs!)
what had we found! While we were embracing a substance we
grasped an empty nothing. The whole amount that was in the nest
of trunks was only one dollar and a half; and all that the man
possessed would not pay for his coffin. Our sudden and exquisite
joy was now succeeded by as sudden and exquisite pain; and my
Captain and I exhibited, for some time, most ridiculous figures –
pictures of chagrin and disappointment! We went away greatly
mortified, and left the deceased to do as well as he could for himself,
as we had taken so good care of him when alive for nothing. We set
sail once more for Montserrat, and arrived there safe; but much out
of humour with our friend the silversmith. When we had unladen
the vessel, and I had sold my venture, finding myself master of
about forty-seven pounds, I consulted my true friend, the Captain,
how I should proceed in offering my master the money for my
freedom. He told me to come on a certain morning, when he and
my master would be at breakfast together. Accordingly, on that
morning I went, and met the Captain there, as he had appointed.
When I went in I made my obeisance to my master, and with my
money in my hand, and many fears in my heart, I prayed him to be
as good as his offer to me, when he was pleased to promise me my
freedom as soon as I could purchase it. This speech seemed to
confound him; he began to recoil: and my heart that instant sank
within me. 'What,' said he, 'give you your freedom? Why, where
did you get the money? Have you got forty pounds sterling? 'Yes,
sir,' I answered. 'How did you get it?' replied he. I told him, very
honestly. The Captain then said he knew I got the money very
honestly and with much industry, and that I was particularly
careful. On which my master replied, I got money much faster than
he did; and said he would not have made me the promise he did if he
had thought I should have got money so soon. 'Come, come,' said
my worthy Captain, clapping my master on the back, 'Come,
Robert, (which was his name) I think you must let him have his
freedom; you have laid your money out very well; you have
received good interest for it all this time, and here is now the
principal at last. I know Gustavus has earned you more than an
hundred a-year, and he will still save you money, as he will not
leave you: – Come, Robert, take the money.' My master then said,
he would not be worse than his promise; and, taking the money,

told me to go to the Secretary at the Register Office, and get my manumission drawn up. These words of my master were like a voice from heaven to me: in an instant all my trepidation was turned into unutterable bliss; and I most reverently bowed myself with gratitude, unable to express my feelings, but by the over-flowing of my eyes, while my true and worthy friend, the Captain, congratulated us both with a peculiar degree of heart-felt pleasure. As soon as the first transports of my joy were over, and that I had expressed my thanks to these my worthy friends in the best manner I was able, I rose with a heart full of affection and reverence, and left the room, in order to obey my master's joyful mandate of going to the Register Office. As I was leaving the house I called to mind the words of the Psalmist, in the 126th Psalm, and like him, 'I glorified God in my heart, in whom I trusted.' These words had been impressed on my mind from the very day I was forced from Deptford to the present hour, and I now saw them, as I thought, fulfilled and verified. My imagination was all rapture as I flew to the Register Office, and in this respect, like the apostle Peter, [Acts, chap. xii, ver. 9] (whose deliverance from prison was so sudden and extraordinary, that he thought he was in a vision) I could scarcely believe I was awake. Heavens! who could do justice to my feelings at this moment! Not conquering heroes themselves, in the midst of a triumph – Not the tender mother who had just regained her long-lost infant, and presses it to her heart – Not the weary hungry mariner, at the sight of the desired friendly port – Not the lover, when he once more embraces his beloved mistress, after she had been ravished from his arms! – All within my breast was tumult, wildness, and delirium! My feet scarcely touched the ground, for they were winged with joy, and, like Elijah, as he rose to Heaven, they 'were with lightning sped as I went on.' Every one I met I told of my happiness, and blazed about the virtue of my amiable master and captain.

When I got to the office and acquainted the Register with my errand he congratulated me on the occasion, and told me he would draw up my manumission for half price, which was a guinea. I thanked him for his kindness; and having received it and paid him, I hastened to my master to get him to sign it, that I might be fully released. Accordingly he signed the manumission that day, so that, before night, I who had been a slave in the morning, trembling at the will of another, was become my own master, and completely free. I thought this was the happiest day I had ever experienced; and my joy was still heightened by the blessings and prayers of the sable race, particularly the aged, to whom my heart had ever been attached with reverence.

As the form of my manumission has something peculiar in it, and expresses the absolute power and dominion one man claims over his fellow, I shall beg leave to present it before my readers at full length:

> *Montserrat.* – To all men unto whom these presents shall come: I Robert King, of the parish of St. Anthony in the said island, merchant, send greeting: Know ye, that I the aforesaid Robert King, for and in consideration of the sum of seventy pounds current money of the said island, to me in hand paid, and to the intent that a negro man-slave, named Gustavus Vassa, shall and may become free, have manumitted, emancipated, enfranchised, and set free, and by these presents do manumit, emancipate, enfranchise, and set free, the aforesaid negro man-slave, named Gustavus Vassa, for ever, hereby giving, granting and releasing unto him, the said Gustavus Vassa, all right, title, dominion, sovereignty, and property, which, as lord and master over the aforesaid Gustavus Vassa, I had, or now I have, or by any means whatsoever I may or can hereafter possibly have over him the aforesaid negro, for ever. In witness whereof I the above-said Robert King have unto these presents set my hand and seal, this tenth day of July, in the year of our Lord one thousand seven hundred and sixty-six.   ROBERT KING

> Signed, sealed, and delivered in the presence of Terrylegay, Montserrat.

> Registered the within manumission at full length, this eleventh day of July, 1766, in liber D.
>   TERRYLEGAY, REGISTER.

In short, the fair as well as black people immediately styled me by a new appellation, to me the most desirable in the world, which was Freeman, and at the dances I gave my Georgia superfine blue clothes made no indifferent appearance, as I thought. Some of the sable females, who formerly stood aloof, now began to relax and appear less coy; but my heart was still fixed on London, where I hoped to be ere long.

(II. 7–19)

e.

For *The Public Advertiser.*
28 January 1788

To J. T. [James Tobin] Esq; Author of the BOOKS called CURSORY REMARKS & REJOINDERS.

Sir,

That to love mercy and judge rightly of things is an honour to man, no body I think will deny, but 'if he understandeth not, nor sheweth compassion to the sufferings of his fellow-creatures, he is like the beasts that perish.' Psalm LIX verse 20.

Excuse me, Sir, if I think you in no better predicament that that exhibited in the latter part of the above clause; for can any man less ferocious than a tiger or a wolf attempt to justify the cruelties inflicted on the [blacks] in the West Indies? You certainly cannot be susceptible of human pity to be so callous to their complicated woes! Who could but the Author of the Cursory Remarks so debase his nature, as not to feel his keenest pangs of heart on reading their deplorable story? I confess my cheek changes colour with resentment against your unrelenting barbarity, and wish you from my soul to run the gauntlet of Lex Talionis at this time; for as you are so fond of flogging others, it is no bad proof of your deserving a flagellation on yourself. Is it not written in the 15th chapter of Numbers, the 15th and 16th verses, that there is the same law for the stranger as for you?

Then, Sir, why do you rob him of the common privilege given to all by the Universal and Almighty Legislator? Why exclude him from the enjoyment of benefits which he has equal right to with yourself? Why treat him as if he was not of like feeling? Does civilization warrant these incursions upon natural justice? No. – Does religion? No. – Benevolence to all is its essence, and do unto others as we would others should do unto us, its grand precept – to Blacks as well as Whites, all being children of the same parent. Those, therefore, who transgress those sacred obligations, and here, Mr. Remarker, I think you are caught, are not superior to brutes which understandeth not, nor to beasts which perish.

From having been in the West Indies, you must know that the facts stated by the Rev. Mr. Ramsay are true; and yet regardless of the truth, you controvert them. This surely is supporting a bad cause at all events, and brandishing falsehood to strengthen the hand

of the oppressor. Recollect, Sir, that you are told in the 17th verse of
the 19th chapter of Leviticus, 'You shall not suffer sin upon your
neighbours', and you will not I am sure, escape the upbraidings of
your conscience, unless you are fortunate enough to have none; and
remember also, that the oppressor and oppressed are in the hands of
the just and awful God, who says, Vengeance is mine and I will
repay – repay the oppressor and the justifier of the oppression.
How dreadful then will your fate be? The studied and torturing
punishments, inhuman, as they are, of a barbarous planter, or a
more barbarous overseer, will be tenderness compared to the
provoked wrath of an angry but righteous God, who will raise, I
have the fullest confidence, many of the sable race to the joys of
Heaven, and cast the oppressive white to that doleful place, where
he will cry, but will cry in vain, for a drop of water!

Your delight seems to be in misrepresentation, else how could
you in page 11 of your Remarks, and in your Rejoinder, page 35,
communicate to the public such a glaring untruth as that the oath of
a free African is equally admissible in several courts with that of a
white person? The contrary of this I know is the fact at every one of
the islands I have been, and I have been at no less than fifteen: But
who will dispute with such an invective fibber? Why nobody to be
sure; for you'll tell, I wish I could say truths, but you oblige me to
use ill manners, you lie faster than Old Nick can hear them. A few
shall stare you in the face:

What is your speaking of the laws in favour of the Blacks?

Your description of the iron muzzle?

That you never saw an infliction of a severe punishment, im-
plying thereby that there is none?

That a [black] has every inducement to wish for a numerous
family?

That in England there are no black labourers?

That those who are not servants, are in rags or thieves?

In a word, the public can bear testimony with me that you are a
malicious slanderer of an honest, industrious, injured people!

From the same source of malevolence the freedom of their
inclinations is to be shackled – it is not sufficient for their bodies to
be oppressed, but their minds must also? Iniquity in the extreme! If
the mind of a black man conceives the passion of love for a fair
female, he is to pine, languish, and even die, sooner than an
intermarriage be allowed, merely because the complexion of the

offspring should be tawney – A more foolish prejudice than this never warped a cultivated mind – for as no contamination of the virtues of the heart would result from the union, the mixture of colour could be of no consequence. God looks with equal good will on all his creatures, whether black or white – let neither, therefore, arrogantly condemn the other.

The mutual commerce of the sexes of both Blacks and Whites, under the restrictions of moderation and law, would yield more benefit than a prohibition – the mind free – would not have such a strong propensity toward the black females as when under restraint: Nature abhors restraint, and for ease either evades or breaks it. Hence arise secret amours, adultery, fornication and all other evils of lasciviousness! hence that most abandoned boasting of the French Planter, who, under the dominion of lust, had the shameless impudence to exult at the violations he had committed against Virtue, Religion, and the Almighty – hence also spring actual murders on infants, the procuring of abortions, enfeebled constitution, disgrace, shame, and a thousand other horrid enormities.

Now, Sir, would it not be more honour to us to have a few darker visages than perhaps yours among us, than inundation of such evils? And to provide effectual remedies, by a liberal policy against evils which may be traced to some of our most wealthy Planters as their fountain, and which may have smeared the purity of even your own chastity?

As the ground work, why not establish intermarriages at home, and in our Colonies? and encourage open, free, and generous loves upon Nature's own wide and extensive plain, subservient only to moral rectitude, without distinction of the colour of a skin?

That ancient most wise, and inspired political Moses, encouraged strangers to unite with the Israelites, upon this maxim, that every addition to their number was an addition to their strength, and as an inducement, admitted them to most of the immunities of his own people. He established marriage with strangers by his own example – The Lord confirmed them – and punished Aaron and Miriam for vexing their brother for marrying the Ethiopian – Away then with your narrow impolitic notion of preventing by law what will be a national honour, national strength, and productive of national virtue – Intermarriages!

Wherefore, to conclude in the words of one of your selected

texts, 'If I come, I will remember the deeds which he doeth, prating against us with malicious words.'

> I am Sir,
> Your fervent Servant,
> GUSTAVUS VASSA, the Ethiopian
> and the King's late Commissary for the
> African Settlement.

Baldwin's Garden, January, 1788.

*f. Letter from Gustavus Vassa, late Commissary for the African
    Settlement, to the Right Honourable Lord Hawkesbury*

My Lord,   London, 13th March 1788.

As the illicit Traffic of Slavery is to be taken into consideration of the British Legislature, I have taken the Liberty of sending you the following Sentiments, which have met the Approbation of many intelligent and commercial Gentlemen.

Sir,

A SYSTEM of commerce once established in Africa, the Demand for Manufactories will most rapidly augment, as the native Inhabitants will sensibly adopt our Fashions, Manner, Customs, &c. &c.

In proportion to the Civilization, so will be the Consumption of British Manufactures.

The Wear and Tear of a Continent, nearly twice as large as Europe, and rich in Vegetable and Mineral Productions, is much easier conceived than calculated. A Case in point. It cost the Aborigines of Britain little or nothing in Cloathing, &c. The Difference between our Forefathers and us in point of Consumption, is literally infinite. The Reason is most obvious. It will be equally immense in Africa. The same Cause, viz. Civilization, will ever produce the same Effect. There are no Book or outstanding Debts, if I may be allowed the Expression. The Word Credit is not to be found in the African Dictionary; it is standing upon safe Ground.

A commercial Intercourse with Africa opens an inexhaustible Source of Wealth to the manufacturing Interest of Great Britain; and to all which the Slave Trade is a physical Obstruction.

If I am not misinformed, the manufacturing Interest is equal, if not superior to the landed Interest as to Value, for Reasons which will soon appear. The Abolition of the diabolical Slavery will give a most rapid and permanent Extension to Manufactures, which is totally and diametrically opposite to what some interested People assert.

The Manufactories of this Country must and will in the nature and Reason of Things have a full and constant Employ by supplying the African Markets. The Population, Bowels, and Surface of Africa abound in valuable and useful Returns; the hidden treasuries of Countries will be brought to Light and into Circulation.

Industry, Enterprise, and Mining will have their full Scope, proportionably as they civilize. In a Word, it lays open an endless Field of Commerce to the British Manufactures and Merchant Adventurer.

The manufacturing Interest and the general Interest of the Enterprise are synonimous; the Abolition of Slavery would be in reality an universal Good, and for which a partial Ill must be supported.

Tortures, Murder, and every other imaginable Barbarity are practised by the West India Planters upon the Slaves with Impunity. I hope the Slave Trade will be abolished: I pray it may be an Event at hand. The great Body of Manufactories, uniting in the Cause, will considerably facilitate and expedite it; and, as I have already stated, it is most substantially their Interest and Advantage, and as such the Nation at large. In a short Space of Time One Sentiment alone will prevail, from Motives of Interest as well as Justice and Humanity.

Europe contains One hundred and Twenty Millions of Inhabitants; Query, How many Millions doth Africa contain? Supposing the Africans, collectively and individually, to expend Five Pounds a Head in Raiment and Furniture yearly, when civilized, &c. – an Immensity beyond the Reach of Imagination: This I conceive to be a Theory founded upon Facts; and therefore an infallible one. If the Blacks were permitted to remain in their own Country they would double themselves every Fifteen Years: In Proportion to such Increase would be the Demand for Manufactures. Cotton and Indigo grow spontaneously in some Parts of Africa: A Consideration this of no small Consequence to the manufacturing Towns of Great Britain.

The Chamber of Manufactories of Great Britain, held in London will be strenuous in the Cause. It opens a most immense, glorious, and happy Prospect.

The Cloathing, &c. of a Continent Ten thousand Miles in Circumference, and immensely rich in Productions of every Demonination, would make an interesting Return indeed for our Manufactories, a free Trade being established.

> I have, my Lord, the Honour to sub-
> scribe myself,
> Your Lordships very humble and de-
> voted Servant,
> GUSTAVUS VASSA,
> the late Commissary for the African
> Settlement.

No. 53, Baldwin's Gardens, Holborn.

g. *Letter to the Rev. G. Walker and family of Nottingham*

London Feby the 27.th———1792

Dr. Revd. & Worthy friends &c.

This with my Best of Respects to you and wife with many Prayers that you both may ever be Well in Souls and Bodys – & also your Little Lovely Daughter – I thank you for all kindnesses which you was please[d] to show me, may God ever Reward you for it – Sir, I went to Ireland & was there 8½ months – & sold 1900 copies of my narrative. I came here on the 10th inst. – & I now mean as it seem Pleasing to my Good God! – to leave London in about 8 – or 10 Days more, & take me a Wife – (one Miss Cullen –) of Soham in Cambridge shire – & when I have given her about 8 or 10 Days Comfort, I mean Directly to go Scotland – and sell my 5th. Editions – I Trust that my going about has been of much use to the Cause of the Abolition of the accu[r]sed Slave Trade – a Gentleman of the Committee the Revd. Dr. Baker has said that I am more use to the Cause than half the People in the Country – I wish to God, I could be so. A noble Earl of Stanhope has Lately Consulted me twice about a Bill which his Ld.ship now mean[s] to bring in to the House to allow the sable People of the wt Indias the Rights of taking an oath against any White Person – I hope it may Pass, tis high time – & will be of much use. – May the Lord Bless all the friends of Humanity. Pray Pardon what ever you here see amiss – I will be Glad to see you at my Wedg. – Pray give my best Love To the Worthy & Revd. Mr. Robinson, & his – also to my friends Coltman – and Mr. & Mrs. Buxton – I Pray that the Good Lord may make all of that family Rich in faith as in the things of this World – I have [a] Great Deal to say if I ever have the Pleasure to see you again – I have been in the uttermust hurry ever since I have being in this wickd.

Town. – & I only came now to save if I can, £232, I Lent to a man, who [is] now Dying. Pray Excuse ha[ste] – will be Glad to hear from you – & do very much beg your Prayers as you ever have mine – & if I see you no more here Below may I see you all at Last at Gods Right Hand – where parting will be no more – Glory to God that J. Christ is yet all, & in all, to my Poor Soul –

    I am with all Due Respects
      yours to Command –
        Gustavus Vassa
        The African
      ——————at Mr. Hardys No. 4 Taylors Building
        Chandos street, Covent Garden

6

JULIUS SOUBISE

born Jamaica c.1750, died Madras 1780

A Love Letter, from Anon., *Nocturnal Revels,* or the History of King's Place, London, 1779, II 210–232

Soubise was a favoured African youth in the service of the Duchess of Queensbury, whose esteem with the Duchess was such that she was found in her boudoir, according to the journal of Lady Mary Coke in March 1767, 'half-dressed and half-undressed ... talking to her Black Boy, who indeed seemed to have an extraordinary capacity, something very uncommon. She told me she had taught him everything he had a mind to learn.' According to contemporary reports, usually rather less enamoured of Soubise than was the Duchess, the art of seduction appears to have been an important part of his education, which included a spell at Eton, as usher to the elder Henry Angelo, the distinguished riding-master, whom the Duchess employed to train Soubise in horsemanship and fencing. Soubise gained a notorious reputation as a dandy and womaniser, but having fallen from grace after seducing the Duchess's maidservant he was ultimately disowned, and in 1777 sent to teach at a riding school in Madras. He died there a few years later of a fall from a horse.

Sancho wrote to him affectionately (see Sancho, letters 5 and 6), but Soubise was treated less kindly by some contemporaries. The satirical portrait of him given by the anonymous author of *Nocturnal Revels*, includes the following letter to a young woman to whom Soubise had taken a fancy. Though printed by the anonymous author in the spirit of mockery against Soubise, it seems to us to convey the stylish self-mockery of an ironic jester more than the vanity of the buffoon the author of the portrait wishes us to see. We regret that it is the only surviving fragment from the pen of this rascally charmer.

The text of the letter is from the chapters on Soubise in *Nocturnal Revels*, reprinted in Edwards and Walvin, *Black*

Personalities in the Era of the Slave Trade 230–237, which quotes further contemporary accounts of Soubise. Information is also to be found in Shyllon, *Black People in Britain* 41–3.

Dear Miss,

I have often beheld you in public with rapture; indeed it is impossible to view you without such emotions as must animate every man of sentiment. In a word, Madam, you have seized my heart, and I dare tell you, I am your *Negro Slave*. You startle at this expression, Madam; but I love to be sincere. I am of that swarthy race of ADAM, whom some despise on account of their complexion; but I begin to find from experience, that even this trial of our patience may last but for a time, as Providence has given such knowledge to Man, as to remedy all the evils of this life. There is not a disorder under the sun which may not, by the skill and industry of the learned, be removed: so do I find, that similar applications in the researches of medicine, have brought to bear such discoveries, as to remove the tawny hue of any complexion, if applied with skill and perseverance. In this pursuit, my dear Miss, I am resolutely engaged, and hope, in a few weeks, I may be able to throw myself at your feet, in as agreeable a form as you can desire; in the mean time, believe me with the greatest sincerity,

> Your's most devotedly,
> My Lovely Angel,
> Soubise.

7

The Sierra Leone Settlers' Letters

1791–1800

In 1786, Granville Sharp's scheme to settle the English Black Poor in Sierra Leone, called 'The Province of Freedom', was sufficiently advanced for ships to set out to establish the Freetown colony. As a result of bad weather, and ill-health, they initially got no further than Plymouth, where Equiano, who had been appointed Commissary for Stores by the Admiralty, was dismissed, though the evidence suggests he had done nothing worse than stand up for the settlers, and complain about inefficient and possibly dishonest administration. After they reached their destination in 1787, things went from bad to worse, and in the early years of the settlement, the criticisms of the planning voiced by Equiano and Cugoano seemed justified. But the small colony managed to survive, and by 1791 it was proposed to introduce new blood.

The American War of Independence had ended in 1783, and many American slaves had seized their freedom, numbers of men joining the British Army. At the end of the war some 3,000 men, women and children were allowed to settle in Nova Scotia, where they were unhappy for various reasons, the coldness of the climate being one; but more serious was that slavery was still legal in Nova Scotia, and they believed that only by way of secure land ownership could they feel confident of achieving true freedom. One of their community, Thomas Peters, a former slave who had been a Sergeant in the British Army during the war, crossed to London to initiate discussions with the Sierra Leone Company for the resettling of the Nova Scotians in Freetown, for which in 1791 they set sail.

They had negotiated terms with the Company's representative, John Clarkson, brother of the great abolitionist Thomas, and in his enthusiasm Clarkson had promised more than the Company Directors had placed on offer. Clarkson had promised property, rent-free, but the Company had drawn up an offer which involved quit-rents. There were also complaints of overcharging by the Company store. When Clarkson went on leave to England to marry, the settlers grew even more dissatisfied, feeling that the one voice of authority sympathetic to them had been silenced. In 1793 the settlers sent two representatives to London, Cato Perkins and Isaac Anderson, to negotiate further with the Company, and seek the aid of Clarkson, to whom they sent a copy of the Settlers' Petition, one of the letters included below. Clarkson on his part wrote back to Perkins and Anderson on November 3 1793 'altho you may have misunderstood me in one or two instances, yet on the whole you appear right – I should be ashamed of myself were I to be neglectful in doing my utmost to bring about a right understanding between you and the Directors of the Sierra Leone Company and therefore I am ready to meet you before the whole of them . . . to endeavour to settle everything.' But the Directors, he wrote on November 11 1793, 'seem unwilling that I should see you before them', adding that he wished 'to convince you that the promises I made you were from authority given me by the Sierra Leone Company, and that you have a just right to their performance – this will I hope convince you, as well as those you represent, that I have done all in *my power* to perform them.'

The Company, apparently displeased with Clarkson's hand-ling of the situation, dismissed him. Though he had been in the wrong to offer the settlers more than the Company had agreed to, he remained the settlers' hero, and the Company, aggres-sive, paternalistic and tactless, established itself as villain of the piece. The journey of Perkins and Anderson 'home' as one letter calls it, to London was of no avail. The Company and the settlers were on a collision course that ended in tragedy, with open armed rebellion, and the capture, trial and execution of some of the settlers' leaders. These included Isaac Anderson, whose final unsigned letter was his death warrant, charged as he was under English law with what then amounted to a capital offence, sending an anonymous and threatening letter to the governor.

In this correspondence we see a very early instance of a black community using their new, limited, but growing literacy to defend their rights and articulate a political aim, beginning with simple everyday requests for fresh beef or soap, to radical demands for just treatment. The reader may find that the voice of true feeling struggling to break through the limitations of its control of the language, speaks to us more powerfully than formal eloquence. The brutal response of the Company did not prevent that small community from becoming the leader in educational development and West Africa's first seat of uni-versity learning.

The texts have been edited by Christopher Fyfe and are selected from his volume in this series,'*Our Children Free and Happy*', which also contains a study by Professor Charles Jones of the use of language in the letters. In preparing this brief introduction and selection, we have drawn upon Mr. Fyfe's scholarship, not only his draft edition of the letters but also his *History of Sierra Leone* (see bibliography). We must also thank the British Library for permission to print the letters from the Clarkson Papers, Add. Ms. 41,262A and Ms. 41,263, the University of Illinois, Chicago, for permission to print the Farewell Petition, letter no. 3, and the Public Record Office, London, for the list of grievances, letter no. 11, from the Colonial Office papers, 270/5.

a. Thomas Peters and David Edmon, 23 December 1791

halefax   december the 23, 1791
the humble petion of the Black pepel lying in mr wisdoms Store Called the anoplus¹ Compnay humbely bag that if it is Consent to your honer as it is the larst Christmas day that we ever shall see in the amaraca that it may please your honer to grant us one days alowance of frish Beef for a Christmas diner that if it is agreabel to you and the rest of the Gentlemon to whom it may Consern

thomas petus [Peters]
david Edmon

b. Susana Smith, 12 May 1792

Sierra Leone May 12th 1792
Sir I your hum bel Servent begs the faver of your Excelence to See if you will Pleas to Let me hav Som Sope for I am in great want of Som I hav not had aney Since I hav bin to this plais I hav bin Sick and I want to git Som Sope verry much to wash my family Clos for we ar not fit to be Sean for dirt
   your hum   Susana Smith
   bel Servet

c. Farewell Petition, 28 November 1792

Sierraleon Freetown November the 28 1792
we the humble pittioners we the Black pepol that Came from novascotia to this place under our agent John Clarkson and from the time he met with us in novascotia he ever did behave to us as a

gentilmon in everey rescpt he provided every thing for our parshige as wors in his pour to make us comfortable till we arrived at Sierraleon and his behaveor heath benge with such a regard to to us his advice his Concil his patience his love in general to us all both men and wemen and Children and thearfour to the gentilmon of the Sierloen Companey in England we thy humbel pittioners wold desier to render thanks to the honerabl gentilmon of the Sierraleon Companey that it heth pleased allmighty god to put it into the hearts to think of them on us when we war in destress and we wold wish that it might please the gentilmon of the Companey as our govenor is a goin to take his leave of us and a goin to England thearfour we wold Bee under stud by the gentilmon that our ardent desier is that the Same John Clarkeson Shold returen Back to bee our goverener our had Comander in Chef for the time to com and we will obay him as our governer and will hold to the laws of England as far as lys in our pour and as for his promis to us in giting our lands it is the peopel agree to take parte of thear land now at present and the remander as soon as posable and we pray that his Excelency John Clarkson might Be preserved safe over the sea to his frinds and return to us again and we thy humbel pittioners is in duty Bound and will ever pray
witness our hands to the sine

David George	George Weeks	Ely Ackim
Richard Corankeapon	Joseph Williams	Kasscey Cranpone
Catrin Bartley	Hector Peters	Lazarus Jones
wider	Jane Richard	John Manuell
Lucy Whiteford	Elizabeth Wite	George Williams
wider	Cato Linas	Jane Humans wider
John Frinken	Joseph Ramsey	Philish Halsted wider
Boston King	John Demps	Janey Marshel
Thomas London	Jacb Wigfall	Isaac Streeter
Francis Worak	Samson Heywood	John Bevis his mark
Jacob Smith	Stephen Ficklin	John Gray his Brick Layer
Francis Partrick	William Taylor	Robert Robertson his
Capt Stpen Peters	John Cuthworth	Josep Lonard his mark
Benjamin Francis	Charity Macgriger	Thomas Godfrey his mark
his mark	a widow	Thomas Sandas
Jess George	Henry Lawrance	Pheby Linch
John Johnson	Cato Burdan	Georg Black
Charles Jones	John Kizell	

d. Cato Perkins and Isaac Anderson, 25 October 1793

London Octr 26. 1793

Sir

We are very sorry indeed that we have not had the happiness to see you since we came to this Country as we expected to find a great friend in you and was in hopes we should have got you to go out to Sierra Leone again for we assure you Sir all the people there have been much put upon since you came away and we wanted you to go out that you might see justice done us as we had no one besides to look to but you but we are sorry to tell you that the Gentlemen you left behind you speaks mightily against you and we was present when Mr Pepys told all the people that you had no authority for the Promises you made us in Nova Scotia but that you did it of your own accord and that the Company could not perform what you had promised and this bred a great disturbance in the Colony and the people send us home to know from the directors here what they had to depend upon but the Gentlemen have not used us well, and we are sorry for it as we are there things will not go well in the Colony unless the people you brought with you from nova Scotia have justice done them, we did not know where to write to you till Mr Duboz[2] let us and as he is going down we send it by him and we would be very glad to hear from you I have some advice from you we would have been there before now but our expenses would not bear it there If it suit you to Come down we should be very happy to se you, we have heard that your Lady is ill we are sorry for it,

And we are Sir your humble and Faithful Servts

Cato Perkins &
Isaac Anderson

e. Settlers' Petition

To the Hble the Chairman & Court of Directors of the Sierra Leone Company London

The Petition and Representation of the Settlers at the New Colony of Sierra Leone most humbly sheweth That your Petitioners the Black Settlers of this Place beg leave to assure your Honours that they are sincerely thankful for the good they know your Honrs wished to do by bringing them from Nova Scotia to this Country & that they in their hearts admire the wonderful blessing you wish to spread by Settling this Place   And we wish to assure your Honrs that there is nothing in our Power that we would not be very glad to do to help your Honrs good intentions   But we are much grieved to see your Honrs and yourselves so much imposed upon and tho we have bore our hardships a long time now without groaning but very little We at last feel ourselves so oppressed that we are forced to trouble your Honrs that your Eyes as well as ours may be open   The hopes of helping your Honrs schemes of enjoying the Priviledges of Freemen of Reaping the benefits accruing from Religion Industry and Virtue and with the help of God and your kindness to receive Temporal advantages better than those we had in Nova Scotia induced us to leave that Country and come here   The Promises made us by your Agents in Nova Scotia were very good and far better than we ever had before from White People and no man can help saying But Mr Clarkson behaved as kind and tender to us as if he was our Father and he did so many humane tender acts of goodness that we can never forget them and notwithstanding we have suffered a great many hardships before he left this Country yet we were willing to look over every thing rather than trouble your Honours in hopes before this Rainy Season came on we would have our Land and be able to make a Crop to support us next year But in Place of that the Rains is now set in and the Lands is not all given out yet so we have no time to clear any for this year to come. Health and life may it please your Honrs is very uncertain and we have not the Education which White Men have yet we have feeling the same as other Human Beings and would wish to do every thing we can for to make our Children free and happy after us but as we feel our selves much put upon & distressed by your Council here we are afraid if such conduct continues we shall be unhappy while we live and our Children may be in bondage after us But as we all understand your Honrs intentions towards us to be very good and as we hear that you are amongst the best People in England living always with the Fear of God before your Eyes we think we may let you know how we are put upon and tell all our Greevances to you in sure hopes that God will incline your hearts to listen to us & make us Comfortable. In Nova Scotia we were very poor but at the time we left that Country we were just getting into a comfortable way of living and what little we had to send for ourselves and Families we could carry to a great many Stores and lay it out as we pleased and get double as much for it in many things as we can get here   There is no Store here but the Company's and the extortionate Price we are obliged to pay for every thing we have out of it keeps us always behind hand so that we have nothing to lay out for a Rainy Day or for our Children after us and we are sorry to tell your Honrs that tho Mr Clarkson promised us in Nova Scotia that we should not pay more than Ten Pounds advance on every Hundred that we are charged from 50 to 100 pr Cent on almost every thing we buy since Mr Clarkson went from this Place and we know of a very bad dishonest action which was done by Mr Dawe's[3] order which was to put Thirty Gals of Water into a Pun^n of Rum not one Punch^n but several & then sell it to us for a Shilling a Gall^n more than we had ever paid before And please your Honrs we have no Place to Work but in the Company's Works and we are just at the mercy of the People you send here to give us what Wages they Please & charge us what they like for their Goods and tho we know your Honrs wishes us to be happy but we are sorry to tell you we are just the reverse. There is please your Honrs People punished here without a Cause they are turned out of the Service & afterwards not suffered to buy any Provisions from the Store & where else can they buy any thing for all the Money we have is Paper Money or such other Money as will not pass any where else and Mr Dawe's who is the Governor at present shows so much partiality to some People & so much dislike to others and he does so many things which seems to us to be very much out of the Character of a Governor that we do not think your Colony will ever be settled unless you out some Person besides and Mr Dawes seems to wish to rule us just as bad as if we were all Slaves which we cannot bear but we do not wish to make any disturbance in the Colony but would chuse that every thing should go on quietly till we hear from you as we are sure we will then have Justice shown us for we have a great deal of Confidence in you and we have never known since we came here what footing we are on but are afraid concerning the happiness of our Children for as we have not Justice shewn us we do not expect our Children after us will unless your Honrs will look into the matter

When Governor Clarkson left us he told us that Mr Pepys would give us all our Lots of Land in two Weeks after he went away and he called upon us all and took leave of us and told us that was to be the case and we were contented tho we were to get but one Fifth part of what we were promised but that we were willing to look over knowing that your Honrs were imposed upon about the Land here and as we made ourselves certain that your Honrs would make up all that to us by and by but we are afraid these things are not told to your Honrs as they are here and we are doubtful about our Fate and the Fate of our Children as the Promises made us has not been perform'd and some of the White Gentlemen here has told us that all Mr Clarkson promised us he had no authority for doing & we wish to know if that is the case for we do not believe it as we have a great opinion of Mr Clarkson and do not think he would say any thing he had not authority for and if your Honours would give us leave to chuse a Governor for our selves we would chuse Mr Clarkson for he knows us better than any Gentleman & he would see every thing he Promised us Performed as so clear up his own Character for when the Gentlemen you send here talks one against another and does not agree among themselves we cannot think things are going on right and we wish your Honrs to know all these things and we wish your Honrs to know that we might have had our Lands long ago if Mr Pepys had done as he ought to do and if there had been no White Man here we could have laid out the Lots our selves for many of us have been used to Surveying and we could have laid out all the Lots in Two Months in place of that Mr Pepys has been Ten Months and not done them yet and we are afraid they have cost your Honrs a great deal of Money but Mr Pepys might have had them done according to his Promise to Mr Clarkson but he took off the People that was working on them to build a Fort which please your Honrs we do not think will ever be done but will cost your Honrs a great deal of Money and we think it is a great pity that your Money should be thrown away but Mr Dawes says he would not mind to lose One Thousand Pound of your Honours money rather than not do what he wishes and this expression was made by Mr Dawes because we complained that our wages was low and the Goods was high & he refused to raise our Wages but put a higher price on the Goods and we are sorry to tell your Honours that we feel ourselves so distressed because we are not treated as Freemen that we do not know what to do and nothing but the fear of God makes us support it until we know from your Honrs what footing we are upon and please your Honrs we wish you to know that the Land Mr Pepys has laid out for us is in most Places so very bad and Rocky that we never can make a living on it and we wish your Honrs could take all these things into Consideration for we

would not trouble you if we had not very good cause and the Minds
of every body here is so distressed about their situation & about the
fate of their Children that we have chosen Mr Isaac Anderson and
Mr Cato Perkins who is a Preacher of the Gospel to take this
Petition to England and lay our distressed Case before your Honrs
they are both very good Men and whatever your Honrs agree upon
with them we will be satisfied with And if your Honours will take
compassion on us and look into our Case and see us done Justice by
we will always pray to God to bless you and everything belonging
to you and we will let our Children know the good you do us that
they may Pray for you after it please God to call our Souls and we
the following Hundreds and Tythings and Preachers of the Gospel
do sign this Petition in behalf of all the Settlers in this Place.[4]

f. Cato Perkins and Isaac Anderson, 30 October 1793

Mr John Clarkson   London Octr 30 1793
                                                    No 13 Finch Lane

Hon^d. Sir
        We send you the Petition which we brought from our
Fellow Settlers at Free Town and we hope you will not see any
thing in it that is not true for we declare Sir we want nothing but
what you Promised us and we look upon you so much our Friend
that we think you will see us done Justice by
Lady Ann Huntingdon has put Mr Perkins to Colledge till he leaves
this Country   We are
            Sir your Faithful Humble Servants
                    Cato Perkins
                    Isaac Anderson

g. Isaac Anderson and Cato Perkins, 9 November 1793

                                            London Novr. 9th 1793
Hon^d. Sir
        We are much obliged to you for the answer you sent to
our Petition and we want to see you very much for we understand
that the Company intend to send us out in the Amy and they will
not give us any answer but send us back like Fools and we are
certain Sir that if they serve us so that the Company will lose their
Colony as nothing kept the People quiet but the thoughts that when

the Company heard their Grievances they would see Justice done them – and we should be sorry any thing bad should happend but we are afraid if the Company does not see Justice done to us they will not have Justice done to them so we want to see you very much as we think you wish us so well that you could keep us from being wronged if you can

> We are Hon^d. Sir
> Your Obedt Serts
> Isaac Anderson
> Cato Perkins

No 13 Finch Lane

h. James Liaster, 30 March 1796

Free Town Sierra Leone March 30 1796

To
    the honourable Jno. Clarkson
honoured Sir this is from me your humble Servant and fellow Sufferer

Oh may it please your honour that you ever leaved this Colony. for the day that you leaved it we was very much Oppress by Goverment and many that did not wish your honour well wish that you was at this time here. for many of us is sorely repented that we ever Came to this place but by a feeling that your honour would be here with us made many of us. We Believe that it was the handy work of Almighty God – that you should be our leader as Mosis and Joshua was bringing the Children of Esaral to the promise land – kind Sir and honoured Sir be not Angry with us all but Oh that God would Once more Give you A Desire to come & visit us here. which we expect if it was not the Goodness of God to give us Our Mother wit we would be all Slaves. but Blessed be unto his holy Name they have took all of my property land and house Only On Suspetion that I had some Goods when they gave up the Colony to the French in A most Scandolas Manner which if we Even had Arms they mought took the place but Never landed but theese things was kept back and by Seeing Our Selfe so much Oppress we have Got A Considarable Quantity of land at Pirots bay from prince George[5] and a Grant giving unto us by the heads for ever which we are now Cutting down the Town ready to move Next dry[6] – Which we have Oppointed Mr Snowball Jurdan & Glasgow heads of Settlement

Which you will your selfe here further About it from them by the Jane Vessel. Which if you think it is better send us Word.

   and hoping my letter will find you and your Good lady well and all All of your Relations beging to be remembered to them And so no more from me But God Bless you & all your Good family

            I am Sir & what is more to your honour
            Your most Obt humble Servt James Liaster
Farewell
God Bless you
God Bless you
   and prosper you that you may have
   A Crown in Heaven laid up for you

i. *Luke Jordan and Nathaniel Snowball, 29 July, 1796*

   Freetown July 29, 1796
Very Dear & Honored Sir
                  We are persuaded from that affection which you have already discovered towards us that you will be Glad to hear we & the Colony people at large are in good health & spirits. We have to lament that such an union as is very desireable for persons in our situation does not exist among us. There are as there always have been divisions among us; indeed Mr George & some of his people seem to think they can do no greater service for the Company or Colony than to invent & carry all the lies in their Power to the Governor against those who differ from them in things which pertain to religion.
The land which we understand you gave us we have had difficulty to hold in our possession.
There have been two tryals concerning it & in the last the jury gave it in our favour but as yet the matter is not quite settled.
We could say many things but after all it will amount to no more than this that we love you, and remember your Labours of love & compassion towards us with Gratitude, & pray and Heaven may always smile on you & yours. We have the honor & happiness to be, Sir your
Most obedient & humble servants
                  Luke Jordan
                  Nathaniel Snowball
Daddy Moses wishes his love to you

j. Isaac Anderson, 21 January 1798

Hon^d Sir

this come with my best Repect to you hopping they will find you and Your in good health as these leave me at Pressent and Mt family. I have sent Your Hon^d a small Barrl of Rice Of my own produce, which I hope your Hon^d will Except of for it is said Thou shall not mushel the ox that Treadet out the Corn & If so how much More is Your Hon^d ought to be Estened More them an ox hond have sheaw the same affection with ous all in this Place as well as in Amarica then for in all thing it is Rasonable that the Husbanman ought first to Pertak of the Fruth. the friends joine with me to you & Mr King Have sent you a letter with a Phemplet by Peter Corner

I am Dear Sir your Affectionate Friend
Isaiah Anderson
January the 21 1798
Sierra Leone
Africa

k. Minutes of Governor and Council, 4 March 1800. List of grievances presented by the Hundredors and Tythingmen to the Governor and Council.

Feby 13th 1800

Sir

We take an occasion to shew the hurt according to Mr Ludlam's[7] request. Mr Ludlam's request was to shew every particulars wherein we were injured.

1. We are willing to shew that we cannot get justice from the White people. Because the time of the man beating Mr York & like to have drowned him. Mr York came up and made a regular complaint to Mr Gray thinking at the present they they were my superior officers. Mr Ludlam and Mr Gray both turned against me & plead for the man at the same time Having sufficient witnesses that I never opened my mouth to the man & the Man confessing himself that I never said a word to him. That is one plain matter to shew that we stand in need of Judges & Justices. If there was a place of an appeal I should have recompence fully.

2 I have been much opposed by Mr Macaulay[8] at the time when I was robed of an 100 and odd Dollars who shall I go to seek Recompence for a fals accusation That is another hurt to shew you

that we stand in need of Judges & Justices 3 I have another thing to shew you that we settlers will take our money and go to the store and we will be turned away with our paper money that they make in our hands and Cannot get such things as we want At the same time the slave traders can come and be supplied when ever they think proper. 4. Sir We would not wish to entrude upon the Company's store for any thing without money no further than the Gentlemen of the store saw proper. But we would wish to be used according to the Company's promise beleiving every thing they said at the time. But for the unjust usage we now doubts and we hault upon the oppinion. But when we come to consider the Matter is great that a White man will always follow a Blackman Because it is for their own ends they expects gains Because we are ignorant –

5 I have another thing to ask Sir Did you ever know in Ireland in Scotland or in England that a Gentleman at a public auction will till another Gentleman that is a freeholder that he will not take his bid. We have been used as such at the Company's stores selling of damaged goods. Thats one point of Unjustice. 6 We would wish to explain this. We do not think it is proper that a Company servant should stand up among a parcel of men and Rebuke them But if they have ought against any man to mention his name to let him come Forth and answer for himself and not to harber tail bearing and News carrying Because Sir where there are such things Harbered and carried forward there can be no peace in that place Neither can the place prosper but hard thoughts and murmurings arises by such traduction and all these traduction proceed from the Companys Servents and it is very hard to think that a man will not take what he makes.

7. Because we perceive that the place grows worse and worse every day the time of Mr Clarkson and Mr Dawses present Shiping was not allowed to come here to shew any authority Neither to caninade the place raising of a Mutiny and Disturbing of the Native Chief and the Settlers which is liable to bring on War upon the Settlers Neither in the time of Mr Clarkson and Mr Dawes proceeding they did not refuse taking the money that they made for any thing at all that they had in their Stores it is so here and carried on in these days and we think that is a hard pint of unjustice View England Scotland and Ireland and consider which is your native Country if they was to deny their own coin how would they live I am sorry to see that the white people strives to blind the eys of the Simple which we

have seen them endeavoured from our youth. I address you with this I am your most humble Servent

Nathaniel Wansey Chairmon of the Tything Mon

l. Paper of Laws, 3 September 1800

Paper of Laws stuck up at Abram Smith's house by the Hundredors and Tythingmen.[9]

Sept 3rd 1800. – If any one shall deny the Settlers of any thing that is to be exposed of in the Colony, and after that shall be found carrying it out of the Colony to sell to any one else, shall be fined £20 or else leave the Colony, and for Palm Oil 1/–[10] Quart, whose ever is found selling for more than 1/– Quart is fined 20/– Salt Beef 6d.lb. any one selling for more shall pay the fine of 40/– and Salt pork 9d.lb. shall pay the fine of 40/– and for rice 50 cwt. to a Dollar 5/– and whosoever is found selling for less than for a Dollar shall pay the fine of £10 and Rum is to be 5/– Galln.at the wholesale and any one that sells for more than 5/– shall pay the fine of £3 and the Retailer is not to sell for more than 6/3 by the Gallon and to sell as low as a Gill at 6/3 Gallon as low [*sic*] a single glass as 3 Cents and if any one should sell for more than that shall pay the fine of £3 Soap at 15d.lb. and whosoever shall sell for more than 15d. shall pay the fine of 20/–. Salt Butter 15d.lb. and if any more than 15d.lb. shall pay the fine of 20/– and if any one found keeping a bad house is fined 20/– or for abuse £1 for trespass 10/– for stealing shall pay for twice the value for stealing, a blow £5 for removing his neighbour's landmark shall pay £5 for cutting timber or wattles on any person's land without their leave shall pay £5 for drawing a weapon or any edge tool shall pay £5 and for threatening shall pay £2.10 and for lying or scandalizing without proof shall pay £2.10 for Sabbath breaking shall pay the fine of 10/– Cheese to be sold at 1/– lb. and if more than 1/– shall pay the fine of 20/– Sugar 15d.lb. and whosoever is found selling for more than 15d. is fined of 20. And if any man shall serve a summons or warrant or execution without orders from the hundredors and Tythingmen must pay the fine of £20. And if any person shall kill a goat, hog, or sheep or cause her to slink[11] her young shall pay the fine of £5 or shall kill Cow or Horse shall pay the fine of £5, and if a man's fence is not lawful he cannot recover any damage, and if a man that has a wife shall leave her and go to another woman, shall pay the fine of £10 and if a woman leave her husband and take up with another man he shall pay £10, and if

Children shall misbehave they shall pay a fine of 10/– or otherwise be severely corrected by their parents.

And this is to give notice by the Hundredors and Tythingmen that the laws they have made that if the Settlers shall owe a debt to the Company they shall come to the Hundredors and Tythingmen and prove their account, and swear to it and swear to every article agreeable to the proclamation that they shall take the produce for their goods and not for their goods pay any per Cent on it, and all that come from Nova Scotia, shall be under this law or quit the place. – The Governor and Council shall not have any thing to do with the Colony no farther than the Company's affairs, and if any man shall side with the Governor, etc against this law shall pay £20.

This is to give notice that the law is signed by the Hundredors and Tythingmen and Chairman they approve it to be just before God and Man.

Given under our hands this 3rd September 1800.

James Roberson, Hundr. Ansel Zizer, Hundr. Isaac Anderson, Hundr. and Nathl. Wansey, Chairman signed this as a law in Sierra Leone.

m. Notice, 10 September 1800

September 10th 1800
        This is to give notis that the law of the Sierra leone Setler is to tak place the 25 of this mounth. By the orders of the Hundred and tyding all complant is to go of Be given in to James robenson ancel Zyzer I Suck anderson Hundreds

n. Isaac Anderson, unsigned

September Sunday Mr Ludlow Sir we we de sire to now wether you will let our Mends out if not turn out the womans and Chill Dren

Notes

1. The People from Annapolis, Nova Scotia.
2. Isaac Duboz, a white loyalist from N. carolina and a friend of Clarkson, dismissed with him by the Sierra Leone Company in 1793.
3. Mr Dawes: Governor of the Company.
4. No signatures appear on the copy in the Clarkson papers.
5. Prince George: a local chief.

6. Next dry: next dry season.
7. Mr. Ludlam: the Company's Governor.
8. Mr. Macaulay: former Governor.
9. Hundredors and Tythingmen: representatives of the settlers, their titles derived from old English ones.
10. The signs '1/–' and 'd.' refer to shilling(s) and pence (old) respectively.
11. Slink: abort.

8

JOHN HENRY NAIMBANNA
1767–1793

Extempore speech made after visiting the House of Commons to hear a debate on the Slave Trade

As we said in our introduction, some of the texts included are not from printed books, but from speeches recorded verbatim in court proceedings: or, as in this case, in the form of notes taken by companions. Several of the authors we have included were also well known as public speakers – Equiano and Wedderburn, for instance – and for the Black community in Britain, articulate self-expression by way of the spoken word would have been of the greatest importance. This passage comes from a short account of the life of this intelligent and sensitive young man, son of King Naimbanna of Sierra Leone. He came to London in 1791 to be educated in English, and after proving a most promising scholar, sadly died almost immediately on his return.

The African Prince, the account of his life, was published in 1796 by Zachary Macaulay, father of Lord Macaulay. It is reproduced in full in Edwards and Walvin, *Black Personalities*, (see bibliography) 204–210. Macaulay's account is based on Henry Thornton's *Report on the Sierra Leone Company* (London 1794) 155–60; another, slightly different version is to be found in Prince Hoare, *Memoirs of Granville Sharp* (London 1820) 364–71.

He was present once at the House of Commons during a debate on the Slave Trade. He there heard a gentleman who spoke in favour of the trade, say some things very degrading to the characters of his countrymen. He was so enraged at this, that on coming out of the House, he cried out with great vehemence, 'I will kill that fellow wherever I meet him, for he has told lies of my country;' he was put in mind of the christian duty of forgiving his enemies; on which he answered nearly in the following words: ... 'If a man should rob me of my money, I can forgive him; if a man should shoot at me, I can forgive him: if a man should sell me and all my family to a slave ship, so that we should pass all the rest of our lives in slavery in the West Indies, I can forgive him; but, (added he with much emotion) if a man takes away the character of the people of my country, I never can forgive him.' Being asked why he would not extend his forgiveness to one who took away the character of the people of his country, he answered – 'If a man should try to kill me, or should sell my family for slaves, he would do an injury to as many as he might kill or sell, but if any one takes away the character of black people, that man injures black people all over the world; and when he has once taken away their character, there is nothing which he may not do to black people ever after. That man, for instance, will beat black men, and say, 'O, it is only a black man, why should I not beat him?' 'That man will make slaves of black people; for when he has taken away their character, he will say, 'O, they are only black people, why should not I make them slaves?' That man will take away all the people of Africa, if he can catch them, and if you ask him, 'Why do you take away all those people,' he will say, 'O, they are only black people, they are not like white people, why should not I take them? That is the reason why I cannot forgive the man who takes away the character of the people of my country.'

He was then told that it would be very wicked to kill this gentleman, or even not to forgive him, seeing the Scriptures said, 'Forgive your enemies.' – 'Vengeance is mine, I will repay, saith the Lord.' This immediately quieted his rage, and he became as calm as a lamb, nor was used afterwards to express the least anger against the gentleman who had so much offended him.

At another time, when he saw a man beat his horse about the head and otherwise use it ill, he became very angry, and talked of getting a gun to shoot the man, for he was sure he deserved it, and also of carrying a gun always about him to shoot such bad people. As soon, however, as a passage of Scripture, which condemned such violence was mentioned to him, his anger ceased, and he became sorry for it.

9

PHILIP QUAQUE

born Cape Coast, Gold Coast (Ghana) c.1741,
died Cape Coast 1816

Letters to the Society for the Propagation of the Gospel

1765–1816

Philip Quaque was a member of the family of the leading local
Chieftain or Caboceer named Cudjo in the town of Cape
Coast. Though it is possible that Cudjo was his actual father, it
seems more likely that that as Margaret Priestley says (Curtin,
106) 'Quaque was a "son" only in the classificatory sense of the
Fanti kinship system.' At birth, he was given the Fanti name,
Kweku. At the age of about thirteen he was recommended by
the Caboceer with two more of Cudjo's young relatives to
travel to England for an education, at the expense of the
Society for the Propagation of the Gospel (S.P.G.) where they
were placed under the tutorship of the Rev. John Moore, at
whose London home in Charterhouse Street, Philip lived for
over ten years: his African name was converted to Quaque,
and he was given the Christian name Philip. He was baptised in
1759. One of the three died of consumption in 1758. Of Philip
Quaque and his surviving companion we learn from a letter
written by John Moore to the Secretary of the S.P.G.

> One of them [Quaque] has rewarded my Labours by
> improving in every Branch of Knowledge necessary to the
> station for which he was designed, and it is hoped will
> prove a worthy Missionary. The other [William Cudjo]
> who never discovered any real talent for Learning, tho'
> otherwise well-behaved, was put out of reach of instruc-
> tion by a Lunacy which seized him in December 1764. He
> has been confined near twelve Months in St. Luke's and
> by the Rules of the Hospital must be returned upon my
> hands in a few days. (Letters to S.P.G. no. 6, January 15th,
> 1766)

Moore goes on to say that William might remain in hospital, if
the S.P.G. will cover expenses. He died in Guy's Hospital
shortly after. William's father tried to arrange to bring him
home – see Letter b. below, note 1 – but died before anything

could be done to help his son, as Quaque records in the final paragraph of the second letter included here.

Philip, however, was ordained a Minister of the Church of England, married a white woman, Catherine Blunt, and sailed shortly after, in 1766, to his birthplace in Africa as Chaplain to Cape Coast Castle, the British settlement and trading station. There his wife grew sick and died. He remarried locally, though he was critical of local customs, and planned to have his children educated in England

> to secure their tender Minds from receiving the bad Impressions of the Country, the vile Customs and Practices, & above all, the losing of their Mother's vile Jargon, the only obstacles of Learning in these Parts. Besides, I may yet hope that this will be an Everlasting Provision for 'em after I am annihilated and intered [sic] in the Sepulchre of my Ancestors. (Letter 37, Oct. 20th, 1781)

The last phrase sorts a little oddly with Quaque's low opinion of pagan custom and belief within his own extended family, and though he saw English Christian education as the only answer to the errors of paganism, there were possibly more tensions at work that appear on the surface (see, for instance, note 3 to letter d.). He retained a little of his mother tongue, and occasionally attempted to use it, but normally employed the services of his interpreters, John Aqua and Frederic Adoy. There is a very human scene in the second of the letters which follow, when he tries to persuade his 'father', the Caboceer to commit himself wholly to the Christian God.

> I have since many times reason'd with the Cabosheer on the Ordinance of Baptism, telling him what a great Joy & Comfort it would be, for him to enter into that Covenant with God; likewise that the only affection he can shew or do for me is to be Baptized, by wch. means says I, if you willingly become so, by yr. good example no doubt but all yr. Subjects will in all propibility become so too: but the only Answer I could get, or draw out of the old Man was, in his asking me, (says he), Pray Son, don't you think I am too old to enter into Covenant with God? I immediately made a reply, that he was not, and that a voluntary Act was more acceptable in the sight of God, than those of a forced Nature. And as for the young Children having Sureties to stand for them, was only for a time till they come to Years of Maturity to take the Vow and Promises made for them by their Godfathers and Godmothers. Upon the strength of this he remained silence (sic), and no further stir was made.

In the same letter, while Quaque complains that 'Here also is no real marriage', he adds that the local people 'do modestly allow the reasonableness of our way of Marriage'. It is the

Europeans' loose behaviour that gives him most offence:
> But for the Europeans to defile themselves with such sort
> of Notions, nay even partaking with them, and disdaining
> not to turn them away [i.e. their 'local wives'] at Pleasure
> for the least trifle of Misdemeanour, and soon after taking
> another at Will, I cannot away with it.

But he sees his London Christian upbringing as rescue from
barbarism, what he calls in Letter 1 'the Bondage of Sin and
Satan', and there appears less than is the case with Equiano to
suggest a more complex view. Though Quaque suffered at
times from public mockery of his pious concern for church-
going and the sacraments, and from indifference or conden-
scension, his values remain essentially those of a conventional,
stubborn, high-minded, not always very successful Church of
England minister disappointed by the vagaries of his flock. He
writes fairly competent, fluent English, sometimes fussy,
overelaborate and tangled, with occasional lapses and eccentri-
cities of grammar and spelling. As Margaret Priestley concludes:
> Considered as literature, Quaque's letters undoubtedly
> have shortcomings. But they still convey a realistic and
> informative picture of life on the West Coast in the
> eighteenth century, from the point of view of an African
> who was caught up in the problem of bridging two
> worlds. (Curtin ed., *Africa Remembered*, 112)

The text is from the manuscripts C/AFR/W1, in the records of
the S.P.G. held at the Rhodes House Library, Oxford. The
letters are on loose sheets, boxed and numbered, and the
number of each letter printed below is given with the heading.
We must thank both the Society, for permission to print a
small sample of the letters, and the Librarian, Alan Bell, and his
Staff, for their kind and generous assistance. Essential material
for the study of Quaque will be found listed in the bibliography, under Curtin (for the invaluable selection by Margaret
Priestley in *Africa Remembered*), Pascoe, and Bartels.

*a. Letter 1. A Request for Assistance. Written at the home of his
tutor, the Rev John Moore, Charterhouse Square, London, on
March 13th, 1765: to the Secretary of the Society for the
Propagation of the Gospel (S.P.G.)*

Hond. Sir,
As Time would not then conveniently permit me to suggest to You
my real Intentions when I waited on you last, makes me take this
earliest opportunity of troubling You with these Lines, to impor-

tune your further Aid & Assistance on the interesting Topic; a subject which I hope will meet with your kind Approbation. I need not therefore present You with a tedious Detail; knowing that you are very sensible of my present State of incapacity to provide for myself. The Venerable Society the Fruit of whose Benevolence I have enjoyed ever since their Compassion snatched me from the Bondage of Sin & Satan, and that miserable Condition I was then involved in for all which, I hope to make hereafter the warmest Acknowledgements imaginable that a heart susceptible of Gratitude is capable of making, so as to be deem'd worthy of their future Patronage. For I scruple not, but that my generous Benefactors will after I am advanced to the Office of Priesthood, handsomely furnish me with all necessary & useful Books of Divinity as well as those bright ornaments that may be requisite to that glorious, tho' awful & laborious Charge. A Vocation which I flatter myself thro' the divine Blessing to walk worthy in. This also, I doubt not but that, that respectable Body will out of their Arms of Benevolence settle a sufficient Maintenance and at the same time I hope a generous One. And now I must beg your attention to the point in question: My design at present is, to crave your further Goodness to me, that your tender Bowels may yearn towards helping the doleful cries of the Indigent, in using your Influence with His Grace, so as to consider my Necessitous State, as well as things of greater Moment: I mean Household Utensils, such as for instance a Bed, Chair, &c., &c. These and the rest of the things cannot Revd: Dr: be obtained in the Situation that Providence has thought to place me. It may likewise not be amiss particularly to give You a hint with effect to the ill-conveniency my Ministry will be attended [with], if the Society doth not take into due Consideration to make an early Application to the African Committee for their charitable Assistance, to enable them to erect a commodious Place to resort unto for the due Attendance of the Worship of Almighty God, together with a convenient Dwell[ing]-House & a Glebe for the reception of the Pastor, in like manner as is appropriated to all other Missionaries for there is no conveniency except a spacious Hall in the Factory,[1] wherein all the Affairs of that Committee are transacted, which, serves also for the Officers common Place of daily food & banqueting, and then on the Lord's Day is made to serve for the publick Administration of the Word. The hearty zeal that I have for the Work of the Gospel, presses me to mention these things by way of an immediate antidote against the ensuing Malady, so as that it may not be hereafter an hinderance to earnest endeavours & progress of the Labourer in the Lord's Vineyard: These things I shall wholly resign to your superior Skill & judicious Management: And shall lastly beg leave to make this one Observation more, which is, how extremely hard would it be after so many Years of experience of that Venerable Body's Benevolence to commission at last a Youth, and then to send him into the wide World to summount [sic] the difficulties without so much as the common Conveniencies of Life. I hope your Goodness will abundantly excuse this Freedom, and that this Representation will not be lookt upon as too bold an Intrusion, or be thought too hard upon the Society, when if rightly considered the greatest Difficulty & Hardships without them will lodge upon me. I must not forget by the way to assure You, as I am credibly inform'd, that the Conveyance of the Convoy will be going out in June next: Your speedy Influence in this Request, which, I hope your sagacity will render it so effectual as to state these things before the Board next Friday in the hearing of the Society that there may be no delay, as the time You see is so very short; will be graciously embraced: and whose daily Prayer shall be offered up to the Throne of Grace on your behalf, &c. The success of the Society in the Work of the Ministry, that the Kingdom of our God may soon be made known in the remotest Regions of the Universe; that those wretched Creatures who are now languishing under despair, & in the shadow of Death may soon be brought to the Truth of the Glorious light of the Gospel of our Lord & Saviour. A Name which they have not known, nor yet ever heard of. In doing which Act of Christian Benevolence & Brotherly kindness as the Apostle stiles it, to the relief of him who stands in need of your Assistance will be greatly esteemed & always acknowledged by

Yr most dutiful & Obed't
Hmble Servant

b. Letter 10. Early Problems at the Cape Coast Mission.
To the Secretary of the S.P.G. in London from
Cape Coast Castle on September 28th, 1766

Revd. Sir,
Since my late Letter to the Venerable Body dated in Feb: 1766, I am induced to acquaint them that all my hopes I am afraid are in

vain: Govr. Hippisley Esqr. whom Mr. Thompson[3] was so kind as to recommend us to, is very lately dead, after having been stationed here only five Months & Eleven Days, with a very short illness. He indeed proved to us in all points a worthy Friend, as was described by Mr. Thompson to the Society. He shewed himself a Man of feeling for the Distresses of others, very humain and hospitable, a sincere lover of his Profession, & a great observant of the publick Worship of Almighty God. For the little time he abode with us, & we became acquainted & familiar with him, he laid all the Scheme that was in his power as a Govr. to make Religion flourish & abound in these parts, who also did daily expostulate with the Cabosheer[4] to use his utmost effort that Nothing be wanting on his part that may conduce to adorn my laudable Undertaking. But since he is dead, all my expectations are foil[ed], & are also buried with him. [We] have no other whom we can call a Friend, that wishes us Health & Prosperity. And as for those faire promises of the Cabosheer's mention'd in my last, I am greatly afraid that all that will now dwindle into Nothing as my chief Agent is now no more: and the only reason & inducement of his then fare promises, I since find to have been Nothing else, but a senister view of getting from Me if possible, the little Income I have from the African Committee into his own Custody, notwithstanding he being a Person of great Repute & Substance, & I being then only as a New-comer, not knowing the manners & Customs of my native Place, made him proceed to such unreasonable steps. But seeing himself with all my numerous Family greatly disappointed in their aim, are therefore become very careless and thoughtless about us.

Now with respect to all most all the Successors of our late worthy Govr. I believe I shall have very little or scarce any Pretensions at all with them, they being all Scotch and Irish People, rank Presbyterians; the present Govr. whose Name is Gilbert Petree Esq. is a very rank Presbyterian born and breed. However there are two or three minor Govrs. who are Englishmen, whose turn as residence here will not be in all propibility these Nine or Ten Years to come, and in all that while shall live in Misery & doubt of performing the publick Duty: there are also some few Factors, Officers, & some Guards & Soldiers that are British by birth, but how many in number, I have not yet made it a point of enquiry. The Factory at present is in very poor Condition, all falling down over our Heads, it's a very antient Building, upwards of Hundred & Eleven Years standing in these parts, so at the time of our severe rainny Season every individual are almost drowned in their Apartments by leeking; during which I was forced to strip and quite my two Rooms of all my Furniture, & incumbering others who were in a better Condition than I, with them; & I & my Spouse partaking with whomsoever we could: this Accident & trouble of moving we shall be liable to every season, if no Remedy is found in time to prevent it. My poor Spouse & Bosom Companion, has been but very indifferent since we came upon the Coast who now lies at the point of Death, & every moment expecting it to be her last.[5]

I would willingly send her or else take a trip with her Home again, but the Difficulty at present is, the getting leave from the considerate Society or a faithful Captn. to trust her with, for her perfect health, if in case there should be a change for the better. Now if leave cannot be obtained & no known Captn. to convey her to, she must inevitably perish as here is no proper Remedy for female Sex.

At the Feast of Easter there was no Duty, owing to a great indisposition of Body I was in by a severe fit of the flux & fever; but all the other festivals following were duly performed to the best of my power with universal Satisfaction, but still found none of what sect or Denomination soever, that was willing or disposed to commence Communicants, and the only plea they offer is, that while they are here acting against Light & Conscience, they dare not come to, that holy Table, so that while I remain in these remote Soil, that branch of Duty will never be exercised in publick, unless it be to myself & Spouse.

Here also is no real Marriage, except that which they term consoring [consorting?], wch. answers to the description of my Predecessor's Celebacy; the reasonable[ness?] of this I have expounded to them in a[s] familiar style as possible, shewing them the utility of having no more than one Wife; but all in vain and their Custom they will follow; yet at the same time do modestly allow the reasonableness of our way of Marriage. But for the Europeans to defile themselves with such sort of Notions, nay even partaking with them, and disdaining not to turn them away at Pleasure for the least trifle of Misdemeanour, and soon after taking another at Will, I cannot away with it: and to their shame be it spoken, it is not so rigorous with the poor Natives themselves.

I have since many times reason'd with the Cabosheer on the

Ordinance of Baptism, telling him what great Joy & Comfort it
would be, for him to enter into that Covenant with God; likewise
that the only affection he can shew or do for me is to be baptized,
by wch. means says I, if you willingly become so, by yr. good
example no doubt but all yr. Subjects will in all propibility become
so too: but the only Answer I could get, or draw out of the old Man
was, in his asking Me, (says he,) Pray Son don't you think I am too
old to enter into Covenant with God? I immediately made a reply,
that he was not, and that a voluntary Act was more acceptable in the
sight of God, than those of a forced Nature. And as for the young
Children having Sureties to stand for them, was only for a time till
they come to Years of Maturity to take the Vow and Promises made
for them by their Godfathers & Godmothers. Upon the strength of
this he remained silence, and no further stir was made; but have
since made a small beginning. On Sunday the 22. of June 1766 I
baptized two little Infants belonging to one John Conrade Piende-
man a Dutch Sergt. but is since made a bum-boy[6] to this Fort; One
a Boy & the other a Girl. And on the 29th. baptized also the son of
the deceased John Hippisley Esqr. aged 12 Years, who was called
after the Name of his Father; he was by the desires of his Father
under my inspection long before, & after his Baptism, but since the
Death of his Father he has quite deserted me. Now with regard to
the Baptism of Infants here, I shall be glad to know from the
Respectable Society whether it will be deemed lawful for me to
baptized them without Sponsors, or whether the Standard of
Heathens Parents will be altogether sufficient on that Head &
Likewise, whether it will be granted on ye other Hand requisite for
me in these parts to omit wholly the Communion Service, when
officiating in Publick? Tho' perhaps it will not be in my power
much I am afraid to officiate in Publick, being apprehensive of
continuing long under the usurping & arbitrary Power of Scotch
and Irish People. Thro' a great indisposition of Body by repeated
Sicknesses, the state of my Constitution is very much altered for the
worse, and the fatigue of performing every part of the Service on
the Lord's Day, and all by standing in one posture almost without
ease, has contributed in a great measure towards it.

This country is very destructive to the Health to many of the
British Constitutions: & tho' myself being a Native by Birth, yet
am not exempted from undergoing the common fate equally with
those who are not: and as a prove of this Assertion, we have had for

the little time we have been here, the third part out of five & twenty Soldiers dead; a Factor the Nephew of the present Bishop of Waterford, & a Surveyor. Several others very sick, & infirm, besides many others of an older standing, together with six or seven Captns. of Ships suddenly cut off by a very short illness.

Numbers of Communicants none, Visitance [visitants] since are Ten; Buried fourteen; Papists, Quakers, & Annabaptists none here: Now the Consideration of the things that has been alledged will, I hope, be duly lookt upon, & noticed by my great Benefactors, the Venerable Society.

And now beg leave to mention to the Society that Mr. Cudjo's Father died soon after my Letter was sent to beg for his return, and do take upon me the liberty to speak to the Society, that since he is dead, it will be much better in my weak opinion to let him remain in the Place as he now is, rather than send him over: for there will be none here that will hardly look upon him, & much more if he should be in the same Situation, nay scarce will give him the proper attendance, as all those who fall under the like accident in the Garrison are obliged to be sent Home; His Relations are almost [all] dead, & even those who are left, will I am Certain do Nothing for him.

And believe me to be with the utmost Respect & Esteem
      Rev. Sir,
      Your most dutiful Bror. & Obedt. Servant

c. Letter 28: A Letter to America. To the Rev. Ed. Bass of Massachusetts, from Cape Coast Castle, July 31st 1775. (Presented to the S.P.G. by J. Whitney Esq. of Boston Mass, 30 January, 1931)[7]

Dear & Revd. Sir

I have had the pleasure of perusing your much esteemed [. . . . . ?] of a long Season forwarded [to] me by my friend Captain John Hay which came to hand the [10th?] January [1775?] at Dixcove Fort. Believe me that your long Season of Silence encouraged me to despair the thought of my ever hearing from you: but the renewal of that friendly Correspondance once established, fills me now big with hopes of Joy unspeakable and full of Glory. I am sorry that I have an Occasion to make a Repitition of the like Complaint which one of my Letters ala[rmed?] You of sometime ago telling you that I still labor under the same dis[advantage?] if any, worse than ever. Yet [to remain?] confident is Indispensably Necessary and the only sure means of Introducing the true Religion and civil manners among a Nation void of Sense both towards their Creator and their Eternal In[tere]st: but my School instead of being an Ornament and doing me Service or Credit, declines daily and doth not cut that formidable figure as I could wish: owing thro' a mistakened Notion imbibed in their Tender Minds by their Inconsiderate and thought-less Parents. This way of Reasoning most assuredly gives Room for Children to become Indolent and [care]less and rather then pur-suing good Principles arising from Education, they therefore couch themselves under Military Discipline and sewing, which they look upon more advantageous in their manner of Life then sound Learning. In Consequence of which these Scholars who consisted chiefly of the Mulattoe kind, not one of them, that have not listed themselves as Soldiers and Fifers in the Service of the African Committee, which turn of Mind have reduced my Seminary to the lowest Ebb that can possibly be, only but two in Number. As to the Administration of Baptism, I have Baptized about five and Twenty both Young and Old. I am I assure You much ashamed of myself in not answering yours much sooner, and was I to advance any Thing in Vindication of myself will not perhaps find Acceptance. How-ever with Presumption do I attempt it; When I had yours, it was at a Time when I was as far as thirty or forty Leagues from my District: where I remain for the space of Ten Months, acting in my own Province, and also as Ad interim Chief in the absence of the Chief of the Fort to whom I was but a visiter. I was in hopes during my Emigration up to Windward of meeting with som[e] [sca]ttered Sheep, but all Ineffectual, altho' encouraged by many [Dutch][8] Chiefs to no Success. In your Epistle You seem to lament bitterly of your Mother Country for Universal Liberty. You upon whom the light of the Gospel flourishes and abound, and if I may be allowed the Expression, as it were advancing daily towards the seat of Bliss, find the Hardships of Bondage and Oppression! Good God can this be possible when I behold with Sorrowful sighing, my poor abject Countrymen over whom You without the Bowels of Christian Love and Pity, hold in Cruel Bondage. This Iniquitous Practice methinks seems to set Religion aside and only making Room for the height of Ambition and Grandeur, the pride of Monarchs &c. to enter. I could wish that the Conviction of this Practice would spring first from the Breast of us all, particularly *You* since We know perfectly well the hainousness of it and may we be diligent to put it in practice by encoraging the Heathen World to partake of the brightness of God's Glory and the Precious Promises of the Gospel. May We with unanimous Consc[ience?] beseech the God of all Grace and Mercy, to open the dark Minds of my benighted Countrymen to see those things that belongeth to their Peace and that instead of continuing in the wretched state of *Lo-ruhamah*, not having obtained Mercy, and *Lo-ammi*, exclusion from being the People of the living God, on the contrary shine bright as the Sun and [.....] partaking of the Appellations *Ammi* and *Ruhamah*[9] having at last obtained Favor from the hands of that being [who] was the Cause of their Existence. May it be pronounced [.....] in the Language of the Prophet, that instead of the Place wh[ere it] was said unto them, ye are not my People, there it shall I hope [be revealed?] or made known to them to be the Sons of the living God. Ma[y they] soon find that Mercy in the [holy?] Description still exten[ded] towards them by the same [Christ] as the Language [.....] of all Consolation, I will have Mercy on Her, that had not obtained Mercy, and I will say to them, which were not my People, thou art my People. Oh God! May they soon feel the benefit of this gracious Call, and truly confess him also with St. Thomas. Thou art also our Lord and our God from Eternity.

I leave you now to meditate on these Sayings, in your private House. In the mean Time I remain with my Spouse,[10] who joins me in sincere Respects to You and Yours, and Prosperity in all
And am, Dear & revd. Sir
Your most Obedt. &
most Hble. Servt.

d. Letter 30: The Funeral of Caboceer Cudjo. A letter to the Secretary of the S.P.G. written on January 17th 1778

Reverend Doctor.
Since my last Notitia of the 11th. of April last to the Venerable Society by Captain Charles Hope, Commander of His Britannic Majesty's Sloop the Weazle Man of War, I have anxious Eyes and confident hope, expected to have been honored with their most gracious Indulgence ere now. But fallen short of my expectation, due Obedience of Orders and Love of Duty therefore inspires me to send in this Narrative, which I confess ought to have pursued its Travels two months sooner, but considering the Lamentableness of the Times, the Uncertainty of a safe Passage, together with

the melancholy News of the African Merchant Ships being apprehended and Properties confiscated, as well as Letters of private Persons seized and destroyed by the [Americans],[11] was the sole Reason of my not expediting this sooner, and even the Safety of this, I have my doubts about me. However since the Appointment of Richard Miles Esqr. to the Command of the African Committee's Affairs here as a successor to David Mill Esqr. late Governor of this Castle, who is since Dead, and whose untimely End we here learn was Occasioned by the Accident of his falling into the hands of the Rebels after his Departure from the Coast, and conveyed to the Iland of Antigua where he died with immence Property totally lost, I have no small Satisfaction in acquainting Them, that the true Spirit of Devotion and due Observance of a Sabboath holy to God, much neglected in the former Governor's time, begins under the present One (tho' not yet confirmed) to illumine the Mind as the Morning Sun enlightens the fertile Earth. I hail its approach and Continuance and invoke the Almighty to touch irresistibly the Hearts of all those that are Enemies to the Faith. The Number of Baptized Infants last Year were only but three; and my School which is my own single Chamber in the Fort, consists also but three Scholars; and as to the Number of Burials the white People amounts to sixteen Persons and three Mulattoes, some of those that comes immediately under my Cognizance. There are yet several Children belonging to different Gentlemn of this Castle unbaptized notwithstanding the many Remonstrances made, touching the utility of their Admission into that sacred Function both in Public and Private, but it has not as yet had any impression. Trusting therefore to that powerful Agency, voluntary Choice I hope it will Hereafter have the desired Influence upon their Hearts and Minds and that process of Time will discover.

The Funeral Ceremony of the late Cudjoe Cabbocier, whose Death I mentioned in my last Account was pompously exhibited on the 20th. Day of October last after the Blacks usual Custom or manner of burying their Deceased. This Performance or Funeral grandeur was accompanied with incessant firing of Musquets from that time successfully [successively?] for eight Days together with little or no Intermission. But the Society will please to observe, that this mighty Exhibition could not well be acted without Songs of Shouting, Drinking and that to a very great Excess, with Dancing and all kinds of Juvenile Festivity: which Scene appeared to me

more like their Harvest Festival than that of Mourning or Neigh-
bouring Cabbociers from the Inland Countries and Villages adjacent. The Computation of the Number of Souls that came to
Perpetuate the Memory of their deceased Monarch might be
upwards of a Million.[12] But the manner in which they make their
public Enterance on these Occasions deserves a place in this cursory
Description, as it is not only laughable but curious withal: in which
Drama You will find the Generality of them equiped with their
Warlike Apparel, Some are covered with a Cap of a Tyger's skin,
others again with Deer's, a third the Skins of Monkies, the fourth &
fifth have on Porcupine's skins and also wild Boar's, and on the
sixth Straw Bonnets and Cuckle Shells strung and ornamented
about their Necks and Legs, together with their numerous Charms;
with these various colours they form their Powder horns and yet
after all, there is no kind of Decorum observed whilst they are
displaying these their Apish Dexterity, but rather great Confusion
and Irregularity. They likewise paint Themselves both Men and
Women, some with white Chaulk, others Yellow Earth; and a
number of others in order to make their Hue appear more odious,
daub themselves with powdered charcoal &c. But the most detestable Scene in all their actions is the Barbarious and Inhuman
practice of Sacrifycing innocent Lives as attendances to the Great
Folks only in the other World, which Diabolical custom and a
mistakened vile Notion seems to prevail much with them when any
of their reputed Head dies: so that all the Recent attempts that has
been heretofore made, nay not even the most forcible Arguments
still advancing towards extirpating this horrid and cruel Tradition,
has had no Impression at all on their Lives and Morals but to make
the Deed still more direful, the Heroes or Principals of them boasts
and glory in torturing their fellow Creatures; and a Thousand other
Infamous Rites held by them which absolutely shews the Depravity
and Obduracy of their Stubborn Hearts: so that Nothing but the
forces of Events predicted must perfect the Work thro' the Grace of
God, the searcher of the Intents of Mankind, and the prevailing
Operations of the Holy Spirit. They also have some faint idea of an
Election, because on the 15th. Day of last December, the supposed
Heir to the Stool so called (or in other words) the Crown of the late
Cudjoe Cabboceer, was publicly installed by a grand Procession in
their own way, by the Consent both of the Town's People, the
Principals of Annamaboe and Elmina. People and Properties of the

Stool, with Songs of shouting, dancing and drinking as before described, decorated with all their usual Apparatus's. He then passes thro' a kind of Oath of Supremacy before the Concourse of both Strangers and has his own Alliances publickly Assembled; after which he and his attendant Train comes into the Castle to pay his Respects, where he takes upon himself the oath of Allegiance before the Governor, cloathed in his War Robe, and having in his Right Hand three edged Sword, with which he swears himself faithfully the Subject of Great Britain, binding the same with a sacred Oath to defend the Rights and Privileges belonging thereto by Night or Day. On leaving the Fort he and his numerous retinue receive a Customary Gratuity granted on these Occasions from the Governor, with the Honor of Nine saluting Guns as a Compliment from the Castle, denoting I imagine the public Consent as well as the British Attachment and Protection of Them. The Society may also Remember of my hinting to them in my last Favor the unavoidable Expence I was likely to be involved in by the Death of this great Man, which so poor as I am amounts to £127.7.6. I mention this merely to shew Them the Difficulties I frequently labor under thro' numerous Family Connections, whose sole Dependance rests entirely upon me; exclusive of Domestic Care, a Wife and two Children and another shortly expected by God's Blessing.[13]

By the paper on which I write, you may easily perceive how short I am of for Stationary; and if I recollect aright I think you promised to indulge me with the Anniversary Sermons preached at St. Martin's Le-bow Yearly: since which I have petitioned your further Indulgance of some small matter of Stationary of all kinds as I am continually Troubling others for what I often write upon, and that even with some Difficulty that I do procure so much as will answer my purposes. Pray may I also presume so far as to ascertain from You of what is become of the Reverend Mr. John Moore? Son of my Worthy Tutor the late Reverend John Moore Lecturer of St. Sepulchre's Parish Snowhill. Excuse this my Impertinent Question, but the Reason which led me to it is, the several Letters I have lately written to him, some of which inclosing Bills on the Society's Treasurer in Favor of some Friends who have been of great Assistance to me; whether these Letters have reached him or Bills drawn, answered to him to settle the Balance of my Accounts with such and such People. Letters of Information have not so regularly appeared from him as usual, which make me uneasiness and very apprehensive of the Accident incident to Man have befallen him; in that case I shall be greatly distressed for want of a Confident, but hope that my Distress will prove to me a Blessing, and that my unhappy Surmize will turn out from you a more favourable Account of his Well Being in Life. Likewise shall shall (sic) be infinitely indebted to you to be informed, whether the Reverend Thomas Thompson my Predecessor is still in Being or Translated to the Bliss above, there to receive the Recompence of his Labor reserved for him in the Kingdom of our Father. The Knowledge of these, and the above Requests, will for ever confer an Additional Duty and Brotherly Love on him, who ardently wishes You all desireable Health and every valuable Blessing this Sublunary Para-dice of Ours is capable of affording, and remain with Love unfeigned always in due submission to your Commands

Reverend Doctor,

Your most Obedient and

most Devoted Hble. Servt.

Notes

1. Factory: the Storehouse and Offices of a Trading Settlement, in the charge of a 'factor' or agent.
2. The letter to which Quaque refers, number 9 in the manuscripts, was the first he wrote from Africa, principally concerned with the distress of the father of his fellow student William Cudjo, who when Quaque left England, had lost his sanity, and was later to die in Guy's Hospital. William Cudjo's father wished both for news of his son, and, at his own expense if necessary, for him to be provided with a return passage 'by the next Committee Ship'. Letter 7 in the manuscripts is from John Moore, the tutor, giving an account of Cudjo's sickness, and is quoted in the introduction.
3. Governor Hippisley and Quaque's predecessor as Chaplain, the Rev. Thomas Thompson, for all their virtues recorded by Quaque, differed from him in one important respect – they were both defenders of the slave trade on economic grounds. (See Margaret Priestley's note in Philip Curtin, ed., *Africa remembered*, 114 n.37. For Quaque's view of American slavery see Letter 28 below to the Rev. Ed. Bass.)
4. Cabosheer: usually 'Caboceer', Head Man, from Portuguese *Cabeceira*.
5. His wife Catherine died in November 1766.
6. Bum-boy: an inferior rank of bailiff.

7. This letter is in a very battered condition. Its particular interest lies in its criticism of the attitude of the American states towards slavery, that at the very time they are fighting a revolutionary war for freedom they should impose 'the Hardships of Bondage and Oppression' upon 'my poor abject Countrymen'.

8. Dutch Chiefs: Chiefs from the area of Dixcove, where there were Dutch forts. In a letter of July 30th 1775, Quaque had written, 'Being weary of confining my time to one spot, to no secret Satisfaction was Obliged, one Day, to acept an invitation from a Friend, one of our Chiefs, belonging to Dixcove Castle, with whom I Resided Happily upwards of eight months.'

9. *Ammi, Ruhamah*: Lo-ruhamah, Lo-ammi? See *The Bible*, Book of Hosea:

   1.6: And God said unto him, call her name Lo-ru-ha-mah ... [That is, Not having obtained mercy].

   1.9: The said *God*, call his name Lo-ammi, for ye *are* not my people, and I will not be your *God*.

   2.1: Say unto your brethren, Am-mi [That is, My people]; and to your sisters, Ru-ha-mah [That is, Having obtained mercy].

10. By this time, Quaque had remarried locally. See letter 37, October 20th, 1781, quoted in the introduction to this section. He writes of his at that time having three children by his African wife, and is planning to have them educated in England in order that they might lose 'their mother's vile jargon.'

11. American: Quaque writes 'African' but this is clearly a slip of the pen. He refers to the activity of American privateers attacking British shipping during the American War of Independence, mentioned in the previous letter.

12. A Million: an exaggeration, but perhaps a reflection of Quaque's astonished recognition of the size of the local population when it is gathered together.

13. Quaque says that he is not referring to his own immediate family expenses, so this presumably refers to his extended African family, which would be making demands on him at the time of his close kinsman the Caboceer Codjo's death, when they would have to bear much of the burden of the cost of the celebrations described. This again suggests an involvement with the African family not brought out in his letters.

10

JOHN JEA

born Old Calabar, Nigeria 1773, date of death unknown

The Life, History and Sufferings of John Jea, the African Preacher

Portsea n.d., c.1815

Unlike most slave narratives, John Jea's contains sparse auto-biographical material, consisting instead of a series of sermons, meditations on Christianity and dozens of lengthy biblical quotations. Its opening words are about all we know of his African origins:

> I, John Jea, the subject of this narrative, was born in the town of Old Callabar, in Africa, in the year 1773. My father's name was Hambleton Robert Jea, my mother's name Margaret Jea. They were of poor but industrious parents. At two years and a half old, I and my father, mother, brothers, and sisters, were stolen, and conveyed to North America, and sold for slaves.

His father, whose name seems, to say the least, improbable in a native African, is never mentioned again in the few brief references made to his family, and the date is one of only two given in the narrative to a specific year. It is evident that he was proud of his native African origins from the way he identifies himself in his book as 'the African Preacher' and 'a black African', and his silhouette portrait emphasises his African features, unlike the engraved portraits of, for instance, Wedderburn and Phillis Wheatley, which play down the physical features of racial diferentiation. Nevertheless, Jea's narrative conveys nothing of any awareness of Africa derived from his parents or other slaves.

As a young field slave in New York, Jea attended chapel and grew to be obsessed with the sinfulness of the human condition. His conversion to Christianity was as intense as it was strange. He managed to get himself baptised secretly, on learning of which his master beat and threatened him, fearing that Jea would claim that his baptism gave him ground for demanding his freedom, a widespread belief amongst the slaves, but rarely confirmed by law. Rather surprisingly, his master's fears were soon realized when Jea made a successful appeal for his freedom to the local magistrates. Soon afterwards, Jea claims, an angel appeared to him:

> The Lord was pleased in his infinite mercy, to send an angel, in a vision, in shining raiment, and his countenance shining as the sun ... although the place was as dark as a dungeon, I awoke, as the Scripture saith, and found it illuminated with the light of the glory of God, and the angel standing by me, with the large book open, which was the Holy Bible, and said to me, 'Thou hath desired to read and understand this book, and to speak the language of it both in English and Dutch; I will therefore teach thee and now read.'

Needless to say, Jea's sudden literacy was cause for wonder, he tells us, not only among his fellow slaves, but all over the city of New York, especially since he could only read the Bible, other books remaining incomprehensible to him.

> From that hour, in which the Lord taught me to read, until the present, I have not been able to read in any book, nor any reading whatever, but such as contain the word of God.

Jea married an American Indian, and went about New York and Boston preaching the Gospel, until domestic tragedy struck. His wife, according to Jea, developed a hatred for the church and reverted to her heathen ways, and 'led astray by the temptations of Satan ... thought it no harm to sing songs', (Jea's stern disapproval of 'songs', as distinct from 'hymns' is a clear indication of his own morbid obsession with righteousness). In her desperate frustration, she killed her mother and strangled her young daughter, She was convicted of murder and executed. She refused to repent, cursing Jea instead: 'I have killed the child, and I mean to kill you, if I possibly can.'

Jea shows no contrition or gives any hint that his own religious inflexibility might have played a part in this tragedy, but it seems apparent that his wife's insanity was in some way a reaction against his obsessive immersion in the Bible, and the sinfulness of man. Reading Jea's account, it is impossible to imagine his displaying any sympathy for common cheerfulness, laughter, song and sexual love.

Jea continued preaching in America for two years before setting sail for Britain, where he spent an unspecified period preaching, he says, to large and enthusiastic crowds in Liverpool, Manchester, Limerick and Cork. In Ireland he married for the third time, his second wife having been, he tells us hurriedly, a Maltese woman, who died 'a natural death.' He ended this period of preaching in Portsmouth, and after a return visit to America and a stay in France, he settled in

Portsmouth where, some time around 1815, his narrative was published. In 1816 he published *A Collection of Hymns*, also in Portsmouth. The only known extant copy was discovered by David Dabydeen in 1983 in the Bodleian Library, Oxford. Apart from a mention in the *Hampshire Telegraph*, October 28, 1816, on the occasion of his fourth marriage, and some documents in Portsmouth City Records, (CHU 5/1A/4), relating to the baptism of a child in September 1817, nothing more is known of his life.

The text is taken from the original edition, published in Portsea, undated, around 1815.

a. *A Puzzle: Whites*

Seeing them act in such a wicked manner. I was encouraged to go on in my sins, being subject to all manner of iniquity that could be mentioned, not knowing there was a God, for they told us that we poor slaves had no God. As I grew up, my desire to know who their God was increased, but I did not know who to apply to, not being allowed to be taught by any one whatever, which caused me to watch their actions very closely: and in so doing, I, at one time, perceived that something was going forward which I could not comprehend, at last I found out that they were burying a slave master, who was very rich; they appeared to mourn and lament for his death, as though he had been a good man, and I asked them why they let him die; they said they could not help it, for God killed him: I said unto them, what, could you not have taken him away from God? They said, no, for he killed whomsoever he pleased. I then said he must be a dreadful God, and was led to fear least he should kill me also; although I had never seen death, but at a distance. But this fear did not last long, for seeing others full of mirth, I became so too.

A short time after this, there were great rejoicings on account of a great victory obtained by the Americans over the poor Indians, who had been so unfortunate as to lose their possessions, and they strove against the Americans, but they over-powered and killed thousands of them, and numbers were taken prisoners, and for this cause they greatly rejoiced. They expressed their joy by the ringing of bells, firing of guns, dancing and singing, while we poor slaves were hard at work. When I was informed of the cause of these rejoicings, I thought, *these* people made a great mourning when *God* killed one man, but they rejoice when *they* kill so many.

(7–8)

b. Observing Christians

From my observations of the conduct and conversation of my master and his sons, I was led to hate those who professed themselves christians, and to look upon them as devils; which made me neglect my work, and I told them what I thought of their ways. On this they did beat me in a most dreadful manner; but instead of making me obedient, it made me the more stubborn, not caring whether I lived or died, thinking that after I was dead I should be at rest, and that I should go back again to my native country, Africa (an idea generally entertained by slaves); but when I told them this, they chastised me seven times the more, and kept me short of food. In addition to this punishment, they made me go to a place of worship, while the other slaves enjoyed a rest for an hour or two; I could not bear to be where the word of God was mentioned, for I had seen so much deception in the people that professed to know God, that I could not endure being where there were, nor yet to hear them call upon the name of the Lord; but I was still sent in order to punish me, for when I entered the place I had such malice against God and his people, as showed the depravity of my heart, and verified that Scripture which saith, 'That the natural man understandeth not the things which are of God, for they are foolishness into him; neither doth he know them, because he is not spiritually discerned.'

My rage and malice against every person that was religious was so very great that I would have destroyed them all, had it been in my power; my indignation was so increased on my entering the place of worship, that, 'the form of my visage was changed,' like Nebuchadnezzar's, when he ordered Shadrach, Meshach, and Abednego, to be cast into the fiery furnace. My fury was more particularly kindled against the minister, and I should have killed him, had I not feared the people, it not being in my power to kill him, grieved me very much; and I went home and told my master what the minister had said, and what lies he had told, as I imagined, in hopes that he would send me no more; but he knowing this was a punishment to me, he made me go the more, for it was evident it was not for the good of my soul; this pained me exceedingly, so that I laid the blame to the minister, thinking that it was through his preaching so many lies, as I thought in my foolish opinion, that I was obliged to attend, not knowing that he spoke the truth, and I told the lies. The more I went to hear him preach, the more I wished to lay in wait to take away his life; but, as when the preaching was over, I was forced to return home to my master, and tell him what I had heard, I had no opportunity. At one time, the minister said that God was in the midst of them, which astonished me very much, and I looked all about to see if I could see him, but I could not, and I thought I had as good eyes as any one; not having any idea that 'God is a spirit, and they that worship him, must worship him in spirit and in truth,' John iv. 24; and only to be seen by a spiritual mind in the exercise of faith.

I was thus sent every Sabbath-day, while the other slaves rested, for while the masters go to worship, the slaves are allowed to rest, but thinking I deserved punishment I was compelled to go to the chapel; but instead of being benefited by what I heard, I mocked and persecuted the people of God; and when I went home I told my master of the foolishness of preaching, and that the people were mad, for they cried and beat their hands together. It amazed me very much to think they suffered such a noise in a place which they called *God's house*; on returning home I told my master what I had heard and seen, and what I thought of it, which pleased him very much. My hatred was so much against going to the chapel, that I would rather have received a hundred lashes.

Hearing the minister say that we must pray to God for his presence, I determined when I went away to do the same as I had seen the minister do; so when I got home, I retired into a secret place, and there began folding my hands together, shuttering my eyes, and using many words which I had heard the minister say, not knowing whether they were right or wrong; and thinking for my much speaking, God would hear me, like the pharisees of old: little did I think that prayer was the sincerity of the heart, and such only is accepted of God; not being acquainted with his word; but I was obliged still to go and hear the minister, or else I should not have had my daily allowance, which was very small. So after thinking a short time, I consented to go one week more, and endeavour to find out 'The Lamb of God, that taketh away the sins of the world,' whom the minister pointed out; but all was in vain, for I was so tempted by Satan, that difficulties and troubles, whenever I attempted to pray, attended me. The temptations of the devil were so great, and my repeated attempts to pray so interrupted, that I resolved to go to the minister, and tell him my situation. I therefore went, and told him the state of my mind. He told me it was the works of the devil, to frustrate me in my endeavours to serve the Lord, but bid me go on praying in opposition to him. I thanked him for his kindness in telling me what to do, but believed him not; however, I still continued praying, in order to find out whether there was a God or not, being determined to take the minister's life away, if I could not find God.

Thus I endeavoured to pray, but such was my situation, that sometimes I could not utter a word; often when I began to pray, I fell asleep, which grieved me very much; conscience accusing me of neglect in my seeking after God. One day being sent as usual to the chapel, in order to punish me, the minister was preaching about prayer, my attention was immediately fixed on the minister to hear what he had to say on the subject, when he said that if any of us had been praying to God and found no benefit from it, we should pray again and again, and be more earnest, and the Lord would hear our prayers: for, 'The effectual fervent prayer of a righteous man availeth much.' Not knowing the similarity of experience, I thought the minister was preaching about me, and exposing me to all the people, which so much vexed me, that I could not stay any longer, but left the place of worship, and returned home crying and weeping all the way.

(10–12)

c. Faith

I was now enabled, by the assistance of the Holy Spirit, to go from house to house, and from plantation to plantation, warning sinners, in the name of Jesus, to flee from the wrath to come; teaching and admonishing them to turn from their evil course of life; whilst some mocked and others scoffed at me, many said that I was mad, others pointed at me, and said there goes '*the preacher*,' in a mocking and jeering manner. Sometimes after I had been preaching in a house, and was leaving it, some of the people, who were assembled together, without the door, would beat and use me in a very cruel manner, saying, as the Jews of old did to Jesus Christ, when they smote him with the palms of their hands, '*Prophesy unto us who it was that smote thee?*'

But, for ever blessed be the Lord, he was pleased to give me one soul for my hire, and one seal to my ministry; which caused me to bless the Lord, and ascribe all the honour and glory to his name, for not having let my labours been in vain. This poor soul to whom the Lord was pleased to bless my feeble endeavours, was a poor black slave, the same as I had been; the Lord in infinite mercy, was pleased to liberate his soul from the bondage of sin and Satan, and afterwards from his cruel master.

It was a law of the state of the city of New York, that if any slave could give a satisfactorily account of what he knew of the work of the Lord on his soul he was free from slavery, by the Act of Congress, that was governed by the good people the Quakers, who were made the happy instruments, in the hands of God, of releasing some thousands of us poor black slaves from the galling chains of slavery.

After this poor man had received his liberty from slavery, he joined me in hand and heart, willing '*To follow the Lamb of God whithersoever he goeth.*' His employment while with his master, was sweeping chimnies; but now his master, who was God, had given him his labour to endeavour to sweep the evils out of the hearts of poor slaves. He and I used to go from house to house, and in barns and under hedges, preaching the gospel of Christ, as the Spirit of God gave us utterance; and God added unto our number such as should be saved. In the course of about nineteen months, it pleased the Lord to add to our number about five hundred souls; and when we could not find room enough in the houses, we used to preach out of doors in the fields and woods, which we used to call our large chapel, and there we assembled together on Saturday evenings about eleven o'clock, after the slaves had done their masters' work, and continued until Sunday evening about ten or eleven o'clock. The other black men and myself used to go fourteen miles of a night to preach, and to instruct our poor fellow brethren, and thought ourselves well paid for our trouble in having a congregation together in the name of the Lord.

I knew it was a hard task for the poor slaves to get out, because when I was a slave I had gone fifteen miles to hear preaching, and was obliged to get back before sun rising, to go to my work, and then, if my master knew I had been to hear preaching, he would beat me most unmercifully, so that I encouraged the other poor slaves to seek the Lord, and to be earnest in prayer and supplication, for well I knew that the Lord would hear and deliver them, if they sought him in sincerity and in truth, as the Lord delivered me; for they did not suffer for evil doing, but for doing the will of God.

(37–40)

d. A Rough Sea Voyage

After that time, it pleased God to put it into my mind to cross the Atlantic main; and I embarked on board of a ship for that purpose. The name of the ship was *The Superb of Boston*, and the captain's name was ABLE STOVEY, with whom I agreed to sail with for seventeen dollars per month. I was quite unacquainted with the sea, and was very much pleased in going on board the vessel; but the case was soon altered, for the first day I went on board to work, the captain and the men asked me if I came on board to work. I told them yes. They asked me where my clothes were. I said I had them on my back. They asked me if that was all I had. I told them I thought I had sufficient, for I was not certain of staying longer than one day; for if I did not like it I would not stay out the month; for I thought that a person going to sea, could go one day and return the next.

After they had told me what to do, which was to clean the coppers, I went and looked all about the ship, but could not find them, not knowing what they were; at last I asked one of the sailors where the coppers were, for the captain had ordered me to clean them, so he shewed me where they were. Those which they called coppers, were a couple of black iron things; and they told me I must make them very clean, and that I was to cook the victuals, being cook of the ship. The coppers were very large, for the ship was about four hundred tons burden. I then began to rub the coppers as I was ordered, and the more I rubbed them, the more the rust came off, and the blacker they looked. About two hours after I had began cleaning them, the captain asked me if I had cleaned the coppers; I told him I could not get them clean; but he told me I must be sure to clean them well.

During this time the vessel had got under weigh, and was sailing through the river, which was very pleasant, until we got outside of the light-house, when the ship began to roll about very much, which greatly terrified me. The captain coming to me, said, 'How do you come on?' I told him that I was tired, and that I wanted to get home. He told me that I should soon get home; and asked me how the sailors' suppers got on. I said, 'I cannot get these black things clean; they certainly are not copper.' The captain said, 'Never mind, let them alone, and have another trial to-morrow.' But I said within myself, 'You shall not catch me here to-morrow, if I can get on shore.' The captain seeing how I was, bade me go below, for the men had some cold beef for supper, and that I should rest myself. When I was going below, I looked at the man at the helm with an evil eye, thinking he made the ship to go on one side on purpose to frighten me the more; but before I got down to the hold I fell down, by the vessel rolling, and all the men sung out, 'Hollo, there is a horse down;' and they laughing at me so, made me the more afraid and terrified, and after I had got down into the hold, I was afraid the ship would fall, and I strove to keep her up by pushing, and holding fast by different parts of the ship, and when the waves came dashing against the sides of the ship, I thought they were sea lions, and was afraid they would beat a hole through the ship's side, and would come in and devour me; when day-light appeared, I was very much tired and fatigued, for I had been holding and trying to keep the ship upright all the night, in the morning I asked the sailors why they did not keep the ship upright, and one of the men said, pointing to another, 'That is the man that makes the ship go on one side.' This they said in their scoffing way, to deride me. Having been about eight or ten days at sea, I found out what it was, in some measure. The weather was very boisterous, the sea running very high, and thundering and lightning very much; the reason of which was, I believe, because they so ill-used and abused me, and swore they would throw me overboard, or beat me so that I should jump overboard. When they saw me praying to God, they called me by way of derision, Jonah, because I prayed to God to calm the tempestuous weather. On the contrary, they were making game of the works of the Lord, and said that the old man had fine fire works, for it gave them light to go up on the yards to furl the sails; but to their great terror, after they had furled the sails, it pleased the Lord to send his lightning and thunder directly, which killed two men on the spot. One of them was burnt like a cinder, his clothes were totally consumed, not so much as a bit of a handkerchief nor any thing else being left. His name was George Begann, about thirty-six years of age. The other's name was James Cash, about twenty-five years of age, his body was entirely burnt up, not a single bit of it was to be seen, nothing but the cinders of his clothes, one of his shoes, his knife, his gold ring, and his key.

Seven more were wounded, some in their backs, and others in different parts of their bodies; and appeared to be dead for about ten or fifteen minutes.

At the time this dreadful carnage happened, I was standing about seven or eight feet from them; my eye-sight was taken from me for four or five minutes, but my soul gave glory to God for what was done. When I recovered my sight I saw the captain standing in the cabin gangway, and the cabin-boy and three passengers behind him, lamenting greatly, ringing their hands, and plucking their hair; the captain crying out – 'O! my men, we are all lost!' I then took the boldness to speak unto him, and said, 'Why do you cry and lament? You see that your ship is not hurt, and that the Lord has been pleased to spare your life; and what the Lord has done is right.'

A short time after we had survived this awful scene, the captain exclaimed, 'O! my men, my men, the ship is on fire!' On hearing this, the men that were able to move, were roused to take off the hatches, to see where the fire was. But, blessed be God, the ship was not on fire, for it was part of the men's clothes who were consumed, which had got down into the hold, and was burning, which caused a very great smoke; for the sailors stood round the main-mast (excepting four who were at the helm) which was the most materially injured; that part of the cargo which was near the main-mast, consising of tobacco and staves for casks, was nearly all consumed, but the ship sustained no damage whatsoever.

The captain and ship's crew were very much terrified when they saw the power of God in killing and wounding the men, and destroying the cargo; which judgments were sent on them.

(49–54)

11

WILLIAM DAVIDSON
1786–1820

The Cato Street Conspiracy: Speech from the Dock

During the period of the slave trade, there were many Scottish born residents of the West Indies, both wealthy owners of estates and senior administrators as well as indentured servants whose status might be little better than that of slaves. Two of the mulatto sons of wealthy Scots in Jamaica were William Davidson and Robert Wedderburn, also represented in this collection, both to achieve notoriety in London as radical extremists during the early years of the nineteenth century. The former left little in the way of written records though we do possess the account of his trial for conspiracy to assassinate the Cabinet, and his moving last letter to his wife written before his execution, both of which convey something of his distinctive character.

During the late Georgian and Regency periods, the radicalism of such men as Thomas Spence and Francis Place inevitably appealed to talented and ambitious members of a disaffected working class and what McCalman's book (see bibliography) calls the *Radical Underworld*. Social discontents led to such outbursts as the storming of Newgate Jail in 1770 by a mob of which the poet William Blake was a member, the Gordon Riots of 1780, described with staunch disapproval by Ignatius Sancho in one of his letters included above, and the Nore Mutinty in the Royal Navy in 1798. We know that Black Londoners were involved in these stirrings of popular discontent and such attacks on the authority of the establishment might have come to a spectacular climax in 1820 with the Cato Street Conspiracy, of which Davidson was one of the leaders, to blow up the Cabinet while it was gathered for dinner in Grosvenor Square – a grim irony of the situation is that Davidson was a cabinet maker by profession. The initial scheme, which had been even more ambitious, to blow up Parliament, was dropped as impractical.

Davidson's Jamaican background – he was the acknowledged son of the Attorney General of Jamaica and a black woman – was almost 'respectable', and before coming to

Britain he had already received a local education. He was sent to Aberdeen to study Mathematics, but the course of his life was erratic: earlier, at the age of 14 he seems to have been apprenticed to a Liverpool lawyer, then to have gone to sea, whether taken by a press-gang or a desire for independence is not clear. After the interlude in Aberdeen he apprenticed himself to a cabinet maker in Lichfield and in due course set up in business in Birmingham. He was articulate, courageous and popular, possessing many of the marks of that respectability towards which one group of radicals aspired, as distinct from the far from respectable element, noted by Francis Place (see McCalman 42–5). As Place observed, a number of otherwise radical skilled workers, rather than revolution sought a modest prosperity for themselves. Nor does Davidson appear to have been particularly motivated by racial solidarity: when the government *agent provocateur* who betrayed him invited him to 'have a glass with a countryman' the trial records:

> I said 'What do you mean by a countryman?'
> 'I am not much acquainted with him' he says, 'a man of colour.'
> I had no objection to going in, for though I am a man of colour, I never associated with any of them. I was very well brought up. I found them all very ignorant. (p. 131)

Wedderburn seems to have been something of a divided personality. As we have said, Radicals tended to divide into two camps, the respectable aiming at social justice by way of principled self-improvement, and the extremist seeking the violent overthrow of the establishment. Davidson appears to have had a foot in both camps. After a distressing love affair marred by the racial prejudice of his fiancée's father, Davidson married a poor widow with four children, and set up house in London, where he was a good and faithful husband. Though described by government spies as 'a desperate man', by all accounts he was jovial and companionable, popular with his neighbours, a thrower of wine parties and singer of radical songs. His thinking was deeply affected by reading Thomas Paine's *The Rights of Man* and after the Peterloo Massacre of 1819 he joined the Marylebone Union Reading Society. Equiano's friend Thomas Hardy, with whom he had lodgings in 1792, was founder of the London Corresponding Society. These Reading, or Corresponding Societies often met in taverns and were devoted to the discussion of press reports and political pamphlets. The Marylebone Society, it appears, also supplied Davidson with gunpower to aid the Cato Street Conspiracy, named after the street in which they met. The conspiracy was betrayed by a government agent, and the conspirators apprehended, it is reported, amidst cries of 'Kill the buggers', though it is not clear from which side the shouts came. A Bow Street Runner was killed in the storming of the conspirators' loft, and Davidson was led away 'damning every person who would not die in Liberty's cause' and singing 'Scots wha hae wi' Wallace bled'. Other insurrections in Scotland and Sheffield fizzled out. Davidson was tried and sentenced to be hanged with four of his fellow conspirators, their heads to be severed and their bodies quartered. This final indignity was never carried out, as the King kindly remitted it. At his execution, Davidson bowed to the assembled people, prayed, and shook hands with the chaplain. The five widows begged the King to let them have the 'mutilated remains', but the King was not so kind this time and the bodies were buried in quicklime under the prison floor.

The text of the speech is from T. B. Howell, *State Trials*, London 1826, Vol. 33, 1498–66. Davidson's letter to his wife was published in the *Observer*, no. 1520, May 7, 1820, and is reproduced by Peter Fryer, in *Staying Power* (see bibliography).

a. The Trial of William Davidson

Mr. *Baron Garrow*. – William Davidson, the law of England, in its extraordinary tenderness for persons charged with the crime of high treason, allows to the person accused on opportunity for making full defence by counsel, and you received the great benefit the law has extended to you in this respect; but if, in addition to that which has been urged to the jury by your learned counsel, you wish to make any observations yourself, it is allowed to you to do so, and this is the proper and the only opportunity.

Davidson. – I am extremely obliged to your lordship for the opportunity you have given me; I would call your attention to two particular instances. –

Mr. *Baron Garrow*. – I wish you would do it so that I may hear every word; if you wish it, pause for a moment.

Davidson. – From my life up, it was always my study to earn my bread by honest industry. I had no friends in England, but I always laboured for my family; I have an extensive family, which is my only grief. As to the crime I am charged with, I lay my hand on my heart, and say that I am not guilty of it. With regard to the blunderbuss – I met with Mr. Williams, who is now gone to the Cape of Good Hope, and he had this blunderbuss very rusty; he asked me where I was going to, I said after a job; I have been working for myself for five years, which is the reason I have had no master to come before you. I used to sell my goods at auction rooms, and when I saw the name of Welford put down in the list of witnesses, I meant to appeal to him as being the cashier for Mr. Denew, who sold my goods; he said, he had bought this blunderbuss to take to the Cape of Good Hope, but that he had taken it to a gunsmith, and found he would charge him more than it was worth for repairing it, and if I could get part of his money back, he would be obliged to me; I took the blunderbuss home, and kept it; it is not worth much; I cleaned it, and scraped the stock, and proposed to raffle it; I met with Mr. Edwards, whom I never knew till I dined at the Crown and Anchor, at Mr. Hunt's procession; that is the first time I ever went to a public dinner in my life; Mr. Edwards promised to be one of the members, and promised to get me a considerable number of persons more; there were to be twenty members, at one shilling each, and it was to take place the next Monday. I saw Mr. Thistlewood there the following Monday for the second time; I saw Mr. Adams and several others, but I did not know them again, except Mr. Adams and Mr. Thistlewood; they wished to commence raffling for the blunderbuss; I got up and said it should not be done without the money was tendered, for it was not my property, and it was my duty to be accountable for it; I received bad language; I found the company inconsistent with that I expected; I took the blunderbuss and went away; Mr. Williams called the next morning to know the result; he was disappointed, as he wished to lay out five or six shillings in the west end of the town; I said he might pledge it if he wished; he said he did not know any person in that end of the town; I said I knew Mr. Aldous, I had known him for years; he said, well, you pledge it; I said I would; I then told Mr. Aldous it was not my property; he said he would not have lent me more than five shillings but for knowing me. The vessel in which Mr. Williams is gone, is called the Belle Alliance. Mr. Williams told me, that he could not sell the ticket to his fellow passengers, they were so very poor, but would I accept it.

On the 22nd of February, Mr. Edwards said, he had been to see Mr. Williams, and that he had told him, that by giving me a trifle, he might get the ticket from me. I said, 'he gave me the ticket; but if you wish it, you may have it;' he said, 'Well, I am going to sell it, and shall get ten shillings more, but I should not have called for it, but for having a customer ready;' the same evening he called at my house again at eight o'clock; he said 'Mr. Davidson, if you have no objection to going for this blunderbuss, you had better go as you pledged it, lest the man should object to my having it.' I did not think he intended to forfeit my life; he told me where to meet him the next morning in Oxford-street, and I took the blunderbuss under a gateway in Oxford-street to him; he said, 'will not you walk in, and have a glass with a countryman of your's?' I said, 'what do you mean by a countryman?' I was not much acquainted with him; he says, 'a man of colour.' I had an objection to going in, for though I am a man of colour, I have never associated with any of them. I was very well brought up. I found them all very ignorant; who this man of colour was I do not know. Mr. Edwards promised to meet me the next day, but that night I was apprehended.

Now, my lord, we will pass to the account of the sword. Going about my own concern, I met with a person I knew at Liverpool, of the name of James Goldsworthy; he expressed his surprise at meeting with me in London, and after inquiring about my family. I told him I was very badly off, and that it was very bad to be a master, unless he has full work, for that other masters do not like to employ him; he told me he had set up a business a few miles out of town; it was a pleasant walk, and he would employ me if I liked; I told him, with the greatest pleasure; I asked him what wages I should have; he said, what did I expect; I said, thirty-two shillings a week; he said, he would give me thirty shillings; he said, call at the Horse and Groom. I did not at that time know that Mr. Goldsworthy and Mr. Edwards were acquainted. I now know they lodged in one house. As the officer says, I stopped at the corner, but as to the habiliments I was in, I never had cross belts on; is it possible, that if they had been so conspicuous, Adams would not have seen them in the stable? however I went into the public-house, and did not see Mr. Goldsworthy; I went a bit of a walk, and when I came back in half an hour, I saw several persons passing backwards and forwards; I saw several men looking at me, but I did not see the person I was looking for; I went again and stood at the corner; at a little after eight o'clock I was going down the Edgware-road; but previous to that, the landlord asked me, whether I was looking for any particular person; 'yes,' says I, 'a gentleman I appointed to meet me, but he has not kept his word;' I was going down the Edgware-road, and I saw Mr. Goldsworthy near Queen-street; he said, 'I suppose you are tired of waiting?' 'Yes,' said I, 'if it was not for an anxiety to get work, I would not have stopped so long;' he says, 'go and get a pint of beer, I have to shake hands with a friend;' and he gave me a sword and a bundle; I said, 'what do you want the sword for, are you going to cut my head off?' – 'No, but we have many thieves in our part, and it is for my own protection.' As I am to stand before God, I never meant any bad. I was passing the stable, I saw persons rush in, and very foolishly went in, and I was attacked; I ran away; I never cut at any one; I never had any belt on; I would never plead for my life only, for I have ventured my life fifteen times for my country and my king, and how can it be supposed I would join wicked men, who would attempt to overthrow so well-founded a constitution as the British constitution, and from the little acquaint-ance I have had with any men, save those directly in my business, it is not likely that I should be in any plot. I do not mean to say that I was not apprehended in Cato-street; but I still contend, my lord, that the carbine was not in my possession directly nor indirectly; it was picked up at a distance, and brought to me, and I was asked whether it was not mine; I denied it, but another person said, 'oh, it is surely his, why do you ask him?' I was carried into a chandler's shop; I never was in a public-house; and captain Fitzclarence cleared up that point, though one of the officers swore that I even addressed the people; and said, that the man who would not die in liberty's cause, ought to be damned. I was left in the custody of the officer who took me; and I asked captain Fitzclarence, whether he did not take me directly to Bow-street; what time had I then to address any persons, or to go into any public-house when I was a prisoner; even the landlord of the public-house I would appeal to, to know whether I was a prisoner in his house. I do not mean to say that an existing plot might not have been, but I pretend to say I knew of no existing plot; I was accidently brought into Cato-street as I have laid my story; but I knew nothing of a plot for plunder or massacre.

If my colour should be against, me which perhaps, gentlemen of the jury, you may suppose it to be, and think that because I am a man of colour I am without an understanding or a feeling, and would act the brute; I am not one of that sort; I would wish to wipe off those impressions from those learned gentlemen who have so prosecuted me. When not employed in my business, I have employed myself as a teacher of a Sunday-school, and in that capacity have remained; and I would draw your attention to a simple mistake – there was a person, a man of colour, nearly my stature, insulted one of our female teachers in the Walworth-road; I then lived at Walworth; and though this young lady was a teacher in the same school I was, she so far mistook the person as to make a complaint of me; I found some of them looked cool upon me, and I sent in a letter of resignation, consequently the whole committee waited upon me, and called me from my wife into the front parlour, and expostulated with me upon the impropriety of my conduct, and persisted in it; it struck me with such horror, that I had nothing to answer, but I determined to investigate it, and I sent my wife to the young woman to ask a little information; I traced out the person that had insulted her, brought him to the committee, and he acknowledged his fault, and she came ashamed to look me in the face, and hid her face, and offered me her hand. If any thing I could say would do away these impressions I would proceed, but I would as lief be put to death, if I thought your lordship or the learned gentlemen for the Crown, believed I was that monster that for a moment I could harbour a thought to murder any human being directly or indirectly; if you believe that, I hope your lordship will not shew me the least mercy, for my conscience acquits me; I can stand before my God, and I will stand at his tribunal to assert, my lord, that I am not guilty of doing such a thing, nor deserving it. If your lordship will permit me to have a drink of water.

Mr. *Baron Garrow*. – Oh, certainly, take you refreshment, sit down and compose yourself, and address the jury again, if you desire it, when you are composed, there is no impatience on the part of the Court, take your own time. I would observe to you, upon that which you have said, that you may rest most perfectly assured that with respect to the colour of your countenance, no prejudice either has or will exist in any part of this Court against you; a man of colour is entitled to British justice as much as the fairest British subject that ever came into a court of justice, and will always be sure to obtain it, and this case will be decided upon the facts given in evidence; God forbid that the complexion of the accused should enter, for a single moment, into the consideration of the jury.

Davidson. – My lord, it is but very few words I have got further to say, for as to politics I never troubled my head with it. I have a family of very little children, and a wife that never earned a penny for me since I have had her; it is only the distress of my family I feel; were it not for that, I should quote a passage in Isaiah, 'He was oppressed and he was afflicted, yet he opened not his mouth;' but when I think of the case of my family, for the love I bear my children, I should use the uttermost of my power to prevail upon a British jury, if it were possible, to clear up those black charges which are laid against me. First of all, here is Mr. Adams, he can positively swear that he has not seen me in any warlike appearance whatever. I was down stairs when Mr. Thistlewood numbered his men; he said eighteen and two below; when he was asked whether I was by, he said no, I was down stairs, but my name was put down immediately the officer came up. The next witness, Mr. Monument, comes forward and says, that I addressed the congregation, and told them that any man that was afraid of his life might walk off, and that in a few minutes afterwards the officers came up; now your lordship and the jury must see there is some exaggeration of these things. I do admit I was in Cato-street, by passing through the street, but as to admitting any thing else, it would be against my conscience, it would be wrong in me to say that; I knew nothing of their plans; I now know that Mr. Goldsworthy was an accomplice of Mr. Edwards, they might be the plotters; but I did not expect that he would be that base character, that having been a journeyman in a shop in which I was an apprentice he would have entrapped me. I have served my country, I have done all which an honest man can do; I have supported my family by honest industry, and I can appeal to fifty gentlemen I have dealt with since I have been master, that they never have known me to go to public meetings, except one meeting in Smithfield, as a common spectator. I knew nothing at all of these men till I found myself a prisoner along with them. I had seen Mr. Thistlewood, but I never saw him the night I was apprehended, till I was apprehended; if I had seen Mr. Thistlewood, and Mr. Edwards, it might have led me to suspect, but none spoke to me nor I to them; if I was one in their concern, being such a conspicuous character as I know I am from my colour, can it be supposed that I would stand in a gateway to be seen and identified above all others? It is not for me to say any thing further on my own behalf, my learned counsel, on the points of law have done me justice; and as for those learned gentlemen, the counsel for the Crown, I have nothing to lay to their charge; I admire the way in which they have done their duty, according to their judgment upon the evidences; if those gentlemen knew me better, or it was possible I could have shewn them my former conduct, they would not have pointed me out the character they have done. I never, my lord, have done any man an injury, but I have supported an honest character, for by an honest character I intended to live, and nothing but that; my family was all my society that I kept, neither politics nor laws ever troubled me; as for any thing further that I have got to say, it would be useless.

I would only call the minds of the jury to a few passages I have selected out for that purpose, if it would not be insulting to the Court; I would select this passage in the indictment, in which it is said that I had not the fear of God before my eyes, but was moved and seduced by the instigation of the Devil; now, my lord, I always had the fear of God before my eyes, and it was my constant prayer, and I always used those passages which I have read in some of Mr. Pope's writings:

> 'If I am right thy grace impart,
> Still in the right to stay;
> If I am wrong, oh! teach my heart
> To find that better way!
>
> 'Teach me to feel another's woe,
> To hide the faults I see;
> That mercy I to others shew,
> That mercy shew to me.'

These were always my constant impressions, my lord, and those passages in the indictment may better be applied to those gentlemen who stand there to swear my life away, to the destruction of myself and my family; but here, in the Bible, it is said, 'One witness shall not rise up against a man for any iniquity, or for any sin in any sin that he sinned but at the mouth of two or three witnesses shall the matter be established.' It goes on to the word which is above your lordship's head, 'If a false witness rise up against any man to testify against him that which is wrong, then both the men between whom the controversy is shall stand before the Lord, before the priests and the judges which shall be in those days, and the judges shall make diligent inquisition; and behold, if the witness be a false witness, and hath testified falsely against his brother, then shall ye do unto him as he had thought to have done unto his brother; so shalt thou put the evil away from among you, that innocent blood be not shed in the land which the Lord thy God giveth thee for an inheritance.'

These things I would wish to impress on the jury's mind; I am a stranger to England by birth; but I was educated and brought up in England; my father was an Englishman and my grandfather a Scotchman; I certainly have a little prerogative for claiming to be an Englishman, being here from fourteen years of age; but I have not a friend in England, and it is hard that my life should be taken away; not knowing any thing of the plot made out against his majesty's ministers; the earl of Ilarrowby I knew for years, when I worked at Rugely, in Staffordshire, for Mr. Bullock. I have worked at his lordship's house, and for the regard I have for his lordship, from knowing him personally, I should have shuddered at the thought of taking his life; and if any man would have mentioned such a plan to me, it would have turned upon whether I should have turned a public informer, or have privately informed his lordship; but my conscience does not accuse me of any thing improper, for if I am to die, I can die with a clear conscience, that I know nothing of any assassination plot, nothing of any plunder or burning of the city, for those things I detest; I would get my living by honest industry, but I never was a man known to associate or keep any bad company.

I would have called your attention to several other witnesses, but they did not attend at the time they were called upon. All I have got to say is this; I hope the gentlemen of the jury will weigh the matter well in their minds, seeing it stands only between life and death; and should they harbour an opinion, that I am guilty of treason, though not guilty of murder, though that has been a crime charged – if they think I am a culprit that would stand here to acquit myself against the force of conscience, I am very willing to abide by their judgments.

––––––

On Monday, the 1st of May – Arthur Thistlewood, William Davidson, James Ings, John Thomas Brunt, and Richard Tidd, were brought out to a platform erected in front of the debtors door, Newgate, where they were hanged until they were dead, when they were cut down, and their heads were severed from their bodies, his majesty having been graciously pleased by warrant to remit that part of the sentence which directed that their bodies should be divided into four quarters, and to direct that the bodies, and heads, should be forthwith privately buried.

James William Wilson, John Harrison, Richard Bradburn, John

Shaw Strange, James Gilchrist, and Charles Cooper, received his majesty's pardon, on condition of being transported to such place beyond the seas as his majesty, with the advice of his Privy Council, should be pleased to direct, for life.

b. *Davidson's Last Letter to his Wife, Sarah*

My dear Sarah, – According to the promise your entreaties caused me to make to you concerning matters of counsel, &c. I have sent you here the order I received last night – an order for application to either of the several justices therein mentioned, whereby an order will be granted to the applicant for the free admission of counsel, solicitors, &c. But I would rather, for my part, use such an order for you and my dear children, in preference to counsel, &c.; and would now retain my integrity of not having any, only as it is the first time you ever ask the favour of being dictator, and, as in such considerations, I did grant you that request, I will not now fall from such a promise, to one whose sole interest & young family entirely depends on the result of this trial. Therefore you can be advised how you are to act; for my own part I am careless about it, as I am determined to maintain my integrity as a man against all the swarms of false witnesses; and I hope you will never be persuaded, or suffer the public to be led away with a belief, that I am fallen from that spirit maintained from my youth up, and had so long been in possession of the ancient name of Davidson (Aberdeen's boast), and is now become fables. Death's countenance is familiar to me. I have had him in view fifteen times, and surely he cannot now be terrible. Keep up that noble spirit for the sake of your children, and depend that even in death, it will be maintained, by your ever affectionate husband,

Wm. Davidson

Mrs. Sarah Davidson, 12, Elliott-row, Lord's Old Cricket Ground, St. Mary-le-bone, New Road

12

The Horrors of Slavery

1824

The Trial of the Rev. Robt. Wedderburn for Blasphemy

Edited by Erasmus Perkins, 1820

Like his friend William Davidson (see above), Robert Wedderburn was the mulatto son of a wealthy Scottish Jamaican and one of his slaves. Wedderburn's father, James Wedderburn of Inveresk near Edinburgh, exchanged the comparatively unprofitable profession of medicine for the rich rewards of planter and slave-owner, for which his son detested him enthusiastically:

> I never saw my dear father but once in the island of Jamaica, when I went with my grandmother to know if he meant to do any thing for me, his son. [He] giving her some abusive language, my grandmother called him a mean Scotch rascal, thus to desert his own flesh and blood. This was the parental treatment I experienced from a Scotch West-India planter and slave-dealer.

His grandmother, Talkee Amy, a small trader with a line in smuggling, brought him up after his mother was sold as a troublemaker when five months pregnant with Robert. He never forgot seeing his grandmother whipped publicly by a white youth she herself had reared as an infant. In 1778 Robert came to England, serving as a gunner in the Navy, then sailing as a privateer (virtually as a licensed pirate). Later he settled ashore as a jobbing tailor, and after being deeply moved by a passionate Wesleyan preacher in 1786, and having read Thomas Paine's *The Rights of Man*, took out a licence to practice as a Unitarian preacher. He founded a tavern chapel for a sect which he was later to call 'Christian Diabolists or Devil Worshippers', kept a brothel on the side, lived on the fringes of criminality, and troubled the authorities with his fiery and popular preaching that it was the Christian duty of his flock to do all in their power to bring down the establishment. He was tried and jailed for blasphemy in 1820, and at the age of 68 in 1831, was serving a two-year sentence of hard labour, not simply for running a brothel, but for brawling in the street outside it. His life has been brilliantly researched by Iain McCalman (see bibliography) who has described him and his chapel as follows:

> Debates functioned as a form of theatre intended to ridicule authority and entertain listeners. Part of the chapel's notoriety derived from the reputation of its leading speakers as performers. Wedderburn believed that many had come to see and hear him because 'his name had gone abroad as a strange and curious sort of fellow'. He had, in Richard Carlile's words, 'developed a powerful eccentricity of manner'. His coarse and profane language, his colour and physique (often described as stout): and the spectacular events of his life – the slave background, rejection by a wealthy family, experience as a fighting sailor, criminal pauper – were to say the least, arresting. He displayed the traits of many populist leaders – physical bulk, roguery, flamboyance, bombast, emotional religiosity and a thirst for martyrdom. (McCalman, *Radical Underworld*, 148–9)

At his trials he spiritedly undertook his own defence and McCalman writes in the introduction to his edition of *The Horrors of Slavery* etc. (see note on the text below), that when charged in his late-sixties with running a brothel,

> Wedderburn's court defence was all his own, and it showed that he had lost neither his old anti-establishment pugnacity nor his flair for Rabelaisian burlesque. He accused one member of the court of himself frequenting the establishment, supposedly attracted by one 'Carroty Eliza' who was usually to be found 'padding the hoof' in Fleet Street. He also argued, somewhat inconsistently, that the Featherbed Lane premises were used not for prostitution, but as a refuge for destitute women.

We include two extracts from Wedderburn, the first from *The Horrors of Slavery*, the second from his defence at this trial for blasphemy. The latter was in the form of a written statement, of which he said 'that he had a defence which a gentleman' (George Cannon, alias Erasmus Perkins) 'had committed to paper for him, but being a superannuated tailor, his sight was too bad to suffer him to read it, and he therefore begged, as a particular favour, that it might be read by some person more qualified than himself' (8). The Lord Chief Justice, Sir Charles Abbott said, 'By all means if it contains nothing objectionable' and it was read by the Clerk of the Court. Its tone is consequently comparatively restrained, but

we gain an impression of his urgent breathless rhetorical style
from the evidence of a witness and informer who quoted in
evidence words from a sermon in which Wedderburn spoke of
inconsistencies in the Bible, essentially an attack upon authority in religion and the state, and significantly, in view of his
own history, of fathers.

> Oh, how unfortunate for them that parsons or priests
> should leave this for us to find out; but as religion is part
> of parcel of the law of the land, (as our friend says) your
> fat-gutted parsons, priests, or Bishops, would rather see
> Jesus Christ d—d, or God Almighty either, than give up
> their twenty or thirty thousand a year, and become poor
> curates at twenty pounds per annum. Jesus Christ, by the
> new testament, taught the Christian religion; but what did
> he teach us, what did he say, 'acknowledge no king.' He
> was a reformer: now every king is a lord. Then he meant,
> acknowledge no lord, because every king is a lord, every
> person is the same, that bears the name, as he lords over
> us, but then he is the Lord's anointed. Jesus Christ says,
> acknowledge no rabbi (no priest:) no! he knew their tricks
> and says, stand it no longer. Then Jesus Christ says,
> acknowledge no father; why? because fathers in those
> days were allowed to thrash their sons at any age ...
> (*Trial*, 5)

The texts are taken from the 1824 edition of *The Horrors of
Slavery*, soon to be reissued in this series along with selections
from his other writings edited by Iain McCalman; and from
Erasmus Perkin's pamphlet, *The Trial of the Rev. Robt.
Wedderburn for Blasphemy* (1820). Wedderburn was literate,
but his style was rough (see Fryer, *Staying Power*, Appendix C
for a letter from his own hand) and, like Cugoano, his writing
was given a polish by others, such as his shady friend, George
Cannon, alias Erasmus Perkins, preacher and pornographer, or
his fellow prisoner in Dorchester Jail, Richard Carlile, the
radical freethinker.

a. from The Horrors of Slavery

My father's name was JAMES WEDDERBURN, Esq. of Inveresk, in
Scotland, an extensive proprietor, of sugar estates in Jamaica, which
are now in the possession of a younger brother of mine, by name,
A. COLVILLE,[1] Esq. of No. 35, Leadenhall Street.

I must explain at the outset of this history – what will appear
unnatural to some – the reason of my abhorrence and indignation at

the conduct of my father. From him I have received no benefit in the world. By him my mother was made the object of his brutal lust, then insulted, abused, and abandoned, and, within a few weeks from the present time, a younger and more fortunate brother of mine, the aforesaid A. Colville, Esq. has had the insolence to revile her memory in the most abusive language, and to stigmatize her for that which was owing to the deep and dark iniquity of my father. Can I contain myself at this? or, have I not the feelings of human nature within my breast? Oppression I can bear with patience, because it hath always been my lot; but when to this is added insult and reproach from the authors of my miseries, I am forced to take up arms in my own defence, and to abide the issue of the conflict.

My father's name, as I said before, was JAMES WEDDERBURN, of Inveresk, in Scotland, near Musselborough, where, if my information is correct, the Wedderburn family have been seated for a long time. My grandfather was a staunch Jacobite, and exerted himself strenuously in the cause of the Pretender, in the rebellion of the year 1745. For his aiding to restore the exiled family to the throne of England, he was tried, condemned, and executed. He was hung by the neck till he was dead; his head was then cut off, and his body was divided into four quarters. When I first came to England, in the year 1779, I remember seeing the remains of a rebel's skull which had been affixed over Temple Bar; but I never yet could fully ascertain whether it was my dear grandfather's skull, or not. Perhaps my dear brother, A. COLVILLE, can lend me some assistance in this affair. For this act of high treason, our family estates were confiscated to the King, and my dear father found himself destitute in the world, or with no resource but his own industry. He adopted the medical profession; and in Jamaica he was Doctor and Man-Midwife, and turned an honest penny by drugging and physicing the poor blacks, where those that were cured, he had the credit for, and for those he killed, the fault was laid to their own obstinacy. In the course of time, by dint of *booing* and *booing*,[2] my father was restored to his father's property, and he became the proprietor of one of the most extensive sugar estates in Jamaica. While my dear and honoured father was poor, he was chaste as any Scotchman, whose poverty made him virtuous; but the moment he became rich, he gave loose to his carnal appetites, and indulged himself without moderation, but as parsimonious as ever. My father's mental powers were none of the brightest, which may account for his libidinous excess. It is a common practice, as has been stated by Mr. Wilberforce in parliament, for the planters to have lewd intercourse with their female slaves; and so inhuman are many of these said planters, that many well-authenticated instances are known, of their selling their slaves while pregnant, and making that a pretence to enhance their value. A father selling his offspring is no disgrace there. A planter letting out his prettiest female slaves for purposes of lust, is by no means uncommon. My father ranged through the whole of his household for his own lewd purposes; for they being his personal property, cost nothing extra; and if any one proved with child – why, it was an acquisition which might one day fetch something in the market, like a horse or pig in Smithfield. In short, amongst his own slaves my father was a perfect parish bull; and his pleasure was the greater, because he at the same time increased his profits.

I now come to speak of the infamous manner with which JAMES WEDDERBURN, Esq. of Inveresk, and father to A. COLVILLE, Esq. No. 35, Leadenhall Street, entrapped my poor mother in his power. My mother was a lady' maid, and had received an education which perfectly qualified her to conduct a household in the most agreeable manner. She was the property of Lady Douglas, whom I have before mentioned; and, prior to the time she met my father, was chaste and virtuous. After my father had got his estate, he did not renounce the pestle and mortar, but, in the capacity of Doctor, he visited Lady Douglas. He there met my mother for the first time, and was determined to have possession of her. His character was known; and therefore he was obliged to go *covertly* and *falsely* to work. In Jamaica, slaves that are esteemed by their owners have generally the power of refusal, whether they will be sold to a particular planter, or not; and my father was aware, that if *he* offered to purchase her, he would meet with a refusal. But his brutal lust was not to be stopped by trifles; my father's conscience would stretch to any extent; and he was a firm believer in the doctrine of 'grace abounding to the chief of sinners.' For this purpose, he employed a fellow of the name of Cruikshank, a brother doctor and Scotchman, to strike a bargain with Lady Douglas for my mother; and this scoundrel of a Scotchman bought my mother for the use of my father, in the name of another planter, a most respectable and highly esteemed man. I have often heard my mother express her indignation at this base and treacherous conduct of my father – a treachery the more base, as it was so calm and premeditated. Let my brother COLVILLE deny this if he can; let him bring me into court, and I will prove what I here advance. To this present hour, while I think of the treatment of my mother, my blood boils in my veins; and, had I not some connections for which I was bound to live, I should long ago have taken ample revenge of my father. But it is as well as it is; and I will not leave the world without some testimony to the injustice and inhumanity of my father.

From the time my mother became the property of my father, she assumed the direction and management of his house; for which no woman was better qualified. But her station there was very disgusting. My father's house was full of female slaves, all objects of his lusts; amongst whom he strutted like Solomon in his grand seraglio, or like a bantam cock upon his own dunghill. My good father's slaves did increase and multiply, like Jacob's kine; and he cultivated those talents well which God had granted so amply. My poor mother, from being the housekeeper, was the object of their envy, which was increased by her superiority of education over the common herd of female slaves. While in this situation, she bore my father two children, one of whom, my brother James, a millwright, I believe, is now living in Jamaica, upon the estate. Soon after this, my father introduced a new concubine into his seraglio, one ESTHER TROTTER, a free tawny, whom he placed over my mother, and to whom he gave the direction of his affairs. My brother COLVILLE asserts, that my mother was of a violent and rebellious temper. I will leave the reader now to judge for himself, whether she had not some reason for her conduct. Hath not a slave feelings? If you starve them, will they not die? If you wrong them, will they not revenge? Insulted on one hand, and degraded on the other, was it likely that my poor mother could practise the Christian virtue of humility, when her Christian master provoked her to wrath? She shortly afterwards became again pregnant; and I have not the least doubt but that from her rebellious and violent temper during that period, that I have inherited the same disposition – the same desire to see justice overtake the oppressors of my country-men – and the same determination to lose no stone unturned, to accomplish so desirable an object. My mother's state was so unpleasant, that my father at last consented to sell her back to Lady Douglas; but not till the animosity in my father's house had grown to such an extent, that my uncle, Sir JOHN WEDDERBURN, my father's elder brother, had given my mother an asylum in his house, against the brutal treatment of my father. At the time of sale, my mother was five months gone in pregnancy; and one of the stipulations of the bargain was, that the child which she then bore should be FREE from the moment of its birth. I was that child. When about four months old, the ill-treatment my mother had experienced had such an effect upon her, that I was obliged to be weaned, to save her life. Lady Douglas, at my admission into the Christian church, stood my godmother, and, as long as she lived, never deserted me. She died when I was about four years old.

From my mother I was delivered over to the care of my grandmother, who lived in Kingston, and who earned her livelihood by retailing all sorts of goods, hard or soft, smuggled or not, for the merchants of Kingston. My grandmother was the property of one JOSEPH PAYNE, at the east end of Kingston; and her place was to sell his property – cheese, checks, chintz, milk, gingerbread, &c; in doing which, she trafficked on her own account with the goods of other merchants, having an agency of half-a-crown in the pound allowed her for her trouble. No woman was perhaps better known in Kingston than my grandmother, by the name of 'Talkee Amy,' signifying a chattering old woman. Though a slave, such was the confidence the merchants of Kingston had in her honesty, that she could be trusted to any amount; in fact, she was the regular agent for selling smuggled goods.

I never saw my dear father but once in the island of Jamaica, when I went with my grandmother to know if he meant to do anything for me, his son. Giving her some abusive language, my grandmother called him a mean Scotch rascal, thus to desert his own flesh and blood; and declared, that as she had kept me hitherto, so she would yet, without his paltry assistance. This was the parental treatment I experienced from a Scotch West-India planter and slave-dealer.

When I was about eleven years of age, my poor old grandmother was flogged for a witch by her master, the occasion of which I must relate in this place. Joseph Payne, her master, was an old and avaricious merchant, who was concerned in the smuggling trade. He had a vessel manned by his own slaves, and commanded by a Welchman of the name of Lloyd, which had made several profitable voyages to Honduras for mahogany, which was brought to Jamaica, and from thence forwarded to England. The old miser had some notion, that Lloyd cheated him in the adventure, and therefore resolved to go himself as a check upon him. Through what means I know not, but most likely from information given by Lloyd out of revenge and jealousy, the Spaniards surprised and captured the vessel; and poor old Payne, at seventy years of age, was condemned to carry stones at Fort Homea, in the Bay of Honduras, for a year and a day; and his vessel and his slaves were confiscated to the Spaniards. On his way home he died, and was tossed overboard to make food for fishes. His nephew succeeded to his property; and a malicious woman-slave, to curry favour with him, persuaded him, that the illsuccess of old Payne's adventures was owing to my grandmother's having bewitched the vessel. The old miser had liberated five of his slaves before he set out on his unlucky expedition; and my grandmother's new master being a believer in the doctrine of Witchcraft, conceived that my grandmother had bewitched the vessel, out of revenge for her not being liberated also. To punish her, therefore, he tied up the poor old woman of seventy years, and flogged her to that degree, that she would have died, but for the interference of a neighbour. Now, what aggravated the affair was, that my grandmother had brought up this young villain from eight years of age, and, till now, he had treated her as a mother. But my grandmother had full satisfaction soon afterwards. The words of our blessed Lord and Saviour Jesus Christ were fulfilled in this instance: 'Do good to them that despitefully use you, and in so doing you shall heap coals of fire upon their heads.' This woman had an only child, which died soon after this affair took place (plainly a judgment of God); and the mother was forced to come and beg pardon of my grandmother for the injury she had done her, and solicit my grandmother to assist her in the burial of her child. My grandmother replied, 'I can forgive you, but I can never forget the flogging;' and the good old woman instantly set about assisting her in her child's funeral, it being as great an object to have a decent burial with the blacks in Jamaica, as with the lower classes in Ireland. This same woman, who had so wickedly calumniated my grandmother, afterwards made public confession of her guilt in the market-place at Kingston, on purpose to ease her guilty conscience, and to make atonement for the injury she had done. I mention this, to show upon what slight grounds the planters exercise their cowskin whips, not sparing even an old woman of seventy years of age.

b. Extracts from Wedderburn's Speech In His Own Defence Against The Charge Of Blasphemy

May it please your lordship.

Gentlemen of the jury. I am under the necessity of making my own defence for two reasons, first, because I am so poor that I cannot afford to fee counsel; and secondly, because if a barrister would plead my cause gratuitously, he would not dare to do it upon principle. As it is not my wish to occupy the time of the court unnecessarily, nor to launch into matter which would excite too strong a prejudice against me, I have committed my defence to paper; and as I have endeavoured to be as moderate as the nature of the case and my native independence will permit, I trust I shall be indulged with a patient hearing ...

The opinions of judges and other authorities have been cited to prove that christianity is part of the law of the land, and that therefore it must not be reviled; and may not many other opinions or laws be cited, which the progress of human knowledge and civilization have caused to be obsolete and nugatory, although they have never been repealed. There are many enactments still in existence, which, if now resorted to, would be instantly erased from the statute-book as absurd, or inhuman, and totally inconsistent with the enlightenment of the present day. Tyrannical and intolerant laws may exist and be enforced in times of darkness and ignorance, but they will be of little effect when once the human mind is emancipated from the trammels of superstition ... therefore I trust that you will not suffer yourselves to be ensnared by that sophistical mode of reasoning which makes me guilty of a crime, merely, because I have offended against opinions or laws originating in times still more bigotted and superstitious than the present. – You will be told, that because christianity, or what *they* choose to call christianity, is a part of the law of the land, or in other words '*the state religion,*' that those whose opinions differ materially from it, must necessarily be punished if they circulate those opinions; but how inconsistent is their conduct who tell you this! these very people, who contend that it is the greatest of sins to offend against the *state religion*, are warm in their praises of those who have been most conspicuous for having committed the same act.

The established church of this country was once Druidism, after that the mythology of the Romans, then Catholicism, and now, through the mere caprice of that tyrannical monster Henry the Eighth, it is Protestantism— — yet they hold in veneration those who first came to supplant the elegant mythology of the ancient Romans by the religion of the modern Romans, which was equally superstitious. When the Catholic system became firmly settled, they then extolled John Wicklif, and called him the 'morning star of the reformation,' because he preached against the state religion of his day, and exposed the corruptions of the Romish church. The celebrated Galileo, and the martyr Jerome of Prague, are now held in estimation, though they suffered for propagating doctrines contrary to the notions of those in power; and Christ and his apostles are admired for their courage in boldly promulgating what they considered the truth, although diametrically opposite, and peculiarly destructive of the established religions of the countries they over-run.

There is no one who will deny the value and importance of truth, but how is it to be ascertained, if we are not allowed the liberty of free inquiry? Does not Paul tell us to '*prove all things, and to hold fast the best;*' but how are we to be determined in our choice, if we are not allowed to canvas and discuss the merits or demerits of particular systems?

Persecution for religious opinions cannot possibly be defended upon Christian principles; if I am wrong, they ought to pity and pray for me, and endeavour by argument and persuasion to convince me of my error; but all attempts to force me are *absurd*, because *impossible – tyrannical*, because *unjust*.

I am aware that I shall be told, the state religion is not set up as a golden image which I am compelled to worship; but that whatever may be my ideas against it, I must not utter them, lest by possibility they should be construed into ridicule and reviling. How weak one would think must be that cause which is afraid of allowing you to laugh. They say we may discuss theological subjects coolly, seriously, and learnedly; but that we must not treat them with levity or sarcasm. Do *they* act up to the maxim of Christ? – Do *they* do as they would be done by? Do they not, on the contrary, take the liberty to ridicule all the solemn forms, rites, ceremonies, and observances of the Catholic church, and call it superstition, mummery, pantomime, scarlet whore of Babylon, &c.? Do they not call those who have dissented from them, and engrossed two-thirds of the community, fanatics, enthusiasts, and visionaries? – Do they not call Mahomet an impostor, and his religion a cheat? and yet they have the gravity and assurance to forbid the same freedoms being taken with themselves. Archbishop Tillotson, one of the greatest ornaments of their church, said, 'he should be sorry to have sceptics, and those who were inimical to Christianity, prohibited from the use of ridicule in their writings; because, in that case,' says he, 'we could not fairly use it against them; and as it can be directed so powerfully by us to the destruction of their theories, I wish them to be allowed the little advantage they can derive from it on their side.'

I cannot but blush at the weakness and bad policy of those who seek to support their cause by the persecution of an humble individual like myself, when the clergymen of the established church of England alone are 20,000, and their wages amount to two millions annually: in addition to these, there are 50,000 dissenting ministers of different denominations; then, there are bible societies, religious tract societies, and institutions for the promotion of Christian knowledge, in every part of the country: yet all this redoubtable phalanx are not sufficient to defend Christianity, without resorting to the arm of power. Is not this itself a far greater libel on their religion than any thing I have said? Is it not stated to have been built on the rock of ages? – Are they not told that the gates of hell shall not prevail against it? – If they are sincere in their belief that its origin is divine, why fear the efforts of a mortal man? If they cannot protect it by fair means, they should not degrade it by resorting to such unworthy measures. They should *pretend* to treat me with contempt, and *say* I was beneath their notice; that I was a poor deluded enthusiast, whose crucible had only tried, and not evaporated, the pure gold of the Christian faith. They should say with Saint Augustine, 'Shall WE *persecute* whom God *tolerates*?'

Every one will agree that all systems cannot be right. 'Error', says [Mamoutel in his *Belisarius*], 'has an immensity of space, and *truth* is like a mathematical point in the prodigious void.' Now, although every one claims that point to himself, is it not palpable, as TRUTH is *one*, and ERROR *multifarious*, that the greater portion of religious murders, barbarities, robberies, and incarcerations, must have been in defence of error, rather than of truth? How modest, how humble ought such considerations to make us! How cautious ought these reflections to render us of arrogating to ourselves the sole possession of the truth! when we find, that thousands who think different from us, claim the same happiness. Ought it not to make us diffident of ourselves, and forbearing towards others? Those who have studied human nature will have perceived, that this violent animosity, and furious persecuting zeal, does not arise so much from a generous love of virtue, or an enthusiastic admiration of abstract truth, as from the inordinate thirst for power which pervades the heart of every human being. We wish others to think as we do, and the greater part of us would, if we possessed the means, compel them to do it. The sword of *religious persecution* is an instrument upon which every party has played its tune when raised to power.

The celebrated Talleyrand, (in a memoir read at the National Institute of Paris, in the year 1794, concerning the commercial relations of the United States of America with Great Britain) says, 'that religious toleration *in its fullest extent*, is one of the most powerful guarantees of social tranquility; for where *liberty of conscience* is respected, every *other* cannot fail to be so.' A sentiment like this, from a man who stands unrivalled in his knowledge of political science, ought to have some weight. How opposite are the opinions of this enlightened statesman, this second Machiavel, to the blind mistaken notions of those who would fain attempt to produce harmony among the people, by endeavouring to enforce their adherence to one particular mode of faith! How absurd it is to suppose we can make persons of different educations and capacities ever think alike on subjects so entirely speculative! that we can enable those whose understandings are so unequal, to comprehend every thing with the same facility; and to render men of various ages, habits, and temperaments, capable of seeing with the same ease and perspicuity through the same medium.

If kings or priests were the architects of the human brain, they might with some justice dictate its operations; but since our faculties are produced by NATURE, and directed by NECESSITY, uncontrolled by their *fiat*; and since they have no more goverment over their own minds, than they have over ours; it is the most arrogant presumption, the most ridiculous folly, and the most diabolical tyranny to persecute us, for our opinions.

Are not all our ideas the result of impressions received through the medium of the senses, from external objects? are not all our notions the effect either of our education or the circumstances in which we have been placed? Who, then, can command opinion, or constrain belief? Where is the *merit* or the *crime* of BELIEF OR DISBELIEF, since neither of them are in our power, but depend entirely upon the state of our intellects, or the evidence offered to our senses? How childish, too, is the plan of promoting *social order* by force and persecution! Is it not evident that clemency and moderation are far better calculated to produce harmony, loyalty, and peace, than threats and imprisonment.

Many of the most ancient fathers of the church have left behind them, in their writings, the amplest testimonies in favor of religious liberty. TERTULIAN in his Apology says, (chap. 24,) – 'It is the greatest impiety to deprive mankind of liberty in matters of religion, or to hither them from choosing which divinity they may please to worship; neither god, nor man, is desirous of constrained service.' LACTANTIUS says, (Lib. 3,) 'religion by compulsion is no longer religion; it must be by persuasion and not by constraint. Religion is under no controul, and cannot be directed by power. Saint ATHA-NASIUS says 'It is an execrable heresy and crime, to endeavour to compel by force, by blows, or by imprisonment, those who cannot be convinced by reason.' JUSTIN MARTYR says, (Lib. 1.) 'nothing is more contrary to religion than constraint.' ST. HILARY says, (Lib. 5,) 'If we were to use violence in defending the faith, the bishops would oppose it.' And ST. BERNARD in his Letters says. (Lib. 1,) 'Advise but force not.' In addition to the foregoing, I shall give a passage from the late pious and learned Dr. WATSON, the bishop of Landaff's Reply to Mr. GIBBON's Attack on the Christian Religion. He declares, 'It would give me much uneasiness to be reputed an enemy to free enquiry into religious matters, or capable of being animated into any degree of personal malevolence against those who differ from me in opinion. On the contrary, I look upon the right of private judgment in every concern respecting God and ourselves, as *superior to the controul of all human authority*; and I have ever regarded free discussion as the best means of illustrating the doctrine and establishing the truth of Christianity. Let the followers of Mahomet, and the zealots of the church of Rome, support their several religious systems, by damping every effort of the human intellect to pry into the foundation of their faith; but it can never become a Christian to be afraid of being asked a reason of the faith that is in him; nor a Protestant to be studious of enveloping his religion in mystery and ignorance' . . .

– And where, after all, is my crime? – it consists merely in having spoken in the same plain and homely language which Christ and his disciples uniformly used. – Well might Chesterfield say, 'that the manner is of more consequence than the matter,' for if I had asserted the same things a thousand times, in a different phraseology, no notice would have been taken; but because my audience were humble people who would not have understood fine-spun discourses, and delicate allusions, I am to be condemned for addressing them in the vulgar tongue. Indeed there seems to be a conspiracy against the poor, to keep them in ignorance and superstition; the rich may have as many copies as they like of such sceptical writers as Shaftsbury, Bolingbroke, Tindal, Morgan, Hume, and Gibbon, because they are above the reach or comprehension of the lower orders; but if I find two most decided contradictions in the bible, I must not in the language of the same book assert that one or the other is a lie. As I have a far greater respect for Christ than for Moses, my bias is, to believe the former when he asserted what was rational and probable, viz. 'That no man hath seen God' in preference to the latter, who represented himself as having frequent interviews with the Deity, and 'speaking to him face to face, as a man speaketh to his friend.' (Exod. 33.) xi.)

And who will have the presumption to deny, that the story of Saul and the witch of Endor, is not an absurdity? it might have done very well for the time in which it was written, and even in this country at an earlier period, when the very judges themselves who sat in this court believed in witchcraft, and pronounced sentence of condemnation against unfortunate women, who were prosecuted for that supposed crime; but who is there now that has faith in such idle tales, or that can credit the power of a wizard or a witch to raise the prophet Samuel, or any other person from the dead.

And is it not equally absurd to suppose, that the false prophet Balaam should have the Supreme Being so completely at his beck and call, as related in the book of Numbers? (chap. 22.) Is it not far more reasonable to conclude, that being perpetually defeated in his attempts to overthrow the Israelites, he invented the story of his ass's speaking as an excuse for his failure, and to palliate his disgrace.

As to my explanation of the doctrines of Christ, I must still maintain it to be particularly faithful. – He was like myself, one of the lower order, and a genuine radical reformer. Being poor himself, he knew how to feel for the poor, and despised the rich for the hardness of their hearts. His principles were *purely republican*; he told his followers they were all brethren and equals, and inculcated a thorough contempt for all the titles, pomps, and dignities of this world. He established no priesthood, but on the contrary, he said to them, 'Be ye not called rabbi.' (Mat. 23.) He was a mild and amiable man, whose object was to benefit the poor and oppressed; but being cut off in his career through spies and informers, his system was never properly established; and though his name has been made a cloak, and stalking horse, for the worst of purposes, his religion has never been followed. For my part, though I consider Jesus Christ to have been deceived in the application of some passages in the Jewish scriptures to himself, yet I have ever revered his principles, and regretted they were never put in practice; nor am I singular in this opinion, for in the 'Disquisitions' of that elegant writer Soam Jenyns, you will find the following passage: 'pure and genuine Christianity never was, nor ever can be, the national religion of any country upon earth. It is a gold too refined to be worked up with any human institutions, without a large portion of alloy; for no sooner is the small grain of mustard-seed watered by the fertile showers of civil emolument, than it grows up to a large and spreading tree, under the shelter of whose branches the birds of prey and plunder will not fail to make for themselves comfortable habitations, and thence deface its beauty and destroy its fruits.'

Before I conclude, permit me to make one more quotation; – it is from the learned Grotius, whose book on the 'Truth of the Christian Religion' is required to be read by every candidate for holy orders. He says, 'to put men in prison on account of their religious belief or persuasion, is a great oppression, and properly speaking, False Imprisonment; to fine them or to take away their estates for that cause, is Robbery: to put them to death for not acting against their conscience, is Murder. Can any thing be more wicked? is it not then difficult to determine, whether the folly and absurdity, or the tyranny and wickedness of persecution on account of religion, are greater?'

Gentlemen of the jury. – It is customary for persons in my situation to flatter you, and to say every thing they can, to court your verdict in their favor; but all I shall say is, to remind you, that notwithstanding you are sworn on the evangelists, yet, being in this case the judges of both law and fact, you are fully competent to acquit me of having uttered a blasphemous libel; and I shall merely add, that if there is among you but one man, who thoroughly understands and respects the religion of Jesus, one sincere friend to religious liberty, and the universal right of conscience, I shall be acquitted; but if, on the contrary, the spirit of bigotry and religious persecution prevails over you, I shall have this satisfaction, that I suffer like Christ and his disciples, for boldly asserting what I deem to be true; and as NATURE has blest me with a calm and tranquil mind, I shall be far happier in the dungeon to which you may consign me, than my persecutors, on their beds of down.

(8–19)

Notes

1. Robert's brother changed his name by legal process in order to procure an inheritance on his mother's side. His father, James, had also changed his name to Wedderburn-Colville.
2. The meaning is not entirely clear. It appears to mean 'shouting in a bullying fashion.'

13

MARY PRINCE

born Bermuda c.1788

The History of Mary Prince, A West Indian Slave

1831

Mary Prince's autobiography, published in 1831 in London and Edinburgh, represents the first substantial account of black female slave-life. Up to that date, all the Afro-British accounts of or comments on slavery were written by men – Olaudah Equiano, Ignatius Sancho and others included in this volume. Her book was very popular, going into a third edition by the end of 1831.

Born in Bermuda around 1788, Mary was part of a family of seven brothers and three sisters who over the years were sold to different masters and dispersed all over the Caribbean. From an early age she was put to work, as a child minder and domestic servant. Later in life, she worked in the fields, hoeing, planting and looking after sheep and cattle. Among the most physically painful of her experiences as an enslaved woman were the ten years spent on the Turks Island in salt production. This involved standing in salt ponds for many hours, as a consequence of which her feet became deformed with boils which ate down to the bone and caused great torment. In addition she witnessed and experienced beatings and sexual harassment by a sadistic slave owner. When Mary Prince was medically examined in London in 1831, it was found that 'the whole of the back part of her body is distinctly scarred, and, as it were, chequered, with the vestiges of severe floggings. Besides this, there are many large scars on other parts of her person, exhibiting an appearance as if the flesh had been deeply cut, or lacerated with gashes, by some instrument wielded by most unmerciful hands.' She also developed a disease of the eyes which threatened to render her totally blind.

Mary Prince arrived in England in 1828 with her master, John Wood, and his wife, who were visiting so as to put their son into school. Suffering from rheumatism, unable to work to full capacity, subjected to verbal abuse and threats of eviction

154

by the Woods, she decided to make a break from slavery by
leaving the household, come what may.

Some missionaries of the Moravian Church (she had joined
the Church in the West Indies and been baptised in 1817)
offered her shelter, food and clothing, and eventually the
Anti-Slavery Society took up her case. Thomas Pringle, the
Secretary of the Society, employed her as a domestic and made
an effort to procure her freedom by offering to pay the Woods.
The Woods refused, bent on punishing Mary for daring to
claim her freedom and for exposing their cruelty to the
Anti-Slavery Society. Their refusal meant that Mary could not
return to the West Indies as a free women to rejoin her
husband, a free black man called Daniel James, a carpenter and
cooper by trade, whom she had married in 1826. Although a
married woman, Mary was still legally owned by the Woods,
who beat her constantly in front of her husband knowing that
he was helpless to protect her. 'I had not much happiness in my
marriage, owing to my being a slave', Mary confessed in her
autobiography. She was determined to acquire her freedom,
refused to return with the Woods to the West Indies and
remained in England to fight her case in the courts, in
Parliament and in the newspapers. The appearance of her book
sparked off a public debate on the nature of slavery, but in
spite of all the publicity and campaigning, Mary still remained
a slave, legally owned by the Woods until 1833/4, when slavery
was finally abolished in the British Colonies.

Apart from the revelation of the physical brutality of
slavery, Mary Prince's autobiography testifies to other crucial
areas of slave experience – firstly, the utter instability and
unpredictability of her condition. The narrative starts off with
the solid facts of her birth and family: 'I was born at Brackish –
Pond, in Bermuda, on a farm belonging to Mr Charles Myners.
My mother was a household slave; and my father, whose name
was Prince, was a sawyer belonging to Mr Trimmingham, a
shipbuilder at Crow-Lane.' These simple details however are
the only certitudes in her life, for her family is soon divided
and sold to different owners. She settles down with a new
family, but as soon as she grows accustomed to her new
environment, she is sold again: 'a few hours after this I was
taken to a strange house, and found myself among strange
people'. This process of settlement then estrangement afflicts
her throughout her life. In the absence of her own family, she
tries to form new relationships, desperately hoping to find a
mother-figure in her Mistress, and surrogate brother-and-
sister relationships with the white children of the household:

> 'I was truly attached to her, and next to my mother, loved
> her better than any creature in the world;'... 'All my
> employment at this time was nursing a sweet baby, little

Master Daniel; and I grew so fond of my nursling that it was my greatest delight to walk out with him by the sea-shore accompanied by his brother and sister'.

This feature of Mary Prince's narrative is a characteristic of other slave testimonies. Equiano for instance, is always seeking a substitute for his lost family, and the white men who have been kind to him are frequently described in terms of paternal–filial relationships. Speaking of Daniel Queen, a white man who showed great kindness to him, Equiano says, 'he was like a father to me ... indeed I almost loved him with the affection of a son'; one ship's Captain who helped Equiano gain his freedom is described as 'a friend and a father'. Such new kinship patterns are extended to black slaves too. Mary Prince writes that 'poor Hetty, my fellow slave, was very kind to me, and I used to call her my Aunt'. Slavery necessitated new formations of family and community. Anthropologists like Sidney Mintz and Richard Price have written about the 'shipmate relationships developed on board the slave ship between individual Africans, previously strangers to each other. In Jamaica for instance, the term 'shipmate' was the equivalent to 'brother' and 'sister'. It was a bonding which transcended biological kinship. 'Shipmates' considered each others' children as their own. The 'shipmate' relationship in Jamaica (the equivalent of 'sippi' in Surinam and 'mattie' in Guyana) continued for decades and even centuries to shape ongoing social relations.

Another fascinating aspect of Mary Prince's narrative lies in the purpose of its writing, which was 'that good people in England might hear from a slave what a slave felt and suffered.' This desire for self-revelation in words, and revelation of the condition shared with other slaves (in other words, the condition of community), also informs all other slave narratives. White people were exposed to white literature, whether travel books, plays, poems or novels, which overwhelmingly observed and described black people from the outside, seeing them as inferior, often subhuman. These biases had to be countered if black people were to be given just and civilized recognition, and the burden of truth-telling was taken up by such authors as Equiano and Mary Prince who could give internal and lived evidence of their condition. This is why Equiano places his personal experience firmly at the heart of his narrative. He is the dominant observer and witness, authenticity his own special perspective:

'while I was in Montserrat I knew a Negro man ...'; 'I have seen a Negro beaten till some of his bones were broken ...'; 'notwithstanding those human exceptions which I have mentioned, and others I am acquainted with ...'.

The need to tell the experienced truth from the point of view of the black man or women explains why early black writing has to be autobiographical rather than cast in the mould of novels, poems and plays, conveying the felt immediacy and authenticity, of actual lived experience.

The need to describe self and society to hostile outsiders remains a driving force behind the creation of much black literature into our own century: Vic Reid, for instance, the Jamaican novelist, in the Author's Preface to his novel, *New Day* (1949), declares that his purpose in writing was to 'transfer to paper some of the beauty, kindliness, and humour of my people ... creating a tale that will offer as true an impression as fiction can of the way by which Jamaica and its people came to today'. Roger Mais, another Jamaican writer, said of his novel *The Hills Were Joyful Together* (1953), that his intention was 'to give the world·a true picture of the real Jamaica'.

Unlike Equiano, Mary Prince did not write her book by herself. The idea of writing was hers, and she dictated her life-story to a female member of the Anti-Slavery Society. The narrative was then shaped and edited by Thomas Pringle, who in his Preface explained that he retained 'as far as was practicable, Mary's exact expressions and peculiar phraseology. No fact of importance has been omitted, and not a single circumstance or sentiment has been added. It is essentially her own, without any material alterations farther than was requisite to exclude redundancies and gross grammatical errors, so as to render it clearly intelligible.'

The truth of Pringle's editorial statement is borne out by the language of the narrative. Characteristically, Mary Prince's expressions are down-to-earth, without trace of elegant adornment. Sometimes Pringle retains the creolized English of direct speech, as when the slave Hetty is running away from the wrath of her master, 'Oh, Massa! Massa, me dead. Massa! have mercy on me – don't kill me outright', which strikes the West Indian ear as an accurate reproduction of local speech. Similarly, the genuine oral nature of Mary Prince's testimony is evident too in the sense of a 'live' situation conveyed by the vocabulary and repetition of: 'I have seen their flesh ragged and raw with licks. – Lick – lick – they were never secure one moment from the blow;' or 'Part of the roof fell down, and everything in the house went – Clatter, clatter, clatter.' The truthfulness of the narrative is conveyed too by Mary Prince's admissions of the difficulty of expressing herself: 'I wish I could find words to tell you all I then felt and suffered'. Altogether, Pringle's editorial work appears sensitive to the need to refrain from intrusion and preserve the narrative tone of Mary Prince's life story.

The text is from the first edition, London 1831, as reprinted in Henry L. Gates' *The Classic Slave Narratives* (see bibliography). There is also a paperback, edited by Moira Ferguson, with a preface by Ziggi Alexander, published by Pandora Books, London 1987.

The History of Mary Prince

Our mother, weeping as she went, called me away with the children Hannah and Dinah, and we took the road that led to Hamble Town, which we reached about four o'clock in the afternoon. We followed my mother to the market-place, where she placed us in a row against a large house, with our backs to the wall and our arms folded across our breasts. I, as the eldest, stood first, Hannah next to me, then Dinah; and our mother stood beside, crying over us. My heart throbbed with grief and terror so violently, that I pressed my hands quite tightly across my breast, but I could not keep it still, and it continued to leap as though it would burst out of my body. But who cared for that? Did one of the many by-standers, who were looking at us so carlessly, think of the pain that wrung the hearts of the negro woman and her young ones? No, no! They were not all bad, I dare say, but slavery hardens white people's hearts towards the blacks; and many of them were not slow to make their remarks upon us aloud, without regard to our grief – though their light words fell like cayenne on the fresh wounds of our hearts. Oh those white people have small hearts who can only feel for themselves.

At length the vendue master, who was to offer us for sale like sheep or cattle, arrived, and asked my mother which was the eldest. She said nothing, but pointed to me. He took me by the hand, and led me out into the middle of the street, and, turning me slowly round, exposed me to the view of those who attended the vendue. I was soon surrounded by strange men, who examined and handled me in the same manner that a butcher would a calf or a lamb he was about to purchase, and who talked about my shape and size in like words – as if I could no more understand their meaning than the dumb beasts. I was then put up for sale. The bidding commenced at a few pounds, and gradually rose to fifty-seven, when I was knocked down to the highest bidder; and the people who stood by said that I had fetched a great sum for so young a slave.

I then saw my sisters led forth, and sold to different owners; so that we had not the sad satisfaction of being partners in bondage. When the sale was over, my mother hugged and kissed us, and mourned over us, begging of us to keep up a good heart, and do our duty to our new masters. It was a sad parting; one went one way, one another, and our poor mammy went home with nothing.

My new master was a Captain I—, who lived at Spanish Point. After parting with my mother and sisters, I followed him to his store, and he gave me into the charge of his son, a lad about my own age, Master Benjy, who took me to my new home. I did not know where I was going, or what my new master would do with me. My heart was quite broken with grief, and my thoughts went back continually to those from whom I had been so suddenly parted. 'Oh, my mother! my mother!' I kept saying to myself, 'Oh, my mammy and my sisters and my brothers, shall I never see you again!'

Oh, the trials! the trials! they make the salt water come into my eyes when I think of the days in which I was afflicted – the times that are gone; when I mourned and grieved with a young heart for those whom I loved.

It was night when I reached my new home. The house was large, and built at the bottom of a very high hill; but I could not see much of it that night. I saw too much of it afterwards. The stones and the timber were the best things in it; they were not so hard as the hearts of the owners.

Before I entered the house, two slave women, hired from another owner, who were at work in the yard, spoke to me, and asked who I belonged to? I replied, 'I am come to live here.' 'Poor child, poor child!' they both said; 'you must keep a good heart, if you are to live here.' – When I went in, I stood up crying in a corner. Mrs. I— came and took off my hat, a little black silk hat Miss Pruden made for me, and said in rough voice, 'You are not come here to stand up in corners and cry, you are come here to work.' She then put a child into my arms, and, tired as I was, I was forced instantly to take up my old occupation of a nurse. – I could not bear to look at my mistress, her countenance was so stern. She was a stout tall woman with a very dark complexion, and her brows were always drawn together into a frown. I thought of the words of the two slave women when I saw Mrs. I—, and heard the harsh sound of her voice.

The person I took the most notice of that night was a French

Black called Hetty, whom my master took in privateering from another vessel, and made his slave. She was the most active woman I ever saw, and she was tasked to her utmost. A few minutes after my arrival she came in from milking the cows, and put the sweet-potatoes on for supper. She then fetched home the sheep, and penned them in the fold; drove home the cattle, and staked them about the pond side; fed and rubbed down my master's horse, and gave the hog and the fed cow their suppers; prepared the beds, and undressed the children, and laid them to sleep. I liked to look at her and watch all her doings, for her's was the only friendly face I had as yet seen, and I felt glad that she was there. She gave me my supper of potatoes and milk, and a blanket to sleep upon, which she spread for me in the passage before the door of Mrs. I—'s chamber.

I got a sad fright, that night. I was just going to sleep, when I heard a noise in my mistress's room; and she presently called out to inquire if some work was finished that she had ordered Hetty to do. 'No, Ma'am, not yet,' was Hetty's answer from below. On hearing this, my master started up from his bed, and just as he was, in his shirt, ran down stairs with a long cow-skin in his hand. I heard immediately after, the cracking of the thong, and the house rang to the shrieks of poor Hetty, who kept crying out, 'Oh, Massa! Massa! me dead. Massa! have mercy upon me – don't kill me outright. – This was a sad beginning for me. I sat up upon my blanket, trembling with terror, like a frightened hound, and thinking that my turn would come next. At length the house became still, and I forgot for a little while all my sorrows by falling fast asleep.

The next morning my mistress set about instructing me in my tasks. She taught me to do all sorts of household work; to wash and bake, pick cotton and wool, and wash floors, and cook. And she taught me (how can I ever forget it!) more things than these; she caused me to know the exact difference between the smart of the rope, the cart-whip, and the cow-skin, when applied to my naked body by her own cruel hand. And there was scarcely any punishment more dreadful than the blows I received on my face and head from her hard heavy fist. She was a fearful woman, and a savage mistress to her slaves.

There were two little slave boys in the house, on whom she vented her bad temper in a special manner. One of these children was a mulatto, called Cyrus, who had been bought while an infant in his mother's arms; the other, Jack, was an African from the coast

of Guinea, whom a sailor had given or sold to my master. Seldom a
day passed without these boys receiving the most severe treatment,
and often for no fault at all. Both my master and mistress seemed to
think that they had a right to ill-use them at their pleasure; and very
often accompanied their commands with blows, whether the children were behaving well or ill. I have seen their flesh ragged and raw
with licks. – Lick – lick – they were never secure one moment from
a blow, and their lives were passed in continual fear. My mistress
was not contented with using the whip, but often pinched their
cheeks and arms in the most cruel manner. My pity for these poor
boys was soon transferred to myself; for I was licked, and flogged,
and pinched by the pitiless fingers in the neck and arms, exactly as
they were. To strip me naked – to hang me up by the wrists and lay
my flesh open with the cow-skin, was an ordinary punishment for
even a slight offence. My mistress often robbed me too of the hours
that belong to sleep. She used to sit up very late, frequently even
until morning; and I had then to stand at a bench and wash during
the greater part of the night, or pick wool and cotton and often I
have dropped down overcome by sleep, and fatigue, till roused from
a state of stupor by the whip, and forced to start up to my tasks.

Poor Hetty, my fellow slave, was very kind to me, and I used to
call her my Aunt, but she led a most miserable life, and her death
was hastened (at least the slaves all believed and said so,) by the
dreadful chastisement she received from my master during her
pregnancy. It happened as follows. One of the cows had dragged
the rope away from the stake to which Hetty had fastened it, and
got loose. My master flew into a terrible passion, and ordered the
poor creature to be stripped quite naked, notwithstanding her
pregnancy, and to be tied up to a tree in the yard. He then flogged
her as hard as he could lick, both with the whip and cow-skin, till
she was all over streaming with blood. He rested, and then beat her
again and again. Her shrieks were terrible. The consequence was
that poor Hetty was brought to bed before her time, and was
delivered after severe labour of a dead child. She appeared to recover
after her confinement, so far that she was repeatedly flogged by
both master and mistress afterwards; but her former strength never
returned to her. Ere long her body and limbs swelled to a great size;
and she lay on a mat in the kitchen, till the water burst out of her
body and she died. All the slaves said that death was a good thing
for poor Hetty; but I cried very much for her death. The manner of

it filled me with horror. I could not bear to think about it; yet it was always present to my mind for many a day.

After Hetty died all her labours fell upon me, in addition to my own. I had now to milk eleven cows every morning before sunrise, sitting among the damp weeds; to take care of the cattle as well as the children; and to do the work of the house. There was no end to my toils – no end to my blows. I lay down at night and rose up in the morning in fear and sorrow; and often wished that like poor Hetty I could escape from this cruel bondage and be at rest in the grave. But the hand of that God whom then I knew not, was stretched over me; and I was mercifully preserved for better things. It was then, however, my heavy lot to weep, weep, weep, and that for years; to pass from one misery to another, and from one cruel master to a worse. But I must go on with the thread of my story.

One day a heavy squall of wind and rain came on suddenly, and my mistress sent me round the corner of the house to empty a large earthen jar. The jar was already cracked with an old deep crack that divided it in the middle, and in turning it upside down to empty it, it parted in my hand. I could not help the accident, but I was dreadfully frightened, looking forward to a severe punishment. I ran crying to my mistress, 'O mistress, the jar has come in two.' 'You have broken it, have you?' she replied: 'come directly here to me.' I came trembling: she stripped and flogged me long and severely with the cow-skin: as long as she had strength to use the lash, for she did not give over till she was quite tired. – When my master came home at night, she told him of my fault; and oh, frightful! how he fell a swearing. After abusing me with every ill name he could think of, (too, too bad to speak in England,) and giving me several heavy blows with his hand, he said, 'I shall come home to-morrow morning at twelve, on purpose to give you a round hundred.' He kept his word – Oh sad for me! I cannot easily forget it. He tied me up upon a ladder, and gave me a hundred lashes with his own hand, and master Benjy stood by to count them for him. When he had licked me for some time he sat down to take breath; then after resting, he beat me again and again, until he was quite wearied, and so hot (for the weather was very sultry), that he sank back in his chair, almost like to faint. While my mistress went to bring him drink, there was a dreadful earthquake. Part of the roof fell down, and every thing in the house went – clatter, clatter, clatter. Oh I thought the end of all things near at hand; and I was so sore with the flogging, that I scarcely cared whether I lived or died. The earth was groaning and shaking; every thing tumbling about; and my mistress and the slaves were shrieking and crying out, 'The earthquake! the earthquake!' It was an awful day for us all.

During the confusion I crawled away on my hands and knees, and laid myself down under the steps of the piazza, in front of the house. I was in a dreadful state – my body all blood and bruises, and I could not help moaning piteously. The other slaves, when they saw me, shook their heads and said, 'Poor child! poor child' – I lay there till the morning, careless of what might happen, for life was very weak in me, and I wished more than ever to die. But when we are very young, death always seems a great way off, and it would not come that night to me. The next morning I was forced by my master to rise and go about my usual work, though my body and limbs were so stiff and sore, that I could not move without the greatest of pain. – Nevertheless, even after all this severe punishment, I never heard the last of that jar; my mistress was always throwing it in my face.

Some little time after this, one of the cows got loose from the stake, and eat one of the sweet-potatoe slips. I was milking when my master found it out. He came to me, and without any more ado, stooped down, and taking off his heavy boot, he struck me such a severe blow in the small of my back, that I shrieked with agony, and thought I was killed; and I feel a weakness in that part to this day. The cow was frightened by his violence, and kicked down the pail and spilt the milk all about. My master knew that this accident was his own fault, but he was so enraged that he seemed glad of an excuse to go on with his ill usage. I cannot remember how many licks he gave me then, but he beat me till I was unable to stand, and till he himself was weary.

After this I ran away and went to my mother, who was living with Mr. Richard Darrel. My poor mother was both grieved and glad to see me; grieved because I had been so ill used, and glad because she had not seen me for a long, long while. She dared not receive me into the house, but she hid me up in a hole in the rocks near, and brought me food at night, after every body was asleep. My father, who lived at Crow-Lane, over the salt-water channel, at last heard of my being hid up in the cavern, and he came and took me back to my master. Oh I was loth, loth to go back; but as there was no remedy, I was obliged to submit.

When we got home, my poor father said to Capt. I—, 'Sir, I am sorry that my child should be forced to run away from her owner; but the treatment she has received is enough to break her heart. The sight of her wounds has nearly broke mine. – I entreat you, for the love of God, to forgive her for running away, and that you will be a kind master to her in future.' Capt. I— said I was used as well as I deserved, and that I ought to be punished for running away. I then took courage and said that I could stand the floggings no longer; that I was weary of my life, and therefore I had run away to my mother; but mothers could only weep and mourn over their children, they could not save them from cruel masters – from the whip, the rope, and the cow-skin. He told me to hold my tongue and go about my work, or he would find a way to settle me. He did not, however, flog me that day.

(52–60)

14

MARY SEACOLE

born Jamaica 1805, died England 1884

The Wonderful Adventures of Mary Seacole in Many Lands

1857

Black women have been living in Britain at least since the early 16th century, when here was a group of 'moor lassis' at the court of King James IV of Scots, including Elen and Margaret, the two African maidservants to the Queen. We know little of their origins, though they were probably captured from Portuguese ships, but they do not appear to have had the status of slaves, and are recorded as receiving gifts from the King, and lavish payments for clothing, their sartorial elegance indicating that they were part of the aristocratic environment of music banquetting, and tournament games. There is evidence that they had their own servants. The overwhelming experience of black women in Britain, however, has been less glamorous. In the 17th and 18th centuries the records point to employment as domestic servants, seamstresses, laundrymaids, children's nurses, street and fairground performers and the like, though a black actress was playing Shakespeare's Juliet in the 1770's, as well as singing the leading role of Polly in *The Beggar's Opera*. Many were forced into prostitution, some becoming famous courtesans, such as Black Harriet, whose clients are said to have included 20 members of the House of Lords. In the early 17th century there was also a poetic fashion for writing love poems to black ladies. But unlike Equiano and Sancho, they left no written records of their life's experience, women in general at this time having less access than men to literacy, let alone a literary education. The black American poetess Phillis Wheatley, who spent a brief time in London, is the only known black woman writer before the 19th century. Even so, apart from Mary Prince's book, which is in any case a transcript of an oral narrative, Mary Seacole's autobiography is the only other book in English by a black woman in Britain published in the 19th century, though African American women published both autobiography and fiction in the United States.

Mary Seacole, the daughter of a Scottish army officer, and a free black woman, was born in Jamaica in 1805, 29 years before the abolition of slavery throughout the British colonies. Her particular claim to fame lay in her services as a nurse to the British Army during the Crimean war, services which made her a household name. In 1857, a benefit Festival was held in the Royal Surrey Gardens in her honour, taking place over four consecutive nights, attended by over 40,000 people. The *Times* of 28 and 30 July 1857 reporting the occasion wrote:

> Nothing could have been more triumphantly successful
> ... Notwithstanding that the charge for admission was
> quintupled, there was an immense concourse in the hall
> ... Mrs Seacole sat in state in front of the centre gallery,
> supported by Lord Rokeby on one side, by Lord George
> Paget on the other, and surrounded by the members of her
> committee ... Few names were more familiar to the public
> during the late war than that of Mrs Seacole ... At the end
> of both the first and second parts the name of Mrs Seacole
> was shouted by a thousand voices. The genial old lady
> rose from her place and smiled benignantly on the assem-
> bled multitude, amid a tremendous and continued cheer-
> ing. Never did woman seem happier, and never was hearty
> and kindly greeting bestowed upon a worthier object ...
> On no previous occasion have the Royal Surrey Gardens
> been thronged by a greater multitude. The music-hall was
> literally crammed, many hundreds of persons being com-
> pelled to remain in the grounds, unable to penetrate into
> the interior of the building.

In the same month, July 1857, Mary Seacole published her autobiography, which was an instant success, and which was reprinted within the year. When she died in 1881, she left an estate valued at £2,615 – a relatively substantial sum, the equivalent of tens of thousands of pounds today. No less a newspaper than the *Times* announced her death: previously, a variety of newspapers, including the *London Advertiser* and the *Illustrated London News*, had carried accounts of her life and work, and *Punch* published a poem in her honour. Although totally forgotten by the twentieth century British public (in contrast to Florence Nightingale, the other heroine of the Crimea), Mary Seacole remains one of the most significant women of her times. She was extraordinary in terms of her fame and the respect she commanded from British nobility and commoner alike.

Mary Seacole learnt folk medicine from her mother, who was something of a nurse, and she became skilled at treating tropical diseases like cholera and yellow fever. She practiced her skills in Jamaica then in Panama and Columbia, saving many lives and earning the gratitude of many. In 1853 war broke out between Britain and Russia, and in 1854 Britain and France sent troops to the Crimea in defence of the Russian invasion of the Turkish Empire. Mary Seacole set off for London in 1854, then moved to the Crimea where she set up a hotel, the British Hotel, to cater for British Officers, and she spent much time on the battlefield, nursing the wounded and the dying.

This saintliness on the part of Seacole is undermined by her narrowly patriotic and romantic glorification of war. Telling us about her ambition to go to the Crimea to help the British cause she says, 'what delight should I not experience if I could be useful to my own "sons", suffering for a cause it was so glorious to fight and bleed for!' She describes war as a dashing and colourful event:

We saw Russians fall slowly back in good order, while the dark-plumed Sardinians and red-pantalooned French spread out in pursuit, and formed a picture so excitingly beautiful that we forgot the suffering and death they left behind.

Here is her spontaneous reaction on first seeing a battle:

My first experience of battle was pleasant enough ... It was very pretty to see them advance and to watch how every now and then little clouds of white smoke puffed up from behind bushes and crests of hills, and were answered by similar puffs from the long line of busy skirmishers that preceded the main body. This was my first experience of actual battle, and I felt that strange excitement which I do not remember on future occasions, coupled with an earnest longing to see more of warfare, and to share in its hazards. It was not long before my wish was gratified.

Some of her descriptions of the injuries suffered by the soldiers are also full of pomp and circumstance. She depicts the common soldiers as full of patriotic bravado and heroism – one soldier for instance, his leg blown away, is still full of spirit and cheerful and impatient to get back into battle to die for King and Country! In another passage she describes an officer's servant 'lying crouched in a rifle pit, having "pots" at the Russians or keeping watch and ward in the long line of trenches, or stripped to his shirt, shovelling powder and shot into the great guns, whose steady roar broke the evening's calm'. The poetic language (alliteration and rhythm are brilliantly employed in the sentence) no doubt stirred the patriotic emotions of the book's readership.

Underlying all these descriptions of romantic heroism is Mary Seacole's own enduring patriotism. Her devotion to Queen and Country is a dominant feature of the narrative. She speaks proudly of the 'part she bore of the trials and hardships endured on that distant shore, where Britain's best and bravest wrung hardy Sebastapol from the grasp of Britain's foe'. This patriotism is at times embarrassing and gauche. She attends the funeral of Lord Raglan, the Commander in Chief of the British Army, 'that great soldier who had such iron courage', and at the funeral, in pride and sadness, she touches the Union Jack:

> And once again they let me into the room in which the coffin lay, and I timidly stretched out my hand and touched a corner of the union-jack which lay upon it, and then I watched it wind its way through the long lines of soldiery towards Kamiesch, while, ever and anon, the guns thundered forth in sorrow ... And for days after I could not help thinking of the *Caradoc* which was ploughing its way through the sunny sea with its sad burden.

Again we note the poetic nature of the prose, its use of alliteration to heighten the emotion and to bind the sentences together into a measured lament, and the sentimentality and falseness of the idea that the guns themselves were 'sad' in the sounds of violence made by them.

All this patriotic rhetoric and fervour is curious given the fact of Seacole's colour, given the rampant racism of the English towards the blacks in their midst, given the plundering and partitioning of Africa that was being undertaken by Europeans and given the colonial repression in Jamaica which had only just emerged from Slavery. Mary Seacole, however, in her religious fervour, her moral severity (she banned gambling and drinking in her British Hotel in the Crimea) and her militaristic patriotism, is an imperial and Victorian figure, though ludicrously so because of her colour. Seacole indeed relished the fact that she was a servant of Empire. She proudly cites a letter of tribute she received from an officer who said, 'I am sure that when her Gracious Majesty the Queen shall have become acquainted with the service you have rendered to so many of her brave soldiers, her generous heart will thank you. For you have been an instrument in the hands of the Almighty to preserve many a gallant heart to the Empire, to fight and win her battles, if ever again war may become a necessity.' Seacole loved such praise. Indeed, when the Crimean War was over, she set her mind to go to India to serve the British army there against the rebellious hordes of savage natives. 'Give me my needle and thread, my medicine chest, my bandages, my probe and scissors, and I am off to India' she declared to the British Secretary of War.

Fortunately for the Indians Seacole changed her mind.

It is true that Mary Seacole received racial insults during her lifetime, on account of her colour, as a result of which she

defends black people against the racist ideas of whites, and
exhibits a pride in African achievement. She is proud of the fact
that many free Africans in Latin America became civic leaders,
government officials, magistrates, and so on. Although many
in white society saw Seacole as a 'nigger', she is more
ambivalent about her colour. She was proud that she was
half-white. On the first page of her narrative she declares that
the better half of her character is due to her white ancestry:

> I am a Creole, and have good Scotch blood coursing
> through my veins. Many people have traced to my
> Scottish blood that energy and activity which are not
> always found in the Creole race, and which have carried
> me to so many varies scenes: and perhaps they are right.

One white contemporary said of her 'She told me that she had
Scotch blood in her veins. I must say that she did not look
like it, but the old lady spoke proudly of this point in her
genealogy". Throughout the narrative Mrs Seacole proudly
refers to herself as a 'yellow woman' or a 'brown woman'.
Indeed she can sometimes exhibit a vicious contempt for black
people (whom she calls 'niggers') and for all non-British
nationalities. Her stereotypical descriptions of Greeks, Maltese
and Turks would have appealed to the xenophobia of a
Victorian reading public. She speaks of the 'lazy Maltese', of
'cunning-eyed Greeks', dismisses Turks as 'deliberate, slow
and indolent', and Spanish Indians as 'treacherous, passionate
and indolent, with no higher aim or object but simply to enjoy
the present after their own torpid, useless fashion'.

Seacole's patriotism, and her attitude to race, reveal a split
personality. On the other hand, she is sensitive to a black
ancestry and sensitive to the racism directed against blacks. On
the other, she shows contempt for blacks, and non-British
peoples, and is eager to declare her half-whiteness. Uninten-
tionally her narrative yields a valuable insight into the divided
loyalties of colonial people of mixed blood and heritage.

The text is taken from the first edition, London 1857, which
has been reprinted with an introduction by Ziggi Alexander,
Falling Walls Press, Bristol, 1984.

My First Glimpses of War

In the last three chapters, I have attempted, without any consideration of dates, to give my readers some idea of my life in the Crimea.
I am fully aware that I have jumbled up events strangely, talking in
the same page, and even sentence, of events which occurred at
different times; but I have three excuses to offer for my unhistorical

inexactness. In the first place, my memory is far from trustworthy, and I kept no written diary; in the second place, the reader must have had more than enough of journals and chronicles of Crimean life, and I am only the historian of Spring Hill; and in the third place, unless I am allowed to tell the story of my life in my own way, I cannot tell it at all.

I shall now endeavour to describe my out-of-door life as much as possible, and write of those great events in the field of which I was a humble witness. But I shall continue to speak from my own experience simply; and if the reader should be surprised at my leaving any memorable action of the army unnoticed, he may be sure that it is because I was mixing medicines or making good things in the kitchen of the British Hotel, and first heard the particulars of it, perhaps, from the newspapers which came from home. My readers must know, too, that they were much more familiar with the history of the camp at their own firesides, than we who lived in it. Just as a spectator seeing one of the battles from a hill, as I did the Tchernaya, knows more about it than the combatant in the valley below, who only thinks of the enemy whom it is his immediate duty to repel; so you, through the valuable aid of the cleverest man in the whole camp, read in the *Times'* columns the details of that great campaign, while we, the actors in it, had enough to do to discharge our own duties well, and rarely concerned ourselves in what seemed of such importance to you. And so very often a desperate skirmish or hard-fought action, the news of which created so much sensation in England, was but little regarded at Spring Hill.

My first experience of battle was pleasant enough. Before we had been long at Spring Hill, Omar Pasha got something for his Turks to do, and one fine morning they were marched away towards the Russian outposts on the road to Baidar. I accompanied them on horseback, and enjoyed the sight amazingly. English and French cavalry preceded the Turkish infantry over the plain yet full of memorials of the terrible Light Cavalry charge a few months before; and while one detachment of the Turks made a reconnaissance to the right of the Tchernaya, another pushed their way up the hill, towards Kamara, driving in the Russian outposts, after what seemed but a slight resistance. It was very pretty to see them advance, and to watch how every now and then little clouds of white smoke puffed up from behind bushes and the crests of hills, and were answered by similar puffs from the long line of busy skirmishers that preceded the main body. This was my first experience of actual battle, and I felt that strange excitement which I do not remember on future occasions, coupled with an earnest longing to see more of warfare, and to share in its hazards. It was not long before my wish was gratified.

I do not know much of the second bombardment of Sebastopol in the month of April, although I was as assiduous as I could be in my attendance at Cathcart's Hill.[1] I could judge of its severity by the long trains of wounded which passed the British Hotel. I had a stretcher laid near the door, and very often a poor fellow was laid upon it, outwearied by the terrible conveyance from the front.

After this unsuccessful bombardment, it seemed to us that there was a sudden lull in the progress of the siege; and other things began to interest us. There were several arrivals to talk over. Miss Nightingale came to supervise the Balaclava hospitals, and, before long, she had practical experience of Crimean fever. After her, came the Duke of Newcastle, and the great high priest of the mysteries of cookery, Mons. Alexis Soyer.[2] He was often at Spring Hill, with the most smiling of faces and in the most gorgeous of irregular uniforms, and never failed to praise my soups and dainties. I always flattered myself that I was his match, and with our West Indian dishes could of course beat him hollow, and more than once I challenged him to a trial of skill; but the gallant Frenchman only shrugged his shoulders, and disclaimed my challenge with many flourishes of his jewelled hands, declaring that Madame proposed a contest where victory would cost him his reputation for gallantry, and be more disastrous than defeat. And all because I was a woman, forsooth. What nonsense to talk like that, when I was doing the work of half a dozen men. Then he would laugh and declare that, when our campaigns were over, we would render rivalry impossible, by combining to open the first restaurant in Europe. There was always fun in the store when the good-natured Frenchman was there.

One dark, tempestuous night, I was knocked up by the arrival of other visitors. These were the first regiment of Sardinian Grenadiers, who, benighted on their way to the position assigned them, remained at Spring Hill until the morning. We soon turned out our staff, and lighted up the store, and entertained the officers as well as we could inside, while the soldiers bivouacked in the yards around. Not a single thing was stolen or disturbed that night, although they had many opportunities. We all admired and liked the Sardinians; they were honest, well-disciplined fellows, and I wish there had been no worse men or soldiers in the Crimea.

As the season advanced many visitors came to the Crimea from all parts of the world, and many of them were glad to make Spring Hill their head-quarters.[3] We should been better off if some of them had spared us this compliment. A Captain St. Clair, for instance – who could doubt any one with such a name? – stayed some time with us, had the best of everything, and paid us most honourably with one bill upon his agents, while we cashed another to provide him with money for his homeward route. He was an accomplished fellow, and I really liked him; but, unfortunately for us, he was a swindler.

I saw much of another visitor to the camp in the Crimea – an old acquaintance of mine with whom I had had many a hard bout in past times – the cholera. There were many cases in the hospital of the Land Transport Corps opposite, and I prescribed for many others personally. The raki[4] sold in too many of the stores in Balaclava and Kadikoi was most pernicious; and although the authorities forbade the sutlers to sell it under heavy penalties, it found its way into the camp in large quantities.

During May, and while preparations were being made for the third great bombardment of the ill-fated city, summer broke beautifully, and the weather, chequered occasionally by fitful intervals of cold and rain, made us all cheerful. You would scarcely have believed that the happy, good-humoured, and jocular visitors to the British Hotel were the same men who had a few weeks before ridden gloomily through the muddy road to its door. It was a period of relaxation, and they all enjoyed it. Amusement was the order of the day. Races, dog-hunts, cricket matches, and dinner-parties were eagerly indulged in, and in all I could be of use to provide the good cheer which was so essential a part of these entertainments; and when the warm weather came in all its intensity, and I took to manufacturing cooling beverages for my friends and customers, my store was always full. To please all was somewhat difficult, and occasionally some of them were scarcely so polite as they should have been to a perplexed hostess, who could scarcely be expected to remember that Lieutenant A. had bespoken his sangaree[5] an instant before Captain B. and his friends had ordered their claret cup.

In anticipation of the hot weather, I had laid in a large stock of raspberry vinegar, which, properly managed, helps to make a pleasant drink; and there was a great demand for sangaree, claret, and cider cups, the cups being battered pewter pots. Would you like, reader, to know my recipe for the favourite claret cup? It is simple enough. Claret, water, lemon-peel, sugar, nutmeg, and ice — yes, ice, but not often and not for long, for the eager officers soon made an end of it. Sometimes there were dinner-parties at Spring Hill, but of these more hereafter. At one of the earliest, when the *Times'* correspondent was to be present, I rode down to Kadikoi, bought some calico and cut it up into table napkins. They all laughed very heartily, and thought perhaps of a few weeks previously, when every available piece of linen in the camp would have been snapped up for pocket-handkerchiefs.

But the reader must not forget that all this time, although there might be only a few short and sullen roars of the great guns by day, few nights passed without some fighting in the trenches; and very often the news of the morning would be that one or other of those I knew had fallen. These tidings often saddened me, and when I awoke in the night and heard the thunder of the guns fiercer than usual, I have quite dreaded the dawn which might usher in bad news.

The deaths in the trenches touched me deeply, perhaps for this reason. It was very usual, when a young officer was ordered into the trenches, for him to ride down to Spring Hill to dine, or obtain something more than his ordinary fare to brighten his weary hours in those fearful ditches. They seldom failed on these occasions to shake me by the hand at parting, and sometimes would say, 'You see, Mrs. Seacole, I can't say good-bye to the dear ones at home, so I'll bid you good-bye for them. Perhaps you'll see them some day, and if the Russians should knock me over, mother, just tell them I thought of them all – will you?' And although all this might be said in a light-hearted manner, it was rather solemn. I felt it to be so, for I never failed (although who was I, that I should preach?) to say something about God's providence and relying upon it; and they were very good. No army of parsons could be much better than my sons. They would listen very gravely, and shake me by the hand again, while I felt that there was nothing in the world I would not do for them. Then very often the men would say, 'I'm going in with my mater to-night, Mrs. Seacole; come and look after him, if he's hit;' and so often as this happened I would pass the night restlessly, awaiting with anxiety the morning, and yet dreading to hear the news it held in store for me. I used to think it was like having a large family of children ill with fever, and dreading to hear which one had passed away in the night.

And as often as the bad news came, I thought it my duty to ride up to the hut of the sufferer and do my woman's work. But I felt it deeply. How could it be otherwise? There was one poor boy in the Artillery, with blue eyes and light golden hair, whom I nursed through a long and weary sickness, borne with all a man's spirit, and whom I grew to love like a fond old-fashioned mother. I thought if ever angels watched over any life, they would shelter his; but one day, but a short time after he had left his sick-bed, he was struck down on his battery, working like a young hero. It was a long time before I could banish from my mind the thought of him as I saw him last, the yellow hair, stiff and stained with his life-blood, and the blue eyes, closed in the sleep of death. Of course, I saw him buried, as I did poor H—— V——, my old Jamaica friend, whose kind face was so familiar to me of old. Another good friend I mourned bitterly – Captain B——, of the Coldstreams – a great cricketer. He had been with me on the previous evening, had seemed dull, but had supped at my store, and on the following morning a brother officer told me he was shot dead while setting his pickets, which made me ill and unfit for work for the whole day. Mind you, a day was a long time to give to sorrow in the Crimea.

I could give many other similar instances, but why should I sadden myself or my readers? Others have described the horrors of those fatal trenches; but their real history has never been written, and perhaps it is as well that so harrowing a tale should be left in oblivion. Such anecdotes as the following were very current in the Camp, but I have no means of answering for its truth. Two sergeants met in the trenches, who had been schoolmates in their youth; years had passed since they set out for the battle of life by different roads, and now they met again under the fire of a common enemy. With one impulse they started forward to exchange the hearty hand-shake and the mutual greetings, and while their hands were still clasped, a chance shot killed both.

(185–192)

Notes

1. Cathcart's Hill: a look-out post which commanded an excellent view of Sebastopol, and was a favourite resort for off-duty officers. Also on the hill was a cemetery in which many senior officers were buried.
2. Alexis Benoit-Soyer (1809–1858): a renowned chef who used his talent to benefit the poor as well as the rich, starting soup kitchens in London and famine-stricken Ireland. On his own initiative he went out to Scutari to organise the improvement of the kitchens in the two hospitals, and afterwards to the Crimea itself to teach the soldiers to make palatable food from their rations. Soyer revolutionised British army catering.
3. From the spring of 1855 onwards, many visitors arrived in the Crimea. Some were officers' relatives, while others were simply tourists who wanted to see the sites of famous battles which had been fought the previous year. Out of range of the Russian guns, they watched both skirmishes and major battles from any vantage point they could find.
4. Raki: a very strong Turkish drink made from aniseed.
5. Sangaree: a cold drink of wine diluted and spiced.

15

HARRIET JACOBS

alias Linda Brent, c.1815–80

Incidents in the Life of a Slave Girl

Boston 1861

This remarkable autobiography, published by Harriet Jacobs under a pseudonym, was for many years believed to have been written by the white abolitionist L. Maria Child. The events of the narrative were seen as too sensational to be other than fiction, until work by Dorothy Sterling and Jean Yellin Fagan established in the early 1980's that Child's role was no more than she had claimed, advisory and editorial, and that the book was genuinely the work of Harriet Jacobs, who had adopted the pseudonym in modesty, since the story tells of the persistent efforts of Harriet's 'owner' to seduce her. Her response was indeed the stuff of sensational fiction, when as her best revenge and defence she made her own choice to take a white lover, with whom she had two children, both of whom were, in accordance with the laws of slave ownership, the property of the man who had bought Harriet as a slave in her own childhood. The tale is a new departure for the slave narrative, previously told from the male viewpoint with the single exception of that of Mary Prince, and candid and explicit about the threat of sexual harrassment and the vulnerability of motherhood. For many years Harriet had to hide in her 'den', an attic in her grandmother's house, to elude detection when she made her break for freedom. For safety, her children were sent to New York, and in due course, Harriet too travelled north to be united with her children, gaining employment with a kindly Mrs Bruce and laying false trails to confuse her owner, Dr Flint, who was still in pursuit of her. Her daughter Ellen, was lodging with an unreliable woman, Mrs Hobbs, whose drunken brother was to betray Harriet's whereabouts to Flint and it is at this point that the extract begins.

The two chapters included here contrast Harriet's life in the States with her experience in England, where she has been offered a post as a governess. The relief she feels at the removal

176

of the threat of return to slavery is one recorded by a number
of Black American visitors to Britain at this time, such as
William Wells Brown and Alexander Crummell. Despite the
currents of racism, both brutal and 'polite', to be found in
Britain in the 19th century, to Harriet it seems a haven of peace
and security.

The text is from Henry L. Gates' reprint of the 1861 edition in
The Classic Slave Narratives. Details of Jean Fagan Yellin's
edition and her work can be found in the bibliography.

a. The Hairbreadth Escape

After we returned to New York, I took the earliest opportunity to
go and see Ellen. I asked to have her called down stairs; for I
supposed Mrs. Hobbs's southern brother might still be there, and I
was desirous to avoid seeing him, if possible. But Mrs. Hobbs came
to the kitchen, and insisted on my going up stairs. 'My brother
wants to see you,' said she, 'and he is sorry you seem to shun him.
He knows you are living in New York. He told me to say to you
that he owes thanks to good old aunt Martha for too many little acts
of kindness for him to be base enough to betray her grandchild.'

This Mr. Thorne had become poor and reckless long before he
left the south, and such persons had much rather go to one of the
faithful old slaves to borrow a dollar, or get a good dinner, than to
go to one whom they consider an equal. It was such acts of
kindness as these for which he professed to feel grateful to my
grandmother. I wished he had kept at a distance, but as he was here,
and knew where I was, I concluded there was nothing to be gained
by trying to avoid him; on the contrary, it might be the means of
exciting his ill will. I followed his sister up stairs. He met me in a
very friendly manner, congratulated me on my escape from slavery,
and hoped I had a good place, where I felt happy.

I continued to visit Ellen as often as I could. She, good thoughtful
child, never forgot my hazardous situation, but always kept a
vigilant lookout for my safety. She never made any complaint about
her own inconveniences and troubles; but a mother's observing eyes
easily perceived that she was not happy. On the occasion of one of
my visits I found her unusually serious. When I asked her what was
the matter, she said nothing was the matter. But I insisted upon

knowing what made her look so very grave. Finally, I ascertained that she felt troubled about the dissipation that was continually going on in the house. She was sent to the store very often for rum and brandy, and she felt ashamed to ask for it so often; and Mr. Hobbs and Mr. Thorne drank a great deal, and their hands trembled so that they had to call her to pour out the liquor for them. 'But for all that,' said she, 'Mr. Hobbs is good to me, and I can't help liking him. I feel sorry for him.' I tried to comfort her, by telling her that I had laid up a hundred dollars, and that before long I hoped to be able to give her and Benjamin a home, and send them to school. She was always desirous not to add to my troubles more than she could help, and I did not discover till years afterwards that Mr. Thorne's intemperance was not the only annoyance she suffered from him. Though he professed too much gratitude to my grandmother to injure any of her descendants, he had poured vile language into the ears of her innocent great-grandchild.

I usually went to Brooklyn to spend Sunday afternoon. One Sunday, I found Ellen anxiously waiting for me near the house. 'O, mother,' said she, 'I've been waiting for you this long time. I'm afraid Mr. Thorne has written to tell Dr. Flint where you are. Make haste and come in. Mrs. Hobbs will tell you all about it!'

The story was soon told. While the children were playing in the grape-vine arbor, the day before, Mr. Thorne came out with a letter in his hand, which he tore up and scattered about. Ellen was sweeping the yard at the time, and having her mind full of suspicions of him, she picked up the pieces and carried them to the children, saying, 'I wonder who Mr. Thorne has been writing to.'

'I'm sure I don't know, and don't care,' replied the oldest of the children; 'and I don't see how it concerns you.'

'But it does concern me,' replied Ellen' 'for I'm afraid he's been writing to the south about my mother.'

They laughed at her, and called her a silly thing, but good-naturedly put the fragments of writing together, in order to read them to her. They were no sooner arranged, than the little girl exclaimed, 'I declare , Ellen, I believe you are right.'

The contents of Mr. Thorne's letter, as nearly as I can remember, were as follows: 'I have seen your slave, Linda, and conversed with her. She can be taken very easily, if you manage prudently. There are enough of us here to swear to her identity as your property. I am a patriot, a lover of my country, and I do this as an act of justice to the laws.' He concluded by informing the doctor of the street and number where I lived. The children carried the pieces to Mrs. Hobbs, who immediately went to her brother's room for an explanation. He was not to be found. The servants said they saw him go out with a letter in his hand, and they supposed he had gone to the post office. The natural inference was, that he had sent to Dr. Flint a copy of those fragments. When he returned, his sister accused him of it, and he did not deny the charge. He went immediately to his room, and the next morning he was missing. He had gone over to New York, before any of the family were astir.

It was evident that I had no time to lose; and I hastened back to the city with a heavy heart. Again I was to be torn from a comfortable home, and all my plans for the welfare of my children were to be frustrated by that demon Slavery! I now regretted that I never told Mrs. Bruce my story. I had not concealed it merely on account of being a fugitive; that would have made her anxious, but it would have excited sympathy in her kind heart. I valued her good opinion, and I was afraid of losing it, if I told her all the particulars of my sad story. But now I felt that it was necessary for her to know how I was situated. I had once left her abruptly, without explaining the reason, and it would not be proper to do it again. I went home resolved to tell her in the morning. But the sadness of my face attracted her attention, and, in answer to her kind inquiries, I poured out my full heart to her, before bed time. She listened with true womanly sympathy, and told me she would do all she could to protect me. How my heart blessed her!

Early the next morning, Judge Vanderpool and Lawyer Hopper were consulted. They said I had better leave the city at once, as the risk would be great if the case came to trial. Mrs. Bruce took me in a carriage to the house of one of her friends, where she assured me I should be safe until my brother could arrive, which would be in a few days. In the interval my thoughts were much occupied with Ellen. She was mine by birth, and she was, also mine by Southern law, since my grandmother held the bill of sale that made her so. I did not feel that she was safe unless I had her with me. Mrs. Hobbs, who felt badly about her brother's treachery, yielded to my entreaties, on condition that she should return in ten days. I avoided making any promise. She came to me clad in very thin garments, all outgrown, and with a school satchel on her arm, containing a few articles. It was late in October, and I knew the child must suffer;

and not daring to go out in the streets to purchase any thing, I took off my own flannel skirt and converted it into one for her. Kind Mrs. Bruce came to bid me good by, and when she saw that I had taken off my clothing for my child, the tears came to her eyes. She said, 'Wait for me, Linda,' and went out. She soon returned with a nice warm shawl and hood for Ellen. Truly, of such souls as hers are the kingdom of heaven.

My brother reached New York on Wednesday. Lawyer Hopper advised us to go to Boston by the Stonington route, as there was less Southern travel in that direction. Mrs. Bruce directed her servants to tell all inquirers that I formerly lived there, but had gone from the city.

We reached the steamboat Rhode Island in safety. That boat employed colored hands, but I knew that colored passengers were not admitted to the cabin. I was very desirous for the seclusion of the cabin, not only on account of exposure to the night air, but also to avoid observation. Lawyer Hopper was waiting on board for us. He spoke to the stewardess, and asked, as a particular favor, that she would treat us well. He said to me, 'Go and speak to the captain yourself by and by. Take your little girl with you, and I am sure that he will not let her sleep on deck.' With these kind words and a shake of the hand he departed.

The boat was soon on her way, bearing me rapidly from the friendly home where I had hoped to find security and rest. My brother had left me to purchase the tickets, thinking that I might have better success than he would. When the stewardess came to me, I paid what she asked, and she gave me three tickets with clipped corners. In the most unsophisticated manner I said, 'You have made a mistake; I asked you for cabin tickets. I cannot possibly consent to sleep on deck with my little daughter.' She assured me there was no mistake. She said on some of the routes colored people were allowed to sleep in the cabin, but not on this route, which was much travelled by the wealthy. I asked her to show me to the captain's office, and she said she would after tea. When the time came, I took Ellen by the hand and went to the captain, politely requesting him to change our tickets, as we should be very uncomfortable on deck. He said it was contrary to their custom, but he would see that we had berths below; he would also try to obtain comfortable seats for us in the cars; of that he was not certain, but he would speak to the conductor about it, when the boat arrived. I thanked him, and returned to the ladies' cabin. He came afterwards and told me that the conductor of the cars was on board, that he had spoken to him, and he had promised to take care of us. I was very much surprised at receiving so much kindness. I don't know whether the pleasing face of my little girl had won his heart, or whether the stewardess inferred from Lawyer Hopper's manner that I was a fugitive, and had pleaded with him in my behalf.

When the boat arrived at Stonington, the conductor kept his promise, and showed us to seats in the first car, nearest the engine. He asked us to take seats next the door, but as he passed through, we ventured to move on toward the other end of the car. No incivility was offered us, and we reached Boston in safety.

The day after my arrival was one of the happiest of my life. I felt as if I was beyond the reach of the bloodhounds; and, for the first time during many years, I had both my children together with me. They greatly enjoyed their reunion, and laughed and chatted merrily. I watched them with a swelling heart. Their every motion delighted me.

I could not feel safe in New York, and I accepted the offer of a friend, that we should share expenses and keep house together. I represented to Mrs. Hobbs that Ellen must have some schooling, and must remain with me for that purpose. She felt ashamed of being unable to read or spell at her age, so instead of sending her to school with Benny, I instructed her myself till she was fitted to enter an intermediate school. The winter passed pleasantly, while I was busy with my needle, and my children with their books.

(Chapter 36)

b. A Visit to England

In the spring, sad news came to me. Mrs. Bruce was dead. Never again, in the world, should I see her gentle face, or hear her sympathizing voice. I had lost an excellent friend, and little Mary had lost a tender mother. Mr. Bruce wished the child to visit some of her mother's relatives in England, and he was desirous that I should take charge of her. The little motherless one was accustomed to me, and attached to me, and I thought she would be happier in my care than in that of a stranger. I could also earn more in this way than I could by my needle. So I put Benny to a trade, and left Ellen to remain in the house with my friend and go to school.

We sailed from New York, and arrived in Liverpool after a pleasant voyage of twelve days. We proceeded directly to London, and took lodgings at the Adelaide Hotel. The supper seemed to me less luxurious than those I had seen in American hotels; but my situation was indescribably more pleasant. For the first time in my life I was in a place where I was treated according to my deportment, without reference to my complexion. I felt as if a great millstone had been lifted from my breast. Ensconced in a pleasant room, with my dear little charge, I laid my head on my pillow, for the first time, with the delightful consciousness of pure, unadulterated freedom.

As I had constant care of the child, I had little opportunity to see the wonders of that great city; but I watched the tide of life that flowed through the streets, and found it a strange contrast to the stagnation in our Southern towns. Mr. Bruce took his little daughter to spend some days with friends in Oxford Crescent, and of course it was necessary for me to accompany her. I had heard much of the systematic method of English education, and I was very desirous that my dear Mary should steer straight in the midst of much propriety. I closely observed her little playmates and their nurses, being ready to take any lessons in the science of good management. The children were more rosy than American children, but I did not see that they differed materially in other respects. They were like all children – sometimes docile and sometimes wayward.

We next went to Steventon, in Berkshire. It was a small town, said to be the poorest in the county. I saw men working in the fields for six shillings, and seven shillings, a week, and women for sixpence, and sevenpence, a day, out of which they boarded themselves. Of course they lived in the most primitive manner; it could not be otherwise, where a woman's wages for an entire day were not sufficient to buy a pound of meat. They paid very low rents, and their clothes were made of the cheapest fabrics, though much better than could have been procured in the United States for the same money. I had heard much about the oppression of the poor in Europe. The people I saw around me were, many of them, among the poorest poor. But when I visited them in their little thatched cottages, I felt that the condition of even the meanest and most ignorant among them was vastly superior to the condition of the most favoured slaves in America. They labored hard; but they were not ordered out to toil while the stars were in the sky, and driven and slashed by an overseer, through heat and cold, till the stars shone out again. Their homes were very humble; but they were protected by law. No insolent patrols could come, in the dead of night, and flog them at their pleasure. The father, when he closed his cottage door, felt safe with his family around him. No master or overseer could come and take from him his wife, or his daughter. They must separate to earn their living; but the parents knew where their children were going, and could communicate with them by letters. The relations of husband and wife, parent and child, were too sacred for the richest noble in the land to violate with impunity. Much was being done to enlighten these poor people. Schools were established among them, and benevolent societies were active in efforts to ameliorate their condition. There was no law forbidding them to learn to read and write; and if they helped each other in spelling out the Bible, they were in no danger of thirty-nine lashes, as was the case with myself and poor, pious, old uncle Fred. I repeat that the most ignorant and the most destitute of these peasants was a thousand fold better off than the most pampered American slave.

I do not deny that the poor are oppressed in Europe. I am not disposed to paint their condition so rose-colored as the Hon. Miss Murray paints the condition of the slaves in the United States. A small portion of *my* experience would enable her to read her own pages with anointed eyes. If she were to lay aside her title, and instead of visiting among the fashionable, become domesticated, as a poor governess, on some plantation in Louisiana or Alabama, she would see and hear things that would make her tell quite a different story.

My visit to England is a memorable event in my life, from the fact of my having there received strong religious impressions. The contemptuous manner in which the communion had been administered to colored people, in my native place; the church membership of Dr. Flint, and others like him; and the buying and selling of slaves, by professed ministers of the gospel, had given me a prejudice against the Episcopal church. The whole service seemed to me a mockery and a sham. But my home in Steventon was in the family of a clergyman, who was a true disciple of Jesus. The beauty of his daily life inspired me with faith in the genuineness of Christian professions. Grace entered my heart, and I kept at the communion table, I trust in true humility of soul.

I remained abroad ten months, which was much longer than I had anticipated. During all that time, I never saw the slightest sympton of prejudice against color. Indeed, I entirely forgot it, till the time came for us to return to America.

(Chapter 37)

16

JAMES AFRICANUS BEALE HORTON
born Freetown 1835, died Freetown 1883

West African Countries and Peoples

1868

James Africanus Horton was the first African to graduate as a
Doctor of Medicine from Edinburgh University. He was not
the first Doctor of African descent to graduate from Edinburgh: William Fergusson, a West Indian, had done so in 1814,
and John Baptist Phillip of Trinidad in 1815, Fergusson going
on to become Governor of Sierra Leone. Horton's parents,
both Igbo, were 'recaptives', that is, resettled in Africa after
being freed from a slave ship by the Royal Navy, the slave
trade having been declared illegal by Act of Parliament in 1807.
His father was a carpenter from the village of Gloucester in the
hills above Freetown, where James attended the C.M.S. Grammar School, receiving an education closely modelled on the
British system. With the success of Fergusson in mind, and the
need to train West Africans for medical work in view of the toll
taken by the climate on white doctors, the War Office awarded
Horton, along with two fellow Sierra Leonians, Samuel Campbell and William B. Davies a scholarship to study medicine in
King's College, London. After graduation, Horton studied a
fourth year for the M.D. in Edinburgh, where Robert Knox,
whose racist theories Horton was later to take issue with in his
book, had only two years before been teaching Anatomy. He
served as an army surgeon in the Ashanti War of 1863–4, then
was posted to the Gambia. He had published a short geological
study in 1862 and from the Gambia, he published a pamphlet,
Political Economy of West Africa in 1865, the themes of which
were to broaden into his major book. He was transferred to
Accra, and then granted leave which he took in London, where
he stayed a year, completing and publishing two medical
studies and *West African Countries and Peoples*.

The modern reader of the book will find plenty to disagree
with but its impressive principal purpose is laid out on the title
page, printed below, exhibiting all the marks of a manifesto
against the misinformation and racial prejudice of the age. Not

only does it proclaim African self-government as its principal end, but it is significantly sub-titled 'A Vindication of the African Race', and instead of the credentials characteristic of the slave-narratives, prefaces and letters by white ladies and gentlemen confirming the virtues of the author, Horton lists his own credentials, his degrees, publications, and merited distinctions.

The shortcomings of his view are those of his age and the education he received. When he asserts that Africans 'have no history' (189) he reveals that he has not gone beyond the limits of 19th century thought on the subject, which underlies the inadequacy of such bland and absurd generalisations about African social and political life as: 'proper legislative science is entirely unknown to them' (190). He fails to respond in any way to African traditional arts, observing with condescension,

> They amuse themselves by rude dances, consisting of severe athletic pantomimic gymnasium, performed with the hands and feet, accompanied with the clapping of hands and rude dramatic recitations by the bystanders, or musicians ... (191)

He cannot understand why those Africans who have had the benefit of western education should continue to 'look back with a sort of veneration and fear on some of the heathenish customs of their fatherland' (192). One might contrast this with the words of Equiano written nearly a hundred years before about Igbo customs:

> ... they had been implanted in me with great care, and made an impression on my mind which time could not erase ... I still look back with pleasure on the first scenes of my life.   (Narrative, I.46)

For all his limitations, however, like Blyden he was a new force in the process of 'the vindication of the African race' and should be seen in a more positive light than that which the prejudices he inherited from his education and the age in which he lived might indicate.

The text is from the 1968 Edinburgh University Press reprint of the edition of 1868. For biographical information we have drawn upon Christopher Fyfe, *Africanus Horton: West African Scientist and Patriot*.

a. Title Page:

WEST AFRICAN
COUNTRIES AND PEOPLES

BRITISH AND NATIVE

WITH THE

REQUIREMENTS NECESSARY FOR ESTABLISHING THAT SELF
GOVERNMENT RECOMMENDED BY THE COMMITTEE OF
THE HOUSE OF COMMONS, 1865

AND A

VINDICATION OF THE AFRICAN RACE

BY

JAMES AFRICANUS B. HORTON, M.D.Edin., F.R.G.S.

Author of *Physical and Medical Climate and Meteorology of the West Coast of
Africa, Guinea Worm, or Dracunculus*, Etc., Etc., Etc.

*Staff Assistant-Surgeon of H.M. Forces in West Africa; Associate of King's
College London; Foreign Fellow of the Botanical Society of Edinburgh;
Corresponding Member of The Medical Society of King's College
London; Member of the Institute D'Afrique of Paris*, Etc., Etc., Etc.

Africa ought to be allowed to have a fair chance of raising her character in the
scale of the civilized world. – Emperor of Russia.

LONDON
W. J. JOHNSON, 121, FLEET STREET
1868

b. The State of The Native Tribes

Bearing in mind the foregoing, it will be my province to prove the
capability of the African for possessing a real political Government
and national independence; and that a more stable and efficient
Government might yet be formed in Western Africa, under the
supervision of a civilized nation, in conformity with the present
Resolution of the Committee of the House of Commons.

In viewing the map of West Africa, and tracing out those political
communities which are not due to the agency of more civilized
politicians, we affirm that there are amongst them fixed and
established Governments, although rude and barbarous; that the
obedience to the supreme power in many cases is implicit, the right
of property is enforced by adjudicature; and, although the power of
the supreme head has been used with extreme despotism, as in
Dahomey and Ashantee, yet still it is as truly a political Government as that of France or England. By nature the African is a social
being, possessing the capacity of commanding and obeying, and
that type of improvement which advances as the reason is cultivated, which are the essential elements both of a political Government and a political community; and therefore Africans bear no
relation whatever to those gregarious species of animals – apes,
monkeys, &c. – to which some fantastic writers have likened them.

Examining Western Africa in its entirety, we find it to be
composed of a number of political communities, each ruled by a
national Government, formed in many cases of distinct nationalities
occupying determined territory; but some national communities are
broken up into innumerable fractional sections, governed by rebel
chiefs, or satraps; others depend upon a political body whose
soevereign chief rules over life and property; and others, again, are
under well-regulated civilized government. But in order to develop
among these different nationalities a true political science, it is
necessary that the inhabitants should be made acquainted with the
useful arts, and the physical conditions which influence other more
civilized and refined political Governments.

What it may be asked, are the different forms of government now
in existence on the West Coast of Africa? The two principal forms
are the monarchical and the republican.

In the purely native community we observe the recognition of
power, in many cases, vested in a single individual, variously called

by the different tribes, but to which we apply the name of *basileus*, or king; surrounded by a number of headmen, who pledge themselves to do his will. Some of these *basileus*, such as those of Ashantee and Dahomey, have implicit power over life and poverty, and therefore are held in dread by their subjects. Of the tribes who are governed by these autocrats we may well apply the language of Merivale,[1] when speaking of the Asiatic races, that 'they have acquiesced in their own immemorial despotisms to which they have been abandoned. To them the names of liberty and equality, invoked in turn by their neighbours, are unintelligible; their sympathies are centred always in men, and not in government'. A desperate and successful warrior, such as an Owoosookorkor, a Mahbah, and a Gezo, commanded all their devotions, and for them the 'foundation of laws lay in the bosom of the autocrat'.

Among other political native communities we find that in some the form of government resembles very closely a limited monarchy – in others a democracy, in which all the caboceers or head men stand almost on equal terms. Among those tribes who are goaded with religious tenets and infinitesmal rites and ceremonies, who believe implicitly in the supernatural powers of their fetish and medicine man, whom they suppose to have the power of communicating with the world of spirits, and using their agency in human affairs, the population are subject to a spiritual despotism not easily comprehended by civilized nations. In matters of great interest, in many cases a whole nation assemble together for deliberation; but the counsels of the aged, from their experience, especially when backed by previous sage advice and reputation of wisdom, a sober and thoughtful deportment, and a vigorous and energetic character, generally decide the will of the multitude. The authority of a chief is hereditary, but this hereditary descent differs materially from that in civilized countries; the individual to whom the succession falls being, not the eldest son of the chief, but the son of his sister; and this is accounted for by the plurality of wives which each man maintains. But men who have shown themselves to possess great tact, courage, and strength in time of war, although they might have been originally slaves, may in time of peace arrogate to themselves such predominant influence, that they soon create themselves chiefs (such as the present King of Denkera on the Gold Coast).

Not being acquainted with letters, they have no history, and are absolutely ignorant of events for any long period beyond the memory of their head men; successive events once out of sight are for ever lost; they pass away like the spectres in a phantasmagoria, leaving no other trace behind them than a dreamy recollection of some distant circumstances that had taken place. They satisfy the curiosity of their generation by the aged among them giving the oral narration of legendary tales, heroic myths, vague traditions, &c., descriptive of deeds of wonder at an uncertain and undated antiquity, and which forms the only channel by which their 'thoughts can be transmitted from one country and one age to another'. Not knowing anything of the useful arts, their Governments are feeble and unenterprising, and their military organization impotent and inefficient; amongst the higher classes in some of them the head wives occupy important positions in the domestic circle, whilst all the other women occupy a degraded position.

Proper legislative science is entirely unknown to them; they possess no means by which a continuous and profitable revenue can be brought into their imperial coffers; no proper determination of political causes, and, consequently, no established principle which might be made to form a guide to the Legislature in the making of new laws or the alteration of old ones, and thus for ages they have shown no improvement in the executive administration; and possess no proper legal status, and no generalized principle of international law. There is an entire absence of any domestic history amongst them. By them a society is never contemplated, either in its constituent elements or mutual relations; in its private recesses or habitual intercourses. A fact, an anecdote, a speech, or remark, which would illustrate the condition of the common people, or of any rank subordinate to the highest, is considered too insignificant to intrude upon a relation which concerns only grandees and ministers, thrones and imperial powers. Some towns there are which are governed entirely by chiefs, who exercise an uncertain rule over the inhabitants – who are regarded more as a father of the community than a political head; some of them are nomadic in their name, but others constitute themselves into a political society of the most primitive order ...

With those in this primitive state of ignorance and poverty we observe their chief occupation to consist in the cultivation of a small plot of ground, where they plant various species of cereals, besides squash, casada, pumpkins, yams, sweet potato, and several sorts of edible fruits. Not being in connexion with civilized nations, their agricultural instruments consist of large shells, sharpened sticks, or rude iron hoes, all consequently of a barbarous nature. They make baskets and mats from the fibre and hard outer-covering of the bamboo. Their dress is very scanty, and in many instances consists of a small piece of plaited straw placed as a frontal covering. They know no intoxicating liquor except the palm wine, the product of nature, after it has been kept for several hours to undergo fermentation; they amuse themselves by rude dances, consisting of severe athletic pantomimic gymnasium, performed with the hands and feet, accompanied with the clapping of hands, and rude dramatic recitations of the bystanders, or musicians.

They carry on warfare with clubs, bow and arrows, and stones, and their system always is to surprise their enemy. Each warrior and hunter (in some cases) manufacturers for himself his weapons and his implements; his war-clubs of hard and heavy wood, wrought and ornamented with great ingenuity; his bows shaped and polished; his arrows pointed with flints, shells, or sharp bones, which serve as cutting instruments. They reckon by the number of the 'moon', and by the occurrence of some remarkable events; they fell large trees by fire, and in all things exhibit great rudeness and extreme simplicity.

Some, such as the *Fans*, show considerable ingenuity in the manufacture of iron. In their country, interior of the Gaboon, iron ore is found in considerable quantity, cropping out at the surface. To obtain the iron, they 'build a huge pile of wood, heap on this a considerable quantity of the ore broken up, then come with more wood', and apply fire to the whole; wood is continually being thrown into it until the ore becomes fluid, when it is allowed to cool down, and cast iron is obtained. To temper and make it malleable, 'they put through a most tedious series of heating and hammerings, till at last they turn out a very superior article of iron and steel', which is much better than the trade quality brought out from Europe. Of this they make their knives, arrowheads, and swords. They reverence their charms and fetishes, and believe in witchcraft; some are cannibals, and others make very disagreeable enemies, by being very energetic, warlike, fierce, and possessing great courage and ingenuity ...

Although advanced to some degree of civilization, some of these tribes indulge in witchcraft and various superstitious rites and ceremonies. The sickness of a chief might lead to the death of many harmless persons; a professed sorcerer is summoned to find the cause or the individual who has bewitched him; 'this he does by inspecting the inside of a mystic fowl, which has been killed and split into two parts. Blackness or blemish about the wing is supposed to denote treachery in children or kinsmen; in the backbone, it convicts mother and grandmother; in the tail, it accuses the wives; and in the thighs, the concubines; in the shank or feet, it condemns the common slaves. Some are so entirely dominated by the superstitious ideas of their country that even after they have been for years under Christian teaching and civilizing re-agents, they look back with a sort of veneration and fear on some of the heathenish customs of their fatherland. In these semi-savage countries the inhabitants believe that the religious devotees are in league with disembodied spirits, who transfer to them such supernatural powers that they are recognized by every one to have the good fortune of weaving the web of human fate; and these pretenders carry themselves with such striking dignity of look and action, such undoubting confidence, at the same time evincing such strength of language and energy of purpose, that these weak-minded people are involuntarily compelled to cherish a deep veneration for those pretensions to supernatural knowledge, and always to hold them in reverential awe. In those places where religion and knowledge have made some progress, as in the seacoast towns of a part of the Gold Coast, these devotees are regarded with hatred and horror, but in those parts where a higher degree of knowledge is attained, they are regarded in the true light of imposters, and expelled wheresoever they come with their pretensions.

(6–9)

c. Erroneous Views Respecting the African

It cannot be denied by even the most casual observer that the British portion of Western Africa has made a very rapid stride in improvement since Sierra Leone has been formed. Fancy a lot of slaves – unlettered, rude, naked, possessing no knowledge of the useful arts – thrown into a wild country, to cut down the woods and build towns; fancy these ragged, wild natives under British, and, consequently, civilized influences after a lapse of a few years, becoming large landowners, possessing large mercantile establishments and money, claiming a voice in the legislative government, and giving their offspring proper English and foreign education; and dare you tell me that the African is not susceptible of improvement of the highest order, that he does not possess in himself a principle of progression and a desire of perfection far surpassing many existing nations – since it cannot be shown in the world's history that any people with so limited advantages has shown such results within fifty years.

In 1818, the immortal Clarkson, in the Congress of *Aix-la-Chapelle*, exhibited certain articles of native manufacture to the Emperor of Russia, whilst endeavouring to secure support in the suppression of the slave-trade; viewing the articles, the Emperor said:

> You astonish me; you have given me a new idea of the state of these poor people; I was not aware that they were so advanced in society. The works you have shown me are not the works of brutes, but of men endued with natural and intellectual powers, and capable of being brought to as high a degree of proficiency as any other men. *Africa ought to be allowed to have a fair chance of raising her character in the scale of the civilized world.*

> 'They have not,' it must be admitted, as a learned author remarked, contributed much towards the advancement of human art and science, but they have shown themselves willing and able to profit by these advantages when introduced among them. The civilization of many African nations is much superior to that of the aborigines of Europe during the ages which preceded the Goths and Swedes in the north, and the Romans in the southern parts. The old Finnish inhabitants of Scandinavia had long, as it has been proved by the learned investigations of Rütis, the religion of Fetishes, and a vocabulary as scanty as that of the most barbarous Africans.

From ages immemorial they lived without government, laws, or social union; in all matters of domestic or political important each individual was the supreme arbiter of his own actions:

> and they displayed as little capability of emerging from the squalid sloth of their rude and merely animal existence. When conquered by a people of Indo-German origin, who brought with them from the East the rudiments of mental culuture, they emerged more slowly from their pristine barbarism than many of the native African nations have since done. Even at the present day there are hordes in various parts of Northern Asia

whose heads have the form belonging to the Tartars, to the Sclavonians, and other Europeans, but who are below many of the African tribes in civilization.

But with these potent facts in evidence we find that Captain Burton[2] and many others[3] have unblushingly advanced the *theoreticum absurdum*, the jejune and barren generalization or apophthegm, that British civilization and Christian influences have demoralized the native African – that, in fact these institutions were the chimera of a mistaken philanthropy; whilst the very advance of the Africans is a positive proof that they make it their principle that their great and leading object should be to 'illustrate the provision made by nature in the principles of the human mind and in the circumstances of man's external situation, for a gradual and progressive augmentation in the means of national wealth; to demonstrate that the most effectual plan for advancing a people to greatness is to maintain that order of things which nature has pointed out,' by encouraging the development of the useful arts, agriculture, of education in the masses, which will be produced by the governed having a voice in the governing body, and which will lay in the minds of the rising generation a solid foundation of the fundamental principles of political government.

But the committee of the House of Commons, in the summary of their resolutions, seemed to throw some disparaging remarks on the good effects of missionary operations on the native African – the success,' say they, 'of education of the liberated Africans at Sierra Leone seems questionable'. This resolution was deduced from evidence which cannot withstand the test of criticism. Whilst the missionaries assert the success with strong proofs, supported by other able evidence, such as that of the Govenor of the colonies and the Commissioner sent by the Colonial-office expressly to report on colonial affairs, the commitee seemed to be guided rather by the evidence of a few interested mercantile gentlemen, who excluded all consideration of the age of the colony, and certainly did not, as impartial observers would have done, look at the now existing improvement in all its different phases. These witnesses belonged to a country where civilization exists in perfection, and where for the last eighteen hundred years the arts and sciences have been gradually but securely advancing, and they forgot that the country which they now see, and the inhabitants which form the subjects of their observations and report, have only been under civilizing assistance within the last fifty years, which was the only time (and, in many cases, less than that) occupied in bringing them from a state of utter barbarism to that of semi-civilization, in which they are now. They also forgot that the number of civilizing agents were so extremely small, in comparison with the bulk of the liberated population, that they were as one to three or four thousand; and Mr Harris showed that he was extremely narrow in his views when he stated in his evidence that the result of missionary labours upon the natives is not so effective as it ought to be. It would be as absurd to attempt to compare the civilization of Britain fifty years after the landing of Julius Cæsar with the civilization of Rome, then in the zenith of her prosperity, as to attempt to compare the result of civlization of a savage, barbarous race of Africa, during fifty years' feeble attempts at civilization, with the civilization of the nineteenth century in England. And, in fact, if the comparison be made between the degree of improvement exhibited by the two countries, history informs us that the present degree of improvement exhibited by the liberated Africans under missionary influence far exceeds that of Britain under Roman influences during a similar period of time.

(23–26)

Notes

1. *History of the Romans under the Empire*, II.141 (Horton's work).
2. *Wanderings in West Africa*, p. 267 (Horton's note).
3. Lord Stanley, Speech in the House of Commons, Tuesday 21 February 1865. Dr Hunt *On the Negro's Place in Nature*, p. 57. Carl Vogt, *Lecture on Man* (Horton's note).

17

JOHN E. OCANSEY
died Gold Coast 1889

African Trading; or the Trials of William Narh Ocansey

1881

In *Pageant of Ghana*, Freda Wolfson's brief note informs us that John Ocansey was a Fulani from the interior of Ghana, then the Gold Coast, who was a slave in the household of the Ocansey family, prosperous African traders of Addah (Ada). The comparative flexibility of African slavery is indicated by the fact that John was adopted by the Ocanseys, employed in the family trading business, and in due course married the daughter, Salome Ocansey, as he tells us in his book. The book describes the problems arising from some of the Ocansey business ventures which led him to Liverpool and London where he observed a civil lawsuit on the family's behalf. These problems, and the account of the civil action take up half of the book, but of more immediate interest to most readers is his sensitive and uncluttered observation of the Victorian English society in which he found himself, an observant innocent abroad. His descriptions of encounters with English children are particularly striking, and indicate a considerable literary talent, unfortunately never to be developed. His description of the service at the orphan school in Liverpool invites comparison with Blake's 'Holy Thursday' in *Songs of Innocence*, a poem he cannot have read.

As with Equiano, there are several passages which, despite the innocence of manner, appear to carry ironic overtones, which are unlikely to have been designed to do so, but may carry this implication for the modern reader. Just as Equiano does not appear to intend his case for the substitution of trade in goods for trade in slaves to be ironic (see pp. 72–9), so the praise of industrial improvements, which may appear to bear a certain weight of irony in view of the industrial and economic exploitation of Africa which followed upon the period of the slave trade, seems here to be an expression of guileless wonder carrying ironic implications for the modern reader unlikely to have been intended by the author. But Ocansey's eye is nevertheless sharp in its innocence, with its awareness of the poverty of the children of the Blue Coat orphans' school with smart white collars adorning their necks, and old before their time yet still conveying a vision of appealing simplicity in the community of voices raised in song, and their two-by-two march through the church which, though disciplined by stern authority, nevertheless leads the author to observe 'how they touched one another in walking'. When Ocansey is taken to observe 'the dark side of English life' at the out-of-doors popular sermon his attention is drawn by an unsympathetic companion to the fact that the poor people attending are not properly dressed for religious service in 'Sunday clothes', yet what strikes his compassionate eye is the common humanity of the people's lives, the men smoking their pipes and the women bringing along their babies; above all he notes in conclusion, 'I saw many of them wipe the tears from their eyes as they listened to the speakers.' The reader might contrast the cold moralising of Ocansey's friend with Ocansey's own unaffected warmth when the little boy begs from them; the friend tries to blame the child for its poverty, nevertheless, says Ocansey, 'he looked so miserable that I gave him a penny, and he left with thanks.'

Recalling some of Equiano's descriptions of his childhood and first experience of white men, the world of Victorian England is for Ocansey one of wonders, often vividly conveyed: the railway engine which 'rushed and pushed along', the Crystal Palace which was 'full of wonders' (a phrase used by Equiano too of the world of the white men) and the firework display 'curious, grand and frightful', the words suggesting the ambivalence of his own response. It remains a world constantly measured for him in terms of distances remembered from his homeland. 'Liverpool is a very large city. The length of it, I consider, will be as far as from Addah to Weycoomaber, and the breadth from Addah to Lolonar ... it would be two days of African travel to go from one end to the other ...' I consider the distance from Liverpool to London to be equal in length as from Addah to Cape Coast Castle, and that journey by land takes us fourteen days, and now I have travelled it [by train] in four hours and a half!' And as with all good travel writing, it is not just literally the journey which is described, but the experience is recreated of the author's living, excited response to it.

The text is from the Liverpool edition of 1881, the only copy of which we have been able to find being in the New York Public Library. The book has been recently reprinted by the Ghana Academy, Accra and edited by Professor Kwame Arhin of the Centre of African Studies, University of Ghana, Legon.

Extracts and brief comments are to be found in Freda Wolfson, *Pageant of Ghana*, Oxford U.P. 1961, and Paul Edwards, *Through African Eyes*, 2 v., Cambridge U.P. 1967.

a. Liverpool

When I first walked through the streets of Liverpool I thought it was a feast day, because every man and woman I met appeared so well and nicely dressed. So I asked what feast it was to-day that caused everybody to be dressed up and walking about. But I was quickly told it was not a feast, but the usual style and custom of the place, and that if anyone would dare to go without being dressed, they would be punished by the Government. The next day when I went out I saw it was just the same, and large numbers of ladies, very grandly dressed, were walking about, and stopping to look in the large glass windows of the various shops.

The streets are very broad, and are divided or shared into three parts. The middle is made with small paving stones, with sand and tar run in between them, to make them smooth and firm; and this is the part for the horses, carts, and carriages. Each side of this is a wide walk covered with smooth flags for the people only to walk on. Many big coaches called 'omnibuses,' with three and four horses drawing them, run constantly to all parts of the town and to the villages, and the people get inside and on the top. Besides, there are dark streets used only by the railways, that go under the other streets, and they too are crowded with passengers.

Liverpool is a very large city. The length of it, I consider, will be as far as from Addah to Weycoomaber, and the breadth from Addah to Lolonar, all thickly covered with houses. It would be two days of African travel to go from one end to the other.

(pp. 26–7)

b. A Gas-Fire

When I first came to my lodgings at 24, Oxford Street, Liverpool, I was very awkward and shy, but I tried to conceal my ignorance and asked no questions. When I first went into my bedroom, I did not know how to put the gas out, so I blew at it, and put it out! and got into bed, and fell fast asleep! Now I had done a very dangerous thing, and it was by God's providence that I had been preserved. Early the next morning, my landlady, Mrs. Lyle, rose up in great haste and alarm, and began to speak loud, and say that the house was full of gas! and she came trembling to my room door, and said, 'Mr. Ocansey, did you blow out the gas last night?' I said, 'Yes, I did.' She exclaimed, 'Good God!' and she continued, 'I thank God that after that you did not strike or scratch a match, for it you had, the house would have been blown to pieces, and all in it killed. Do you not knew that gas is as dangerous as gunpowder?' I was amazed, and had to confess that I did not know how to put it out. She then called me to look near to the pipe, and shewed me a small screw fastened into it, and she said, 'When you want to put out the gas again, don't blow at it, but turn the screw this way, and it will go out without danger.' I then thanked her, and asked her if there were any other dangerous things in the room? but she said there was nothing more.

(p. 20)

c. An Orphans School

On Sunday the 26th of June, I visited the Blue-coat School where many young orphan boys and girls are taken in and educated. After passing through and inspecting the apartments in which they live, I went into their church to attend the service. It was a large building capable of holding 2,000 persons, besides all the Blue-coat scholars, which number about 300, and 100 lady teachers, singers and servants. The Church was very full, and I was told that the people come to hear the singing which is very fine, for the scholars are well trained. After the people were all seated, the organist came in and began to play a soft sweet exercise, which I thought to be part of the service. The pulpit was there, but there was no one in it, and I began to feel uneasy about the minister – why did he delay? had he not arrived? was he taken ill? Still the organist went on playing what appeared a long time. But see! now he pulls out the stops of the organ and rises to his exercise with great energy and changes the sound of the organ until it is like a large band of music marching. I could hardly think it was the organ, for I thought I heard many instruments, and the drums beating, and it swelled louder and louder in great deep tones until the place shook with the sound. Then he played a fine march and the scholars, boys and girls, came marching in, two by two, so close that they touched each other in walking, and kept step to the music most correctly. Oh, how nice and pleasant it was, and how clean and healthy they all appeared!

Nothing pleased me more than the large white broad collars over
their necks. They came marching on through the middle of the
Church with steady, solid step to the tones of the drum-playing
organ. Then one little boy, about ten years of age, ascended into the
pulpit, and taking the hymn-book, gave out the hymn like an aged
minister. Then the organist, after preparing his stops, began to play,
and all the people rise and sing:

> Before Johovah's awful throne
>   Ye nations bow with sacred joy;
> Know that the Lord is God alone,
>   He can create and He destroy.

After that twelve boys came forward in a line just before the organ
and pulpit, and one of them, taking a book called a Catechism,
asked the others a great many questions which they answered very
willingly, and with great ability. Then six girls came forward, and
they were asked many questions out of the Bible, and they also
answered very correctly and cleverly. A collection was then made,
and afterwards a hymn sung, and the little boy gave the benediction.
Then without the least noise or confusion, they form into procession, and march out to the sound of the organ. We followed them,
and passed through their eating rooms. Their evening meal was then
prepared and on the tables; their bread on wooden plates and their
tea and milk in tin cups. I was told that they were all poor and
destitute children that were taken in, who had no father or mother,
and that the expense of keeping them is defrayed by some of the
people of the city, who give yearly subscriptions, as they think fit.

(pp. 24–31)

d. The Train to London

On the day following my arrival, I made enquiries about Hickson,
Sykes & Co., and then I found they had been declared bankrupt,
and that the 17th of June had been appointed for the meeting of
their creditors. This was terrible news. I felt my heart sink, and I
could not eat for three days. I thought of my dear father and the
heavy loss he would sustain of £2,678 11s. 8d., besides all the delay
in the enlargement of his business for want of the steam launch, for
which he had already paid, and which ought to have been out and in
full working order. I now found that I could do nothing but wait
and attend the meeting of creditors. But I remembered that I had

business in London, and on the 7th June I decided to visit that great city to see some of my firm's agents. At eleven o'clock in the morning we left Lime Street Station, Liverpool, and arrived in Euston Square Station, London, at 3-50 in the afternoon, travelling at some times at the rate of sixty miles in one hour!

When I first went into the railway train, I observed they were like great coaches, mounted on springs, with strong, heavy wheels. Six persons can sit side by side in a row and they are so high that a man can stand upright with his hat on and not touch the top. The seats are cushioned and the carriages have large, strong glass windows at each end, and a lamp at the top to give light when they are rushing through the dark tunnels. Some carriages will carry fifty or more persons, and the carriages can be hooked on, one after the other, according to the number of passengers. A large and powerful engine, with fires burning inside, was fastened to the front of the carriages. The steam was coming out of the top, or chimney, with great force and noise. After I had been inside, and secured my seat, I came out and stood on the platform, near to the door, to look at the large station, and all the people coming and going, and I was greatly astonished to see so large a place. You can walk about for half-an-hour before you can go all round it; and yet this vast place is all covered over with a glass roof, supported and held up by iron beams and pillars. Whilst I was gazing about a gentleman came up, dressed in a blue suit, with silver buttons. I thought he was a soldier; but he shouted out, 'Take your seats, gentlemen; show your tickets.' I immediately jumped inside, and he took my ticket and made a small cut in it, and then shut the door with a loud bang. I then heard a bell ring, and the engine gave a loud screech, or whistle, and began to move very slowly at first, but gradually increased in speed, and we shot into a dark tunnel, which is made under the houses for about two miles, until we came out into the light in the country. I was bewildered with the motion of the carriages, and the great noise they made in rushing through the tunnel. The carriages were certainly very comfortable, and the lamp in the top gave us good light. But it was pleasant to break out into the sunshine again. Then I settled and composed myself to look out of the window on the country, and behold! all the trees of the field seemed to be flying away from us backwards! It was then I saw how swiftly we were going; swifter than a bird can fly through the sky! And thus the engine rushed and pushed away with all its might; and we went dashing along past houses, villages, and through the midst of large towns, and over high bridges, and darted in and out of deep tunnels, with such a loud noise that I could not hear the sound of my own voice. As I looked out on the country it seemed very green and beautiful. There were many cattle in the fields; and all the land is divided by hedges, and long lines of bushes and trees. There were many houses and towns all the way, and large factories with long chimneys.

After we had been flying along in this way for more than four hours, the train began to get quiet and to go slower, until it stopped; and a man, dressed as an officer, came and violently opened the door, and shouted out, 'Tickets, please!' and he took them from us; then I knew I was in the great city of London! But I was not tired of the journey, it was so pleasant, and so short a time in coming such a long distance.

I consider the distance from Liverpool to London to be equal in length as from Addah to Cape Coast Castle, and that journey by land takes us fourteen days, and now I have travelled it in four hours and a half!

Oh, I do pray that I may live to see one of these railways on the West Coast of Africa! What a saving of time and trouble it will be to the poor Africans who have to make their long and weary journeys on foot, carrying their heavy loads on their heads, under a broiling, burning sun! Oh! may God look down in mercy and remember for good the poor Africans, that they also may enjoy the benefits, advantages, and pleasures of knowledge and civilization! Oh! that they would consider and be wise, and rise up like the prodigal son, and say, 'I will arise and go to my Father, and will say unto him, Father, I have sinned against heaven and before thee, and am no more worthy to be called thy son; make me as one of thy hired servants.' And God, our merciful Father, will in no wise cast us out; but He will, instead of servants, make us as His dear children. I have had conversations with many intelligent, high-minded Christian people in England, and they all say that the improvement of the white man is derived from nothing but the Word of God. Africa, I hope, will not cast away this most sacred, precious Word, which is now being preached amongst them in very many places by white men. In some places it has been preached for fifty years, in others forty, thirty, twenty, and ten years, and in all it has produced some precious fruit. Oh! may the knowledge of the Lord spread over

Africa as the waters cover the great deep! Then shall Africa find out her great wealth and riches, – then will the earth yield her increase, and God, even our God, shall bless us.

> 'Come home, come home, you are weary at heart;
> For the way has been dark, and so lonely and wild;
> Oh! prodigal child, come home, oh! come home!
>
> Come home, come home, oh! come home!
>
> 'Come home, come home from the sorrow and blame;
> From the sin and the shame, and the tempter that smiled;
> Oh! prodigal child, come home, oh! come home!'

Africa is rising – she is lifting up her head, and the light is spreading. Not many years back, and but few Africans came to Europe, and those who did were generally from Sierra Leone and connected with the government. But now native African traders and their sons from far away up the coast come on their own business; and the kindness shown to them is so great that they are filled with pleasure and gratitude. They are taken to see anything that is useful or profitable, and they are improved and not spoiled. When they return to their friends and neighbours, they have very much to say, and are listened to with respect and confidence. Then their people are proud and pleased that the English have respected them; and they are far more ready to accept English ways and customs. And thus, little by little, Africa will be changed, as England was changed; for she too has come out of the darkness into God's marvellous light.

(34–8)

e. The Sights of London

As I passed along the streets, I noticed the people looking at me very earnestly. The small boys especially would stand and stare, and would sometimes call out to me, 'Halloa! blacky, can't you wash your face before you come out in the morning, and make it white?' My companion kindly said, 'You must not take notice of them, because they do not know any better.'

The next morning, my kind friend came again for me at my lodgings, and we went to see the Thames embankment, a long, strong wall built alongside the river. We there saw Cleopatra's

Needle, a long upright monument made of marble, and lately brought from Egypt. We then went into the Houses of Parliament, but the members were not there; and we crossed the road and went into Westminster Abbey, which is a grand Church, where they bury the Kings and Queens and all the great men of England. Their monuments are all round on the walls; and are very interesting. We also visited Buckingham Palace, one of the residences of the Queen; and Marlborough House, the residence of the Prince of Wales; and closed a heavy day's work by going to Madame Tussaud's wax-work exhibition. All the figures were dressed up like living men and women. The following day was entirely spent in the Crystal Palace, a very large collection of buildings all covered in by glass roofs. The inside is full of wonders; so many that I am bewildered when I think of them, and I really cannot describe them. There were all kinds of machines working away as if they were in a factory. I stayed all the day looking first at one thing and then another, and yet they said I had not seen half of what there was in. At nine o'clock we all went outside of the building to see the fireworks, which appeared to me very curious, grand, and frightful. Altogether I was eight days in London, and every day I was out seeing some grand thing, until I got as tired as if I had been on a long, weary journey.

London is a very great place; I thought far too big and confusing, and I would not like to stay there. I was glad, therefore, to come back to Liverpool and be quiet.

My friends in Liverpool are very kind to me, and often ask me to their private houses. I went with one friend, and he introduced me to his family, one little boy and two girls. During the evening, one of the little girls, about six years of age, came and said to me, 'Mr. Ocansey, I wish when you go back to Africa that you would send your little black boy here, and then he could carry my books to school for me.' The father said, 'Mary, my love, what are saying? Suppose I give you to Mr. Ocansey, and he will take you to Africa, and then you will have to carry the books for the black boy?' She looked round smart, and said, 'But I shall not go to Africa, the sun will make me a black girl, and you said just now that they have no good schools in Africa.'

On another occasion, as I was going with a friend to his home, we had to go down a street leading to the docks, when a poor white boy came and ran along with us, and sometimes before us, begging for a penny. He looked so beseechingly, and begged so strongly, that I said to him, 'What is it you want?' He said, 'A penny, please!' And I was just going to give him one when my friend said, 'No! do not do it; you encourage begging, and we want to put it down; for no one in England need beg in the street if they are honest and willing to work.' But the boy still followed us, and he looked so miserable that I gave him a penny, and then he left us with his thanks.

My friend now explained to me that every man who lives in a house in England is taxed every year to keep the poor, and the sick, and the cripples in a large house called a work-house, and that when that is too full they give 1s., 2s. or 3s. or more per week to the poor people to keep them in their own houses. And he said they that follow you and beg are idle and very bad, and ought not to be helped, for they spend it in strong drink, and the parents of those ragged children are somewhere near, and take the money from them.

(42–5)

f. More Liverpool Children

A few days after I had been in Liverpool, and was walking down the streets, a small boy ran up to me, and touched his cap to salute me. I thought, perhaps, he knew me. He then pointed down to my boots, and I looked down too, for I began to be uneasy, thinking there was something wrong with my feet; but the boy continued touching his cap and pointing to my boots, and crying out 'Shine, sir!' 'Shine, sir; only a penny!' Then I saw he had blacking and brushes, and a little stand to rest the foot on; and he wanted to earn a penny by blacking my boots!

In the afternoons, and evenings especially, quite a large number of small boys and girls are in the streets selling newspapers. And they are very quick, and watch every person going up or down the street to see if they will buy one. Now I like the newspaper. It is a luxury to me as it is to the white man. It is very cheap, and contains much information from all parts, and about many things. Then I thought I would buy one, and I put my hand in my pocket to seek if I had a copper. Instantly the boys and girls detected my intention, and half-a-dozen came bounding towards me, and thrusting their papers at me, said, 'Please buy from me!' 'Please take mine; I saw you first!' and I could hardly get away from them.

(p. 52)

g. *An Outdoor Service: Abraham*

On Sunday afternoon, July 17th, I was asked along with Mr. Jacobson, to attend a preaching service in the open-air. It was said that it was an old English custom to preach in the open-air, and that it was greatly prized by many, but that other people did not care for it. 'But if you come you will see many English people who do not attend church or chapel, but who have got into bad ways and drink too much. Still, the gospel is for them, and they ought to hear it, and if they will not come to us we must go to them. And besides, we want you to see the dark side of English life as well as the bright.' So I went, and was much pleased with the earnest addresses that were given. There were, I thought, nearly 1,000 persons standing about Gill-street market, and they listened very attentively, and sang some of the hymns. But I saw they were not like the regular chapel-people, some of the men who lived near came out without their coats or hats on, smoking their pipes; and there were many women with babies, but no Sunday clothes on, and I saw many of them wipe the tears from their eyes as they listened to the speakers.

There was a coloured man there, who seemed to be well known by every one, and especially by the small boys who made very free with him, calling him 'Abraham.' Seeing us present, he looked quite pleased, and came smiling up to us, and said that he came from New York, America, and that his people (the coloured people) have fine chapels there. He wanted to have a great deal of talk, but I did not feel towards him, for as I looked at his dirty dress and his face, I thought 'you do not live a good life.' I asked about him after the service, and they told me he was a 'knocker-up,' and they explained it by saying that he lives by going out very early every morning and knocking loudly at the doors of people who have to get up and go to their business, and they pay him so much per week. After the service we went for tea to the house of that mother to all black boys, Mrs. Looney, and there were many friends with us. After tea they were very anxious for me and Mr. Jacobson to sing together, so he played the piano, and we sang a hymn in English, and then I played, and we sang a hymn in our native language. Then the friends all sang, and we had a most enjoyable time.

Although sight-seeing was extremely interesting and instructive to me, I always felt some sensation of the miserable business that had brought me to England. There were times when this depression of feeling came over me like a thick, black cloud, and I could not raise myself above it. I would not come down into the city because I felt I could not mix up in any society with any pleasure. So I remained all day in my lodgings, and very long days and nights they were. And to be true and faithful, I must confess I began to be home-sick, and impatient of every hour's delay that separated me from my home and friends. And what had I to expect from this wretched trial? There was no money to recover. In some foolish or mysterious way, Hickson had either spent or lost all our money, and now our only consolation was that we should uphold the power of the law, and punish a dishonest, fraudulent man. However, I was glad the time was drawing near when we should be done with it, and having come to and known the bitter end, we might start afresh, and endeavour to regain our lost ground in the great battle of life.

(56–8)

18

EDWARD WILMOT BLYDEN

born St Thomas 1832, died Sierra Leone 1912

From West Africa to Palestine

1873

Christianity, Islam and the Negro Race

1887

The story of E. W. Blyden is one of extraordinary achievements: born to humble parents on a Danish Caribbean island, spending his schooldays as a part time apprentice tailor, he was to found newspapers, hold the Chair of Classics and later the Presidency of the University of Liberia, and hold the offices of Director of Mohammedan Education in Sierra Leone, and in Liberia, Secretary of State, Minister of the Interior, and Ambassador to the English Court. He wrote extensively in leading journals, and published many books and essays on African political, religious and racial issues, from two of which we include extracts here.

Yet for all this, his thought remained in certain ways seriously flawed. At his best he is witty, and controlled even in irritation and anger, and in the midst of his enthusiasms he can retain a sense of amused proportion, as the episodes of the mail-boat and the Pyramids demonstrate. But his love of Africa could deteriorate into an alternative racist preoccupation with purity of blood, and a venomous hatred of mulattos. Being received in New York 'by the men of colour [Frederick Douglass among them] ... and others of the mongrel tribe ... they seemed to me as light and empty as men professing to lead a race could be.' So he turns gratefully to R. R. Eliot, 'a pure negro' (see Holden, *Blyden of Liberia*, 501).

He can also indulge in both deliberate falsification and flights of sentimental fancy, such as those of extract 3 below, describing the shortcomings of European attempts to colonize Africa and proposing Black American resettlement. In the middle of this we read of 'The King of the Belgians, in his philanthropic and commercial zeal for the opening and

208

colonizing of Africa' (we know from Blyden's letters that he was aware of the vicious exploitation that was taking place in the Congo), and at the end we are offered a vision of Africa that owes more to the feebler, sentimental side of the Euro-American pastoral tradition than to African life. Asserting the purity and beauty of native African tradition, he can yet write of Africans of the interior, that 'People in a state of barbarism in which the Pagan tribes are usually found, have no proper conception of humanity and its capacities', (*Christianity, Islam* etc. 176) His enthusiasm for Islam can lead him to extremes on the representation of the African in art. He does not present a reasoned case for the Islamic rejection of representational art, but argues that the representation of the Negro is not possible in painting and sculpture, which is patently false.

> Happily for the development of the Negro in Africa ...
> No art can represent him. The 'rich black and richer bronze' of his complexion has never yet been reproduced in marble or on canvas; neither brush nor chisel can give his peculiar expression. Any representation of him must be untrue to Nature.   (ibid. 330)

Like Horton, Blyden had no fondness for energetic dancing, so, in an age which was to have its doubts even about the waltz and the polka, the extravagances of African dancing were unlikely to escape his axe:

> The love of noisy terpsichorean performances, so notice-able in Pagan communities, disappears as the people come under the influence of Mohammedanism. It is not a fact that 'when the sun goes down, all Africa dances', but it might be a fact if it were not for the influence of Islam. Those who would once have sought pleasure in the excitement of the tom-tom, now repair five times a day to the mosque.   (ibid. 6)

In the third extract, the passage from *Christianity, Islam and the Negro Race*, he actually uses one of the common arguments of the racists he is opposing, when he cruelly and snobbishly insists that the slaves were an inferior kind of African anyway – 'nearly all the forty millions who have been brought away – belonged to the servile or criminal classes. Only here and there, by the accident of war, or the misfortunes of politics, was a leading African brought away.'

But whilst it is important to acknowledge these shortcom-ings, it would be unjust not to recognise too the positive impact of Blyden on the thought and feeling of black people. Christopher Fyfe, in his introduction to the 1967 reprint of *Christianity, Islam and the Negro Race*, writes of Blyden's achievement and the importance of his influence in his own time and since, for instance, that which he has had upon the followers of Marcus Garvey, Elijah Muhammad and the

Rastafarians, as well as the founders of West African political independence:

> He, therefore, saw the peoples of Africa not just as Africans, but as members of a dispersed Negro race inhabiting both sides of the Atlantic ... Hence he gave American Negroes a new vision of themselves in relation to their ancestral home. He preached an inner identity with the peoples of Africa – all members of one great Negro race. Even those of them who might remain unconvinced by his theories, could scarcely remain unmoved by the words of a man who wrote 'the political history of the United States is the history of the Negro' (*Christianity, Islam* etc., 119) and insisted that the word 'Negro' be always written with a capital letter (9, note 12).
>
> Africans too were given a new vision of themselves as part of a wider identity than they had hitherto perceived. At a period when the educated inhabitants of the British West African Colonies were becoming conscious of their own achievements and looking forward to self-government, he made them aware of their affinities not only with transatlantic Negroes but with the inhabitants of the vast continent inland. Thus Blyden can be seen as a forerunner of the Pan-African movement.

(xii)

The texts are taken from the 1873 Freetown edition of *From West Africa to Palestine* and the 1967 Edinburgh University Press reprint of *Christianity, Islam and the Negro Race*. For Holden, *Blyden of Liberia*, referred to above, see bibliography.

a. *The Mail-Boat from* From West Africa to Palestine

On the afternoon of Sunday, May 20th, during a drenching rain, I embarked, in company with a large number of passengers, on board the English mail steamer *Lagos*, Captain Croft, homeward bound. The violence of the shower furnished no excuse to the captain, as many hoped it would, to defer his hour of sailing. His first and last signal guns were fired during the heaviest portions of the shower, the water rushing in torrents through the streets. The passengers were therefore obliged hurriedly to take leave of their friends, whose grief at their departure was mingled with the utmost indignation at the rigid and, as it appeared to them, uncalled for punctuality of the captain, imposing upon several invalids the necessity of encountering such inclement weather.

The *Lagos*, then on her first voyage, was the latest improvement of the Royal Mail African Steamship Company. This company, established not many years ago, began at first with very small and inferior boats, but as it grew in resources by superseding, to a great extent, sail vessels in the carrying trade, and by developing a more extensive commerce, it has gradually improved the character and class of its ships. And at this moment it has grown in wealth and power, and, despite the active competition of another line, it yet continues to advance. But, notwithstanding the vast commercial developments, the astounding quantity of produce taken from the coast by every steamer, the Royal Mail Company still retains its device and motto, which, if they were ever appropriate, have now lost their force and significance. The motto of *Spero meliora* – 'I hope for better things' – may always be appropriate on account of the insatiable desire of having more which is characteristic of man; but the figure of Commerce drawing aside a curtain and revealing a 'few melons and small potatoes,' while an African on bended knees is entreating patronage, has entirely lost its truthfulness and significance, and misrepresents the actual facts.

On this occasion the *Lagos* had a goodly number of passengers from various parts of the coast, many of whom seemed to take a senseless delight in casting slurs and insinuations on the African passengers. One of these scoffing passengers, I regret to state, was a professed missionary. He had been on the coast for two years; had been first in connection with one denomination, had left it, and was, at the time I had the misfortune to make his acquaintance, enjoying the confidence of another. He informed me that he was retiring in disgust from the field, regarding the natives as incorrigible. He had a great deal to say of the 'hopeless inferiority' of the negro, and was particularly vehement in his denunciations of the Africans of Sierra Leone. He failed, however, to impress me with his own superiority, which I did not recognise half so distinctly as I did his absolute want of good-breeding, his immense vanity and self-conceit, and his marvellous unsuitableness for the work to which he had been appointed on the coast, and in which he had made no movement so important, prudent, and beneficial as when he removed his baggage and his person from the mission premises to the steamer homeward bound, with the resolution never to return.

All this talk, however, about African inferiority and about the sense of repulsion and radical antagonism experienced by Euro-

peans, growing out of diversity in race, is the most stupendous
nonsense and flimsy pretence, especially considering the character
and habits of the men who generally indulge in such talk. Every one
knows how, at certain times, and under certain circumstances, their
utter antipathy is abated and their radical estrangement is relaxed
even into the utmost intimacy and the closest affection. From such
men, whose work on the coast is the demoralisation of the people, it
is natural that abuse of them should come; but it is melancholy and
mortifying in the extreme when such abuse proceeds from the lips
of a professed missionary.

This man is a type of class of 'false brethren' who come to the
coast of Africa, and who, having not the spirit of their Master, do
more harm than even the thoughtless and unscrupulous trader; for
the latter, making no pretension to philanthropy, carries on *con
amore* his work of demoralisation. Under garb of deep interest in
the cause which they profess to have espoused, the former carry up
an evil report of the land, and paralyse the hands of those at home
who, in true faith and patience, are labouring to send the gospel to
every creature. They find it very convenient to roll from their own
shoulders all their failures and shortcomings upon the scenes and
circumstances of their labour. Their own brethren dread them, and
wordly men despise them. They belong to Dante's despicable herd –

> – 'la setta dei cattivi,
> A Dio spiacenti ed a nemici sui.'

> [– 'the gang of scoundrels
> enemies of God and hateful to Him.'
> Dante, *Inferno* 3, 61–2]

I was put into a large cabin, having accommodations for seven,
with four other African passengers, I suppose on the principle – in
the mind of the purser, or whoever had the assignment of berths –
that 'birds of a feather flock together.' But does it always follow
that, because men wear the same external hue, they are necessarily
'birds of a feather?' On this occasion, however, I think no one was
particularly displeased with the company in which it was his lot to
travel. Of the four who started with me from Sierra Leone one
remained at the Gambia; of the others, two were merchants going to
England for the purpose of enlarging their operations; the third was

an artist who, in the practice of his profession at Sierra Leone, had acquired, within a brief period, sufficient means to enable him to visit Europe in order to perfect his acquaintance with his art, and to add to his stock of working materials. I think that, on the whole, we were the most happy and self-dependent group on the steamer – having everything in our own room necessary for recreation, amusement, and instruction. Nothing in the shape of wit, repartee, exciting stories, music, reading, courtesy, was wanting. And on account of the consequent attractiveness of our room, several of the other passengers were often drawn thither. Ours was literally a *drawing*-room: we welcomed all whom we considered agreeable. Especially were we always glad to admit a Spanish gentleman, an official from Fernando Po on his way to Spain, who could not speak a word of English, but who seemed to like our company because there was one of our number with whom he could converse in his own language. Don Ramon contributed not a little to our amusement by his power of delicious song; and another gentleman from Canada, who called in from time to time, and whom we took to be a 'half-German,' was skilled on the concertina. The whole voyage thus passed pleasantly away.

(26–30)

b. *The Pyramids from* From West Africa to Palestine

On the morning of the 11th of July, at half-past four o'clock, under the guidance of a young Copt named Ibrahim, I set out for the pyramids. Owing to considerable delay in procuring a boat to cross the Nile – for the pyramids are on the other side of the river from Cairo – we did not reach our destination until eleven o'clock, under a broiling sun.

This journey will long be remembered by me, and will ever be the object of delightful reminiscences. I felt as if I were in an entirely new world. My thoughts were partly of the remote past, but mostly of the immediate future. When crossing the river, an island was pointed out to me as the spot where tradition says Moses was concealed by his mother. My interest was intense.

Half an half after crossing the river, we caught a view of the pyramids in the distance. Here was opened to me a wide field of contemplation, and my imagination was complete 'master of the situation.' Though we were in an exposed plain, and my companion complained of the intense heat, I did not notice it, so eager was I to gain the pyramids, which seemed further and further to recede the longer we rode towards them. We saw them for three hours before we came up to them.

Just before reaching the pyramids we passed a small village of Arabs, who make their living, for the most part, by assisting travellers to 'do' the pyramids. About a dozen of them rushed out as, they saw us approaching, with goblets of water, pitchers of coffee, candles, and matches, and engraving knives. The water was very acceptable. I looked at the other articles, and wondered what could be the object of them.

The pyramids stand apparently on a hill of sand, on the borders of the Libyan desert. We had to ascend a considerable elevation – about 130 feet – before getting to the pyramid of Cheops. In the side of this apparent hill of sand, extending from the pyramids of Ghizeh to the smaller pyramids of Abusir and Sakarah, about two miles, are excavated tombs. The pyramids are at the extremities of an immense city of the dead, they themselves forming the imperishable tombs of the mighty monarchs who constructed them.

On reaching the base of the great pyramid I tried to find the shady side, but it was impossible to find any shade. On the north side there were several large stones, taken out at the base – leaving huge spaces. Into one of these Ibrahim, myself, and our donkeys entered and sheltered ourselves. The Arabs crowded about us, and kept asking question after question, suggesting the pleasure we should enjoy in ascending to the top, and the advantage to be reaped by visiting the interior. But I paid very little attention to them. They addressed me in broken English, French, and Italian. Other thoughts were crowding my mind. I thought of the continuous fatigue I had undergone, without eating anything, sustained only by the object I expected to attain in front, viz., a close inspection of the pyramids. And now that I had gained my point, I could not help feeling that my effort was, after all, but a forcible type of our experience in one-half of the pursuits we follow through life. My enchanting dreams and fancies left me completely as, heated and weary and hungry, I sat down to rest. How speedily the most cursory experience of the reality often levels to the dust all the mountains built up by the imagination ...

After recovering myself by about an hour's rest, I suffered the Arabs to persuade me to ascend the great pyramid (Cheops). Three assisted me; one taking hold of each hand, and one supporting me from behind. Before reaching one-third of the way, however, I gave out, changed my mind, and refused to ascend those dizzy heights. The Arabs clung to me, and insisted that I should go up. I could pacify them only by promising to allow them to take me to the interior – preferring then to examine the interior a little more closely from a less elevated and commanding, but to me a more comfortable, position.

After gazing in amazement at the outside, I made up my mind, in consultation with Ibrahim as to the safety of the enterprise, to visit the central hall in the interior. Had I known, however, that the performance required so much nerve and physical strength as I found out during the experiment, I should not have ventured. The entrance is firstly by a very steep and narrow passage, paved with immense stones, which have become dangerously slippery by centuries of use. There are small notches for the toes of those who would achieve the enterprise of entering, distant from each other about four or five feet, showing that they were intended for very tall men who wore no shoes. The modern traveller is obliged to make Hiawathan strides to get the toe of his boot into one of these notches, which are also wearing smooth, so as to make the hold which he gets exceedingly precarious. But for the help of these half-naked, shoeless, and sure-footed Arabs, it would be impossible for Western pilgrims generally to accomplish the feat of visiting the interior. Before entering, the Arabs lighted two candles – an operation which, I confess, somewhat staggered me, as it gave me the idea of sepulchral gloom and ghastliness. I had supposed that the interior of the pyramids was lighted in some way, though I had not stopped to think how. As we had to go down sideways, two attended me, one holding my left hand, and the other my right, so that if one slipped the other would be a support. If we had all slipped at once, it is difficult to imagine what would have been the result. The lighted candles were carried in advance.

In about half an hour, after descending and ascending difficult places, we gained the centre. The feeling in going up to the centre of a pyramid is akin to that which one experiences when ascending a very high hill. When we had accomplished the feat of reaching the centre, the Arabs themselves, who are not unaccustomed to the enterprise, seemed to think it a wonderful achievement, for they burst out into simultaneous and boisterous hurrahs. The floor of the hall was one huge stone. On the sides were engraved the names of visitors who had been there centuries ago. But there were very few names: comparatively few travellers, it would seem, go into the pyramids. In the centre of the hall stands the large porphyry coffer in which the embalmed bodies of the kings were deposited – evidently too large to pass through the narrow passages by which we had entered. How was it brought to this place? The Arabs said it was put there while the pyramid was building . . .

While standing in the central hall of the pyramid I thought of the lines of Teage, the Liberian poet, when urging his countrymen to noble deeds –

> From the pyramidal hall,
> From Karnac's sculptured wall,
> From Thebes they loudly call –
> Retake your fame.

This, thought I, is the work of my African progenitors. Teage was right; they had fame, and their descendants should strive, by nobler deeds, to 'retake' it. Feelings came over me far different from those which I have felt when looking at the mighty works of European genius. I felt that I had a peculiar 'heritage in the Great Pyramid' – built before the tribes of man had been so generally scattered, and therefore, before they had acquired their different geographical characteristics, but built by that branch of the descendants of Noah, the enterprising sons of Ham, from whom I am descended. The blood seemed to flow faster in my veins. I seemed to hear the echo of those illustrious Africans. I seemed to feel the impulse from those stirring characters who sent civilisation into Greece – the teachers of the fathers of poetry, history, and mathematics – Homer, Herodotus, and Euclid . . . I felt lifted out of the commonplace grandeur of modern times; and, could my voice have reached every African in the world, I would have earnestly addressed him in the language of Hilary Teage –

> Retake your fame!

But I must return from my long digression – which my countrymen, I am sure, will forgive, for the honour of the race -- to the interior of the pyramids, looking at which brought on the train of thought which I have indulged.

The heat was not so great within the pyramid as might at first be supposed; it seems to be ventilated from some quarter. Before the Arabs would consent to guide us out they insisted on receiving *bakhshish* – a present, corresponding to *dash* among the aborigines of West Africa. We had to promise them solemnly and earnestly that on gaining the open air we would satisfy all their desires. Had they left us, as they pretended to be about to do, it would have been utterly impossible for us to get out; and the idea of stumbling in the darkness, rolling down slippery places, and falling into deep holes, was harassingly frightful. We were considerably relieved therefore, when they accepted our pledge, and, taking us upon their shoulders, carefully carried us out. And as soon as I breathed once more the pure air I felt how appropriately the words might be written over the narrow entrance, which Dante says he saw inscribed over the gates of everlasting woe: –

Lasciate ogni speranza voi ch'entrate.

['Give up all hope, you who enter.]

On reaching the opening the Arabs sold us coffee, in very small cups, which considerably refreshed us. I felt that my perilous adventure had given me the right of inscribing my name among the hundreds which I saw engraved over and on each side of the entrance, bearing dates as early as the sixteenth century. Borrowing, or rather hiring, for I paid him a shilling for the use of it, an engraving knife from one of the Arabs, I engraved, not far from a name dated 1685, the word LIBERIA, with my name and the date – July 11th, 1866 – immediately under it. There is a tolerable degree of certainty, therefore, that the name at least of that little Republic will go down to posterity.

(95–112)

c. *From* Christianity, Islam and the Negro Race

Africa may yet prove to be the spiritual conservatory of the world. Just as in past times, Egypt proved the stronghold of Christianity after Jerusalem fell, and just as the noblest and greatest of the Fathers of the Christian Church came out of Egypt, so it may be, when the civilized nations, in consequence of their wonderful material development, shall have had their spiritual preceptions darkened and their spiritual susceptibilities blunted through the agency of a captivating and absorbing materialism, it may be, that they may have to resort to Africa to recover some of the simple elements of faith; for the promise of that land is that she shall stretch forth her hands unto God.

And see the wisdom and justice of God. While the Africans have been away rendering service their country has been kept for them. It is a very insignificant portion of that continent, after all, that foreigners have been permitted to occupy. Take any good map of Africa, and you will see that it is blank everywhere almost down to the sea. Senegambia, that important country north of the equator, has been much travelled over, and yet it is only on the coast and in spots here and there that it is occupied by Europeans. Going down along the west coast, we find the French Colonies of Senegal and Goree, the British settlements at the Gambia, Sierra Leone, the Gold Coast and Lagos, the French colony of Gaboon, the Spanish island of Fernando Po, and the Portuguese colony of Loanda. The most important parts of the coast are still in the hands of the aborigines; and civilized and Christian Negroes from the United States occupy six hundred miles of the choicest territory in Africa, called the Republic of Liberia. All travellers along the Coast pronounce the region of country included within the limits of Liberia, as the most fertile and wealthy along the entire coast, and commanding a back country of untold resources. Europeans tried for centuries to get a foothold in that territory; but the natives would never consent to their settlement in it, while they gladly welcomed their brethren returning from exile in this country.

The exiled Negro, then, has a home in Africa. Africa is his, if he will. He may ignore it. He may consider that he is divested of any right to it; but this will not alter his relations to that country, or impair the integrity of his title. He may be content to fight against the fearful odds in this country; but he is the proprietor of a vast domain. He is entitled to a whole continent by his constitution and antecedents. Those who refuse, at the present moment, to avail themselves of their inheritance think they do so because they believe that they are progressing in this country. There has, no doubt, been progress in many respects in their condition here. I would not, for one moment, say anything that would cast a shadow upon their hopes, or blight, in the slightest degree, their anticipations. I could wish that they might realize to the fullest extent their loftiest aspirations. It is indeed impossible not to sympathize with the intelligent Negro, whose imagination, kindled by the prospects and possibilities of this great country, the land of his birth, makes him desire to remain and share in its future struggles and future glories. But he still suffers from many drawbacks. The stranger visiting this land and going among its coloured inhabitants, and reading their newspapers, still hears the wail of slavery. The wail of physical suffering has been exchanged for the groans of an intellectual, social, and ecclesiastical ostracism. Not long since the touching appeal of a coloured man, almost in *forma pauperis*, before a great ecclesiastical assembly for equal rights in the Church, was wafted over the country, and sent its thrilling tones into many a heart, but yet the only response has been the reverberation of the echo. And who cannot understand the meaning of the hesitancy on the part of the powers that be to grant the appeal? 'He who runs may read'.

As a result of their freedom and enlarged education, the descendants of Africa in this country are beginning to feel themselves straitened. They are beginning to feel that only in Africa will they find the sphere of their true activity. And it is a significant fact that this impulse is coming from the Southern States. *There* is the great mass of the race; and there their instincts are less impaired by the infusion of alien blood and by hostile climatic influences. There we find the Negro in the almost unimpaired integrity of his race susceptibility, and he is by an uncontrollable impulse feeling after a congenial atmosphere which his nature tells him he can find only in Africa, *And he is going to Africa.*

As long as he remains in this country, he is hampered both in mind and body. He can conceive of no radiance, no beauty, no inspiration in what are ignorantly called 'the Wilds of Africa'. The society in which he lives in the lands of his exile he supposes, from knowing no other, to be the normal condition of man, and fancies that he will suffer it he leaves it. But when he gets home he finds the atmosphere there a part of himself. He puts off the garment which has hampered his growth here, and he finds that he not only does not take cold, but has a chance for healthful development.

There is not a single Negro in the United States on the road to practical truth, so far as his race is concerned. He feels something in him, his instincts point to it, but he cannot act out what he feels. And when he has made up his mind to remain in America, he has also made up his mind to surrender his race integrity; for he sees no chance of its preservation. There is in him neither hope enough to excite the desire to preserve it, nor desire enough to encourage the hope of its preservation. But, in Africa, he casts off his trammels. His wings develop, and he soars into an atmosphere of exhaustless truth for him. There he becomes a righteous man; he casts off his fears and his doubts. There for him is perpetual health; there he returns to reason and faith. There he feels that nothing can happen to the race. There he is surrounded by millions of men, as far as he can see or hear, just like himself, and he is delivered from the constant dread which harasses him in this country, as to what is to become of the Negro. There the solicitude is in the opposite direction. There he fears for the white man, living in a climate hostile, and often fatal to him.

But there are two other facts, not, perhaps, generally known, to which I would like to call attention. The first is, that, notwithstanding the thousands and millions who, by violence and plunder, have been taken from Africa, she is as populous to-day as she ever was; and the other is, that Africa has never lost the better classes of her people. As a rule, those who were exported – nearly all the forty millions who have been brought away – belonged to the servile and criminal classes. Only here and there, by the accidents of war, or the misfortunes of politics, was a leading African brought away. Africa is often called the Niobe of the nations, in allusion to the fact that her children in such vast numbers have been torn from her bosom; but the analogy is not strictly accurate. The ancient fable tells that Niobe clung to her children with warding arms, while the envious deities shot child after child, daughters and fair sons, till the whole twelve were slain, and the mother, powerless to defend her offspring, herself became a stone. Now this is not the fact with Africa. The children who were torn from her bosom she could well spare. She has not been petrified with grief; she has not become a stone. She is as prolific to-day as in the days of yore. Her greenness and fertility are perennial. It was said of her in the past, and it may be said of her to-day, that she is ever bringing forth something new.

And she has not been entirely bereaved even of those who have been torn from her bosom. In all the countries of their exile, severe as the ordeal has been, they have been preserved. It might be said of them as of the Hebrews in Egypt, 'the more they afflicted them, the more they multiplied and grew'.

No; if we are to gather an analogy to Africa from ancient fable, the Sphinx supplies us with a truer symbol. The Sphinx was said to sit in the road side, and put riddles to every passenger. If the man could not answer, she swallowed him alive. If he could solve the riddle, the Sphinx was slain. Has not Africa been, through the ages, sitting on the highway of the world? There she is, south of Europe, with but a lake between, joined on to Asia, with the most frequented oceans on the east and west of her – accessible to all the races, and yet her secret is unknown. She has swallowed up her thousands. The Sphinx must solve her own riddle at last. The opening up of Africa is to be the work of Africans.

In the Providence of God, it seems that this great and glorious work is reserved for the Negro. Centuries of effort and centuries of failure demonstrate that white men cannot build up colonies there. If we look at the most recent maps of Africa, we see that large tracts have been explored: English, German, Belgian, French and American expeditions have lately described large portions of the continent; but every one must be struck by the enormous gaps that remain to be filled in – the vast portions which the foot of the white man has never trodden. With the exception of the countries south of Egypt, the great lake region, and the strip of country from east to west, containing the routes of Cameron and Stanley, and if we leave out the portion of North Central Africa explored by Barth – the country is still as unknown to foreigners as it has been throughout all history, from the days of Herodotus and Ptolemy to the present. Who knows anything of the mountains of the moon? of all that vast region which lies directly east of Liberia, as far as the Indian Ocean? What foreigner can tell anything of the interior of Bonny, or of Calabar? If we examine the Continent, from the extreme south, from Egypt to Kaffraria or the country of the Zulus, we see very little yet accomplished. The most successful effort yet made in colonizing Africa is in Liberia. This will be permanent, because the colonists are of the indigenous stock. There are six hundred miles of coast, and two hundred miles of breadth, rescued for civilization. I mean, in that extent of country, over a million of people are on the road to self-elevation. They come in contact with an atmosphere of growth.

Now the people who are producing these changes have a peculiar claim upon this country – for they went out from this nation and are carrying American institutions into that Continent. And this great country has peculiar facilities for the work of African civilization.

The nations of Europe are looking for anxious eyes to the 'Dark Continent', as they love to call it, probably for the purpose of kindling their religious zeal, or stimulating their commercial instincts. But not one of them has the opportunity of entering that Continent with the advantages of the United States. They cannot send their citizens there from Europe to colonize – they die. France is now aiming at taking possession, by railroads, of the trade of the Soudan, from Algeria and Senegal. But the success of the scheme, through European agency, is extremely problematical. The question has been mooted of transferring their Negro citizens from the West Indies – from Martinique and Guadaloupe – but they cannot spare them from those islands. England would like to transport to the countries of the Niger, and to the regions interior of Sierra Leone, civilized blacks from her colonies in the Western hemisphere; but to encourage such a movement would be to destroy Barbadoes, Jamaica and Antigua. The King of the Belgians, in his philanthropic and commercial zeal for the opening and colonizing of Africa, has no population available. The United States is the only country which, providentially, can do the work which the whole world now wants done. Entering on the West Coast, through Liberia, she may stretch a chain of colonies of her own citizens through the whole length of the Soudan, from the Niger to the Nile – from the Atlantic to the Indian Ocean.

> This country, said Dr Storrs, has thousands of liberated and Christianized Africans in it, just at the moment when that dark continent is suddenly opened to the access of the Gospel. God has been building here a power, for the glory of His name, and for His service in the earth. I see the stamp held in the hand, and the liquid wax lying before it; and I do not doubt that the purpose is to fix the impression on that wax from the engraved brass or stone. I see the men whom man has brought there, and whom God has converted, and before them those vast outstretching realms made ready for the truth; and I cannot doubt that His purpose is to fix by these men, upon those prepared lands, the inscription of the Gospel and the Cross! And it seems to me that in the end all men must feel this'.[1]

Some have already gone, the pioneers in this great work. Leaving the land of their birth, where they have laboured for generations, they have gone to brave the perils of another wilderness, to cut down forests, to clear away jungles, to make roads, to build towns, to cultivate farms and to teach regular industry to their less favoured brethren; and they ask you to follow these new settlements, as they push into the heart of the continent, with all the aids and appliances of your advanced civilization.

In visions of the future, I behold those beautiful hills – the banks of those charming streams, the verdant plains and flowery fields, the salubrious highlands in primæval innocence and glory, and those fertile districts watered everywhere as the garden of the Lord; I see them all taken possession of by the returning exiles from the West, trained for the work of re-building waste places under severe discipline and hard bondage. I see, too, their brethren hastening to welcome them from the slopes of the Niger, and from its lovely valleys – from many a sequestered nook, and from many a palmy plain – Mohammedans and Pagans, chiefs and people, all coming to catch something of the inspiration the exiles have brought – to share in the borrowed jewels they have imported, and to march back hand-in-hand with their returned brethren towards the sunrise for the regeneration of a continent. And under their united labours, I see the land rapidly reclaimed – raised from the slumber of ages and rescued from a stagnant barbarism; and then to the astonishment of the whole world, in a higher sense than has yet been witnessed, 'Ethiopia shall *suddenly* stretch out her hands unto God'.

(124–9)

Note

1. Discourse before the American Missionary Association, October 1879.

19

J. J. THOMAS
born Trinidad c.1840, died London 1889

Froudacity

1889

J. J. Thomas, born in poverty sometime around 1840 in Trinidad, ended up his life as the nation's best known intellectual of the 19th century. He was a largely self-taught man, with a talent for languages. He learnt French, Greek, Latin, Spanish and Creole and in 1869 published his first book, *The Theory and Practice of Creole Grammer*, which was well received by scholars of linguistics. He was invited to lecture in London and was elected a member of Britain's Philological Society. Thomas, who worked as a primary school teacher and then as a civil servant, was very active in promoting West Indian culture. He became a folklorist, collecting nature songs and proverbs. He was secretary of the *Trinidad Monthly*, a literary journal, and editor of the *Trinidad Review*. He organised the Trinidad Athenaeum, an organisation which held lectures, seminars and debates on literary and educational issues.

In 1888, Thomas visited England to study in the British Museum, his purpose being to write an enlarged version of his book on Creole grammer. In 1889, he published instead another book, *Froudacity*. He died that very year in London of tuberculosis. He was only forty-nine.

Froudacity was written very quickly, in response to J. A. Froude's *The English in the West Indies*, published in 1888. Froude was a distinguished British academic, Regius Professor of Modern History at the University of Oxford. His book is deeply hostile to black West-Indians, tainted with some of the worst examples of Victorian racism. It is a sturdy defence of Imperial rule:

> Under the rule of England, in these islands, the two millions of these brothers-in-law of ours are the most perfectly contented specimens of the human race to be found upon the planet ... If happiness be the satisfaction of every conscious desire, theirs is a condition that admits of no improvement: were they independent, they might

quarrel among themselves, and the weaker become the bondsmen of the stronger; under the beneficent despotism of the English Government, which knows no difference of colour and permits no oppression, they can sleep, lounge, and laugh away their lives as they please, fearing no danger.

Froude's views of the incapacity of black people, their indolence, stupidity, childishness, and so forth, is not mere eccentricity or harmless bigotry from an ageing professor: he is at all stages concerned with racial order. White people are to be in firm control. He despises 'the freedom in which the moderns take delight', promoting instead 'the sharp rule of the strong over the weak' (the word 'sharp' being a sinister understatement of the reality of beatings, hangings and shootings experienced by rebellious blacks. Less than twenty years before Froude's book, Governor Eyre had executed hundreds of black Jamaicans after the Morant Bay rebellion).

Thomas, though physically weak and in pain (he had been ill for several years, on and off) felt obliged to reply, so provoked was he by the ignorance of Froude's utterances. It was a David-and-Goliath contest, the humble, obscure school teacher from Trinidad taking on the mighty and influential Oxford Professor. The result was a triumphant win for the West Indian. *Froudacity* not only exposes gross factual errors in Froude's book, thereby casting doubt on the scholarly abilities of Froude as an historian, but does so in a prose, the elegance and polish of which surpasses that of the Oxford Professor (Froude was noted as a fine and stylish prose writer). In content as well as style, Thomas revealed himself to be a superior talent to Froude. As C. L. R. James puts it, Thomas possessed 'a mind and mentality, a social conception and an historial method, which were vastly superior to that of the highly educated and famous English historian and writer'.

Froudacity ranges over the history, politics, religion and culture of the West Indies, arguing with Froude at crucial points. The book reveals not just the cruelties endured by blacks at the hand of white planters and colonists, but their achievements over the centuries of slavery, their ambition to better their lives and their capacity for hard work. Perhaps the most subtle but devastating of Thomas' comments on Froude is the suggestion that the latter's sympathy for black women, (as against his contempt for black men) is a disguised sexual lust which is as seedy as any planter's. Froude says of the black women of Barbados that 'they were smartly dressed in white calico, scrupulously clean, and tricked out with ribbons and feathers: but their figures were so good, and they carried themselves so well and gracefully, that although they might make themselves absurd, they could not look vulgar.

Black Writers in Britain 1760–1890

Like the Greek and Etrusan women, they are trained from childhood to carry weights on their heads. They are thus perfectly upright, and plant their feet firmly and naturally on the ground. They might serve for sculptors' models ...'

Thomas expresses gratitude for this 'more than chivalrous appreciation of our womenkind', wishing that Froude had observed with like closeness and detail all other aspects of West Indian life. In other words, the Oxford Professor, apart from being a poor scholar, apart from being riddled with bias, is a bit of a dirty old man.

The text is taken from the first edition, London, 1889.

a. The Future of the African

Thus far we have dealt with the main questions raised by Mr. Froude on the lines of his own choosing; lines which demonstrate to the fullest how unsuited his capacity is for appreciating – still less grappling with – the political and social issues he has so confidently undertaken to determine. In vain have we sought throughout his bastard philosophising for any phrase giving promise of an adequate treatment of this important subject. We find paraded ostentatiously enough the doctrine that in the adjustment of human affairs the possession of a white skin should be the strongest recommendation. Wonder might fairly be felt that there is no suggestion of a corresponding advantage being accorded to the possession of a long nose or of auburn hair. Indeed, little or no attention that can be deemed serious is given to the interest of the Blacks, as a large and (out of Africa) no longer despicable section of the human family, in the great world-problems which are so visibly preparing and press for definitive solutions. The intra-African Negro is clearly powerless to struggle successfully against personal enslavement, annexation, or volunteer forcible 'protection' of his territory. What, we ask, will in the coming ages be the opinion and attitude of the extra-African millions – ten millions in the Western Hemisphere – dispersed so widely over the surface of the globe, apt apprentices in every conceivable department of civilised culture? Will these men remain for ever too poor, too isolated from one another for grand racial combinations? Or will the naturally opulent cradle of their people, too long a prey to violence and unholy greed, become at length the sacred watchword of a generation' willing and able to conquer or perish under its inspiration? Such large and interesting questions it was within the province and duty of a famous historian, laying confident claim to prophetic insight, not to propound alone, but also definitely to solve. The sacred power of forecast, however, has been confined to finical pronouncements regarding those for whose special benefit he has exercised it, and to childish insults of the Blacks whose doom must be sealed to secure the precious result which aimed at. In view of this ill-intentioned omission, we shall offer a few cursory remarks bearing on, but not attempting to answer, those grave inquiries concerning the African people. As in our humble opinion these are questions paramount to all the petty local issues finically dilated on by the confident prophet of *The Bow of Ulysses*, we will here briefly devote ourselves to its discussion.

Accepting the theory of human development propounded by our author, let us apply it to the African race. Except, of course, to intelligences having a share in the Councils of Eternity, there can be no attainable knowledge respecting the laws which regulate the growth and progress of civilisation among the races of the earth. That in the existence of the human family every age has been marked by its own essential characteristics with regard to manifestations of intellectual life, however circumscribed, is a proposition too self-evident to require more than the stating. But investigation beyond such evidence as we possess concerning the past – whether recorded by man himself in the written pages of history, or by the Creator on the tablets of nature – would be worse than futile. We see that in the past different races have successively come to the front, as prominent actors on the world's stage. The years of civilised development have dawned in turn on many sections of the human family, and the Anglo-Saxons, who now enjoy pre-eminence, got their turn only after Egypt, Assyria, Babylon, Greece, Rome, and others had successfully held the palm of supremacy. And since these mighty empires have all passed away, may we not then, if the past teaches aught, confidently expect that other racial hegemonies will arise in the future to keep up the ceaseless progression of temporal existence towards the existence that is eternal? What is it in the nature of things that will oust the African race from the right to participate, in times to come, in the high destinies that have been assigned in times past to so many races that have not been in anywise superior to us in the qualifications, physical, moral, and intellectual, that mark out a race for prominence amongst other races?

The normal composition of the typical Negro has the testimony of ages to its essential soundness and nobility. Physically, as an active labourer, he is capable of the most protracted exertion under climatic conditions the most exhausting. By the mere strain of his brawn and sinew he has converted waste tracts of earth into fertile regions of agricultural bountifulness. On the scenes of strife he has in his savage state been known to be indomitable save by the stress of irresistible forces, whether of men or of circumstances. Staunch in his friendship and tender towards the weak directly under his protection, the unvitiated African furnishes in himself the combination of native virtue which in the land of his exile was so prolific of good results for the welfare of the whole slave-class. But distracted at home by the sudden irruptions of skulking foes, he has been robbed, both intellectually and morally, of the immense advantage of Peace, which is the mother of Progress. Transplanted to alien climes, and through centuries of desolating trials, this irrepressible race has bated not one throb of its energy, nor one jot of its heart or hope. In modern times, after his expatriation into dismal bondage, both Britain and America have had occasion to see that even in the paralysing fetters of political and social degradation the right arm of the Ethiop can be a valuable auxiliary on the field of battle. Britain, in her conflict with France for supremacy in the West Indies, did not disdain the aid of the sable arms that struck together with those of Britons for the trophies that furnished the motives for those epic contests.

(179–181)

b. The Inadequacy of Froude

At this point I must pause to express on behalf of the entire coloured population of the West Indies our most heartfelt acknowledgements to Mr. C. Salmon for the luminous and effective vindication of us, in his volume on *West Indian Confederation*, against Mr. Froude's libels. The service thus rendered by Mr. Salmon possesses a double significance and value in my estimation. In the first place, as being the work of a European of high position, quite independent of us (wbo testifies concerning Negroes, not through having gazed at them from balconies, decks of steamers, or the seats of moving carriages, but from actual and long personal intercouse with them, which the internal evidence of his book plainly proves to have been as sympathetic as it was familiar), and, secondly, as the work of an individual entirely outside of our race, it has been gratefully accepted by myself as an incentive to self-help, on the same more formal and permanent lines, in a matter so important to the status which we can justly claim as a progressive, law-abiding, and self-respecting section of Her Majesty's liege subjects.

It behoves me now to say a few words respecting this book as a mere literary production.

Alexander Pope, who, next to Shakespeare and perhaps Butler, was the most copious contributor to the current stock of English maxims, says:

'True ease in writing comes from Art, not Chance,
As those move easiest who have learnt to dance.'

A whole dozen years of bodily sickness and mental tribulation have not been conducive to that regularity of practice in composition which alone can ensure the 'true ease' spoken of by the poet; and therefore is it that my style leaves so much to be desired, and exhibits, perhaps, still more to be pardoned. Happily, a quarrel such as ours with the author of *The English in the West Indies* cannot be finally or even approximately settled on the score of superior literary competency, whether of aggressor or defender. I feel free to ignore whatever verdict might be grounded on a consideration so purely artificial. There ought to be enough, if not in these pages, at any rate in whatever else I have heretofore published, that should prove me not so hopelessly stupid and wanting in self-respect, as would be implied by my undertaking a contest in artistic phrase-weaving with one who, even among the foremost of his literary countrymen, is confessedly a master in that craft. The judges to whom I do submit our case are those Englishmen and others whose conscience blends with their judgement, and who determine such questions as this on their essential rightness which has claim to the first and decisive consideration. For much that is irregular in the arrangement and sequence of the subject-matter, some blame fairly attaches to our assailant. The erratic manner in which he launches his injurious statements against the hapless Blacks, even in the course of passages which no more led up to them than to any other section of mankind, is a very notable feature of his anti-Negro production. As he frequently repeats, very often with cynical aggravations, his charges and sinister prophecies against the sable objects of his aversion, I could see no other course open to me than to take him up on the points whereto I demurred, exactly how, when, and where I found them . . .

We come now to the ingenious and novel fashion in which Mr. Froude carries out his investigations among the black population, and to his dogmatic conclusions concerning them. He says:

'In Trinidad, as everywhere else, my own chief desire was to see the human inhabitants, to learn what they were doing, how they were living, and what they were thinking about, and this could best be done by drives about the town and neighbourhood.'

'Drives about the town and neighbourhood', indeed! To learn and be able to depict with faithful accuracy what people 'were doing, how they were living, and what they were thinking about' – all this being *best* done (domestic circumstances, nay, soul-workings and all!) through fleeting glimpses of shifting panoramas of intelligent human beings! What a bright notion! We have here the suggestion of a capacity too superhuman to be accepted on trust, especially when, as in this case, it is by implication self-arrogated. The modesty of this thaumaturgic traveller in confining the execution of his detailed scrutiny of a whole community to the moderate progression of some conventional vehicle, drawn by some conventional quadruped or the other, does injustice to powers which, if possessed at all, might have compassed the same achievement in the swifter transit of an express train, or, better still perhaps, from the empyrean elevation of a balloon! Yet is Mr. Froude confident that data professed to be thus collected would easily pass muster with the readers of his book! A confidence of this kind is abnormal, and illustrates, we think most fully, all the special characteristics of the man. With his passion for repeating, our author tells us in continuation of a strange rhapsody on Negro felicity:

'Once more, the earth does not contain any peasantry so well off, so well-cared for, as happy, so sleek and contented, as the sons and daughters of the emancipated slaves in the English West Indian Islands.'

Again:

'Under the rule of England, in these islands, the two millions of these brothers-in-law of ours are the most perfectly contented specimens of the human race to be found upon the planet . . . If happiness be the satisfaction of every conscious desire, theirs is a condition that admits of no improvement: were they independent, they might quarrel among themselves, and the weaker become the bondsmen of the stronger; under the beneficent despotism of the English Government, which knows no difference of colour and permits no oppression, they can sleep, lounge, and laugh away their lives as they please, fearing no danger,' etc.

Now, then, let us examine for a while this roseate picture of Arcadian blissfulness said to be enjoyed by British West Indian Negroes in general, and by the Negroes of Trinidad in particular. 'No distinction of colour' under the British rule, and, better still, absolute protection of the weaker against the stronger! This latter consummation especially, Mr. Froude tells us, has been happily secured 'under the beneficent despotism' of the Crown Colony system. However, let the above vague hyperboles be submitted to the test of practical experience, and the abstract government analysed in its concrete relations with the people.

(94–5)

c. Slavery and Empire

In favour of slavery, which has for so many centuries desolated the African family and blighted its every chance of indigenous progress – of slavery whose abolition our author so ostentatiously regrets – only one solitary permanent result, extending in every case over a natural human life, has been paraded by him as a respectable justification. At p. 246, speaking of Negroes met by him during a stroll which he took at Mandeville, Jamaica, he tells us:

'The people had black faces; but even they had shaped their manners in the old English models. The men touched their hats respectfully (as they eminently did not in Kingston and its environs). The women smiled and curtsied, and the children looked shy when once spoke to them. The name of slavery is a horror to us; but there must have been *something human and kindly* about it, too, when it left upon the character *the marks of courtesy and good breeding*'!

Alas for Africa and the sufferings of her desolated millions, in view of so light-hearted an assessment as this! Only think of the ages of outrage, misery, and slaughter – of the countless hecatombs that Mammon is hereby absolved from having directly exacted, since the suflicing expiatory outcome of it all has been only 'marks of courtesy and good breeding'! Marks that are displayed, forsooth, by the survivors of the ghastly experiences or by their descendants! And yet, granting the appreciable ethical value of the hat-touching, the smirking and curtseyings of those Blacks to persons whom they had no reason to suspect of unfriendliness, or whose white face they may in the white man's country have greeted with a civility perhaps only prudential, we fail to discover the necessity of the dreadful agency we have adverted to, for securing the results on manners which are so warmly commended. African explorers, from Mungo Park to Livingstone and Stanley, have all borne sufficient testimony to the world regarding the natural friendliness of the Negro in his ancestral home, when not under the influence of suspicion, anger, or dread.

It behoves us to repeat (for our detractor is a persistent repeater) that the cardinal dodge by which Mr. Froude and his few adherents expect to succeed in obtaining the reversal of the progress of the coloured population is by misrepresenting the elements, and their real attitude towards one another, of the sections composing the British West Indian communities. Everybody knows full well that Englishmen, Scotchmen, and Irishmen (who are not officials), as well as Germans, Spaniards, Italians, Portuguese, and other nation-alities, work in unbroken harmony and, more or less, prosper in these Islands. These are no cherishers of any vain hankering after a state of things in which men felt not the infamy of living not only on the unpaid labour, but at the expense of the sufferings, the blood, and even the life of their fellow-men. These men, honourable by instinct and of independent spirit, depend on their own resources for self-advancement in the world – on their capital either of money in their pockets or of serviceable brains in their heads, energy in their limbs, and on these alone, either singly or more or less in combination. These reputable specimens of manhood have created homes dear to them in these favoured climes; and they, at any rate, being on the very best terms with all sections of the community in which their lot is cast, have a common cause as fellow-sufferers under the *régime* of Mr. Froude's offical 'birds of passage'. The agitation in Trinidad tells its own tale. There is not a single black man – though there should have been many – among the leaders of the movement for Reform. Nevertheless the honourable and truth-ful author of *The English in the West Indies*, in order to invent a plausible pretext for his sinister labours of love on behalf of the poor pro-slavery survivals, and despite his knowledge that sturdy

Britons are at the head of the agitation, coolly tells the world that it
is a struggle to secure 'negro domination'.

(133–5)

d. Conclusions

Thanks to Lord Harris for introducing, and to Sir Arthur Gordon
for extending to the secondary stage, the public education of
Trinidad, there has been since Emancipation, that is, during the last
thirty-seven years, a more effective bringing together in public
schools of various grades, of children of all races and ranks. Rivals at
home, at school and college, in books as well as on the playground,
they have very frequently gone abroad together to learn the
professions they have selected. In this way there is an intercommunion between all the intelligent sections of the inhabitants, based on a
common training and the subtle sympathies usually generated in
enlightened breasts by intimate personal knowledge. In mixed
communities thus circumstanced, there is no possibility of main-
taining distinctions based on mere colour, as advocated by Mr.
Froude.

The following brief summary by the Rev P. H. Doughlin, Rector
of St Clement's, Trinidad, a brilliant star among the sons of Ham,
embodies this fact in language which, so far as it goes, is as
comprehensive as it is weighty:

'Who could, without seeming to insult the intelligence of men,
have predicted on the day of Emancipation that the Negroes
then released from the blight and withering influence of ten
generations of cruel bondage, so weakened and half-destroyed
– so denationalised and demoralised – so despoiled and naked,
would be in the position they are now? In spite of the proud,
supercilious, and dictatorial bearing of their teachers, in spite of
the hampering of unsympathetic, alien oversight, in spite of the
spirit of dependence and servility engendered by slavery, not
only have individual members of the race entered into all the
offices of dignity in Church and State, as subalterns – as hewers
of wood and drawers of water – but they have attained to the
very highest places. Here in the West Indies, and on the West
Coast of Africa, are to be found Surgeons of the Negro Race,
Solicitors, Barristers, Mayors, Councillors, Principals and
Proprietors of Newspapers, Archdeacons, Bishops, Judges,
and Authors – men who not only teach those immediately

around them, but also teach the world. Members of the race have even been entrusted with the administration of Governments. And it is not mere commonplace men that the Negro Race has produced. Not only have the British Universities thought them worthy of their honorary degrees and conferred them on them, but members of the race have won these University degrees. A few years back a full-blooded Negro took the highest degree Oxford has to give to a young man. The European world is looking with wonder and admiration at the progress made by the Negro Race – a progress unparalleled in the annals of the history of any race.'

To this we may add that in the domain of high literature the Blacks of the United States, for the twenty-five years of social emancipation, and despite the lingering obstructions of caste prejudice, have positively achieved wonders. Leaving aside the writings of men of such high calibre as F. Douglass, Dr. Hyland Garnet, Prof. Crummell, Prof. E. Blyden, Dr. Tanner, and others, it is gratifying to be able to chronicle the Ethiopic women of North America as moving shoulder to shoulder with the men in the highest spheres of literary activity. Among a brilliant band of these our sisters, conspicuous no less in poetry than in prose, we single out but a solitary name for the double purpose of preserving brevity and of giving in one embodiment the ideal Afro-American woman of letters. The allusion here can scarcely fail to point to Mrs. S. Harper. This lady's philosophical subtlety of reasoning on grave questions finds effective expression in a prose of singular precision and vigour. But it is as a poet that posterity will hail her in the coming ages of our Race. For pathos, depth of spiritual insight, and magical exercise of a rare power of self-utterance, it will hardly be questioned that she has surpassed every competitor among females – white or black – save and except Elizabeth Barrett Browning, with whom the gifted African stands on much the same plane of poetic excellence.

The above summary of our past vicissitudes and actual position shows that there is nothing in our political circumstances to occasion uneasiness. The miserable skin and race doctrine we have been discussing does not at all prefigure the destinies at all events of the West Indies, or determine the motives that will affect them. With the exception of those belonging to the Southern States of the Union, the vast body of African descendants now dispersed in

various countries of the Western Hemisphere are at sufficient peace
to begin occupying themselves, according to some fixed program-
me, about matters of racial importance. More than ten millions of
Africans are scattered over the wide area indicated, and possess
amongst them instances of mental and other qualifications which
render them remarkable among their fellow-men. But like the
essential parts of a complicated albeit perfect machine, these attain-
ments and qualifications so widely dispersed await, it is evident,
some potential agency to collect and adjust them into the vast
engine essential for executing the true purposes of the civilised
African Race. Already, especially since the late Emancipation
Jubilee, are signs manifest of a desire for intercommunion and
intercomprehension amongst the more distinguished of our people.
With intercourse and unity of purpose will be secured the means to
carry out the obvious duties which are sure to devolve upon us,
especially with reference to the cradle of our Race, which is most
probably destined to be the ultimate resting-place and headquarters
of millions of our posterity. Within the short time that we had to
compass all that we have achieved, there could not have arisen
opportunities for doing more than we have effected. Meanwhile our
present device is: 'Work, Hope, and Wait!'

Finally, it must be borne in mind that the abolition of physical
bondage did not by any means secure all the requisite conditions of
'a fair field and no favour' for the future career of the freedmen. The
remnant of Jacob, on their return from the Captivity, were compelled, whilst rebuilding their Temple, literally to labour with the
working tool in one hand and the sword for personal defence in the
other. Even so have the conditions, figuratively, presented themselves under which the Blacks have been obliged to rear the fabric of
self-elevation since 1838, whilst combating ceaselessly the obstacles
opposed to the realising of their legitimate aspirations. Mental and,
in many cases, material success has been gained, but the machinery
for accumulating and applying the means required for comprehensive racial enterprise is waiting on Providence, time, and circumstances for its establishment and successful working.

(191–4)

Select Bibliography

Texts

BLYDEN, Edward Wilmot, *Christianity, Islam and the Negro Race*, London 1887.

——, the same, with an introduction by C. Fyfe, Edinburgh UP 1967.

——, *From West Africa to Palestine*, Freetown 1873.

CUGOANO, Ottobah (John Stuart), *Thoughts and Sentiments on the Evil and Wicked Traffic of the Slavery and Commerce of the Human Species*, London 1787.

——, the same, in Colonial History Series, Dawsons of Pall Mall, London 1969, ed. Paul Edwards.

EQUIANO, Olaudah, *The Interesting Narrative of the Life of Olaudah Equiano, or Gustavus Vassa, the African*, 2 v., London 1789.

——, the same, ed. with an introduction by Paul Edwards, in Colonial History Series, Dawsons of Pall Mall, London 1969.

——, *Equiano's Travels*, ed. and abridged by Paul Edwards, Heinemann African Writers Series, London 1966.

——, *The Classic Slave Narratives*, New American Library, New York 1987, ed. Henry L. Gates Jr. (Leeds edn., 1814; also includes narratives by Frederick Douglass, Mary Prince, and Harriet Jacobs).

——, *The Life of Olaudah Equiano*, ed. and abridged by Paul Edwards, Longman African Classics Series, Longman, Harlow 1989.

GRONNIOSAW, Ukawsaw (James Albert), *A Narrative of the Most Remarkable Particulars of the Life of James Albert Ukawsaw Gronniosaw, An African Prince*, Bath n.d. [c. 1770] and many subsequent editions.

——, Reprinted in edition of London, 1840 in a collection of early narratives including Hammon (see below), by Kraus Reprint, Nendeln 1972.

HAMMON, Briton, *A Narrative of the Uncommon Sufferings and Surprising Deliverance of Briton Hammon, a Negro Man*, Boston 1760.

——, the same, Kraus Reprint, Nendeln 1972.

HORTON, James Beale Africanus, *West African Countries and Peoples*, London 1868.

——, the same, Edinburgh UP 1967.

——, the same, Kraus Reprint, Nendeln 1970.

JACOBS, Harriet (Linda Brent), *Incidents in the Life of a Slave Girl*, ed. L. Maria Child, Boston 1861.

——, the same, London 1862.

236

——, the same, see under Equiano in *The Classic Slave Narratives* (1987) ed. Gates above.

——, the same, ed. Jean Fagan Yellin, Cambridge, Harvard UP 1987.

——, the same, ed. William L. Andrews, *Six Women's Slave Narratives*, New York, Oxford UP 1988.

JEA, John, *The History and Sufferings of John Jea, the African Preacher*, Portsea n.d. (c. 1815).

PRINCE, Mary, *The History of Mary Prince, a West Indian Slave*, London and Edinburgh 1831.

——, the same, see under Equiano in *The Classic Slave Narratives*, ed. Gates above.

——, the same, ed. Moira Ferguson, with a Preface by Ziggi Alexander, Pandora Books, London 1987.

OCANSEY, John E., *African Trading: or the Trials of William Narh Ocansey*, Liverpool 1881.

——, the same, ed. Kwame Arhin, Ghana Academy Publications, Accra 1989.

QUAQUE, Philip, *Letters to the Secretary of the Society for the Propagation of the Gospel*, mss. in the Rhodes House Library, Oxford, C/AFR/W1.

SANCHO, Ignatius, *The Letters of the late Ignatius Sancho, An African to which are prefixed Memoirs of His Life by Joseph Jekyll, Esq., M.P.*, London 1782.

——, the same reprinted from the 5th edition of 1803, in the Black Heritage Library Collection, Books for Libraries Press, Freeport, New York 1971.

——, the same reprinted from the 5th edition of 1803, with a new introduction by Paul Edwards, in Colonial History Series, Dawsons of Pall Mall, 1969.

——, *Selected Letters of Ignatius Sancho*, ed. and introduced by Paul Edwards, in Early Black Writers Series, Edinburgh UP, to be published 1992.

SEACOLE, Mary, *The Wonderful Adventures of Mary Seacole in Many Lands*, London 1857.

——, the same, with an introduction by Ziggi Alexander, Falling Walls Press, Bristol 1984.

SIERRA LEONE SETTLERS, Letters mainly to Thomas Clarkson, manuscripts at the British Library, Clarkson Papers, Add. Ms. 41,262A and Ms. 41.263. Also the Public Record Office, London, CO 270/5, and the University of Illinois, Chicago.

——, the same, ed. and introduced by Christopher Fyfe, with an essay on the language of the letters by Charles Jones, in Early Black Writers Series, Edinburgh UP 1991.

THOMAS, J. J., *Froudacity*, London 1889.

WEDDERBURN, Robert, *Trial of Robert Wedderburn ... for Blasphemy*, ed. Erasmus Perkins, London 1820.

——, *The Horrors of Slavery*, London 1824.

——, *The Horrors of Slavery and other writings by Robert Wedderburn*, ed. and introduced by Iain McCalman, in Early Black Writers Series, Edinburgh UP 1991.

Historical and Critical Studies

ACHOLONU, Catherine O., *The Igbo Roots of Olaudah Equiano*, Owerri, Nigeria, AFA Publications 1989.

BARTELS, F. L., 'Philip Quaque of Cape Coast, 1742–1816', in *Transactions of the Gold Coast and Togoland Historical Society*, Achimota 1955, 153–177.

COSTANZO, Angelo, *Surprizing Narrative: Olaudah Equiano and the Beginnings of Black Autobiography*, New York and London, Greenwood Press 1987.

CURTIN, Philip ed., *Africa Remembered: Narratives of West Africans from the Era of the Slave Trade*, Madison, Univ. of Wisconsin Press 1967. (Includes extracts from and commentaries on Equiano by G. I. Jones, and on Quaque by Margaret Priestly.)

DABYDEEN, David ed., *The Black Presence in English Literature*, Manchester Univ. Press 1985.

——, *Hogarth's Blacks*, Manchester UP 1987.

DAVIS, Charles T. and GATES, Henry L. Jr. eds, *The Slave's Narrative*, Oxford and New York, Oxford UP 1985. (Includes essays by Edwards on Sancho, Equiano and Cugoano, and by Yellin on Jacobs.)

DUFFIELD, Ian and EDWARDS, Paul, 'Equiano's Turks and Christians: an Eighteenth Century African View of Islam', in *Journal of African Studies* 2, 4, Winter 1975–6, 533–44.

EDWARDS, Paul, and SHAW, Rosalind, 'The Invisible *Chi* in Equiano's *Interesting Narrative*', in *Journal of Religion in Africa*, XIX.2 (1989) 146–55.

EDWARDS, Paul and WALVIN, James, *Black Personalities in the Era of the Slave Trade*, London, Macmillan 1983. (Includes extracts from and comments on Sancho, Equiano, Cugoano, Hammon, Gronniosaw, Soubise and others.)

EDWARDS, Paul, ' "Master" and "Father" in *The Interesting Narrative*', in *Slavery and Abolition* 11.3 (September 1990), 217–27.

——, 'A Descriptive List of Manuscripts in the Cambridgeshire Record Office Relating to the Will of Gustavus Vassa (Olaudah Equiano)', in *Research in African Literatures* 20.3, Fall 1989, 473–80.

FRYER, Peter, *Staying Power: The History of Black People in Britain*, London, Pluto Press 1984. (Includes commentaries on Davidson, Wedderburn, Equiano, Sancho etc.)

FYFE, Christopher, *History of Sierra Leone*, Oxford UP 1962.

——, *Africanus Horton: West African Scientist and Patriot*, Oxford UP 1972.

GATES, Henry L. Jr., *The Signifying Monkey*, New York, Oxford UP 1989. (Includes an essay on 'the talking book' with reference to Equiano, Cugoano, Gronniosaw and Jea.)

HECHT, J. Jean, *Continental and Colonial Servants in 18th Century England*, Northampton, Mass., Dept. of History, Smith College 1954.

HOLDEN, Edith, *Blyden of Liberia*, New York, Vantage Press 1966.

LYNCH, Hollis R., *Edward Wilmot Blyden: Pan-Negro Patriot 1832–1912*, Oxford UP 1967.

MCCALMAN, Iain, *Radical Underworld: Prophets, revolutionaries, and pornographers in London, 1795–1840*, Cambridge UP 1989. (Places Wedderburn and Davidson in the context of British radicalism.)

OGUDE, S. E., 'Facts into Fiction: Equiano's Narrative Revisited' in *Research in African Literatures* 13.1. Spring 1982, 31–43. (Argues that Equiano 'borrowed' from eighteenth-century British travel writers, discussed by Edwards in *The Life of Olaudah Equiano* xx–xxiii.)

PASCOE, C. F., *Two Hundred Years of the Society for the Propagation of the Gospel, 1701–1900*, London 1901. (See pp. 254–9 for Philip Quaque.)

SAMUELS, Wilfred D., 'The Disguised Voice in *The Interesting Narrative of Olaudah Equiano*' in *Black American Literature Forum*, 19.2, Summer 1985, 64–9.

SANDIFORD, Keith A., *Measuring the Moment: Strategies of Protest in Eighteenth-Century Afro-English Writing*, Selinsgrove, Susquehanna UP 1988. (An excellent survey of the Black British contribution to the period, and of three principal authors, Equiano, Sancho and Cugoano.)

SEKORA, John, and TURNER, Darwin T. eds, *The Art of Slave Narrative: Original Essays in Criticism and Theory*, Macomb, Univ. of Western Illinois Press 1982. (Contains a good essay on Equiano by Chinosole.)

SHYLLON, Folarin, *Black People in Britain, 1555–1833*, Oxford UP 1977.

WALVIN, James, *Black and White: The Negro and English Society, 1555–1945*, London, Penguin Press 1973.